TRUTH GIVES STRENGTH TO WINGS

It's All in The Journal

Katy Sudano and Ginger Green

TRUTH GIVES STRENGTH TO WINGS
It's All In the Journal
www.AllintheJournal.com

Published by TopShelf Publishing
An imprint of TopShelf Authors & Books, LLC
www.topshelfmagazine.net

Book Design by Katy Sudano
Photos Copyright © 2020, Katy Sudano

Special Thanks to Christine Boswell
for her help with editing and proofreading

ISBN 978-1-64184-307-2 (Paperback)
ISBN 978-1-64184-306-5 (Hardcover)
ISBN 978-1-64184-308-9 (Ebook)

Our books may be purchased in any quantities through INGRAM

First Edition: March 2020

0   9   8   7   6   5   4   3   2   1

Contents

Katy's Dedications

First and foremost, I dedicate this work to God, who guides, protects, and supports my journey.

To my loving and super supportive husband: A man who has been there for me through all my phases of healing, creating a solid foundation of unconditional love. He is my rock; a man who has shown a loyalty I have never known. He is an amazing provider and father. Thank you for showing me that abandonment is not in your vocabulary. I am stronger because of you!

Wito — the only father figure who mattered.

Wita — the woman who showed me that family always comes first and taught me how to get my point across with "Ay no!"

My mother — whom I will always love.

My son — who showed me a strength within myself I would have never otherwise known, and a love that runs deeper than I could imagine. He is unapologetically sensitive, yet strong. We have shared so much laughter. He has surprised me in many ways. But mostly he is loyal, appreciative, and caring.

My daughters — my source of light who made my dreams a reality. We have shared so much laughter, fun, and adventure. They exemplify what it looks like to grow up independent, strong, and secure. It is so fun to see them express their thoughts and dreams with me. I feel honored to experience how well-rounded, caring, smart, open, and loving my girls have become.

Ginger — the woman who eloquently articulated and made my story a written reality. Her incredible talent, spiritual sense, and support nurtured and brought forth my true essence through countless hours of writing, uplifting and sharing with me.

Ginger's Dedications

Casteneda, Seth, and Abraham for confirming how human senses and imagination barely scratch the surface of the immersive reality from which we emerge.

Linda Freeman — a former boss and mentor who saw my potential and taught me more about writing than I ever learned in classrooms.

My loving family and friends — for believing in me and respectfully asking for ten years, "How's the book coming?"

Katy — for the precious gift of letting me help tell her story.

My World of Normal

With respect for Joseph Campbell and *The Hero's Journey*.

My world of normal is silence. We live in Colorado and ski the Rocky Mountains. Normal begins when we get into the car and drive. Mom, Peter, and his kids talk and gesture; their voices are muffled in my head. Nothing else matters — we are going to the top of the mountain. I look up at the trees and clouds and watch our progress. Light flickers through the window. I seem calm because I can't give myself away. Somewhere I'm tingling because I can't help it. I see snow, and creek water winding through crystal surfaces. I am already alone, about to be free. I know there is a God because this mountain is here.

Pull on the gloves and hat, wriggle and stomp everything into place. Get the tickets and stand in line. Wait for the chair lift to hit my butt. I relent, sit, and the silence is complete. I climb slowly and lean forward to get there faster. My face is cold wind. My eyes are ice. I am in my world of normal.

Silence, stillness. People are on the mountain but there is no sound. I'm wound up and need to spring open. My skis on the edge of the cliff are a commitment. I poise for flight, grip the poles. Now. Pushing off the little ramp, I take a breath. The mountain peaks glare at me as I select the slope I want to play on — usually the one others don't. I alone can do this, and no one can criticize me, judge me. It's perfect. I'm perfect. I go off path and soar through a green blur of trees.

My power is live — I am on. There are no thoughts, no words, no chatter. I can do anything on the planet. I am the best, the strongest ever. Most 12-year olds don't go down this hill. It is a short run and a lifetime. I glide through the end and boys watch me fling off my hat. I see their faces. I am a girl with long flowing brown hair. I like the attention but do not talk to them. It's enough that they notice and wonder. They cannot know how. Especially not why.

Some sounds now, but I am free and climbing again. By the end of the weekend, I have enough normal to live through another week of Peter.

Relationships: An Introduction

Life is about relationships. Who you think you are, your ability to thrive and express yourself, depends upon your relationship with other people. Your beliefs about the universe, nature, fear, war, worthiness, happiness, and your role in the world grow in the fertile soil of your relationships. Relationships of all kinds, and most importantly the relationship you have with your own heart, teach you *who you really are.*

As a child, those who care for you and control you are usually the same people. Those who encourage you to do what seems right *to you* may be the ones who loved you the most. As an adult, a loving partner can hold you down, a critical boss can lift you up. Nothing is black or white. It's all relative.

From the earliest histories shared around ancient campfires to the overwhelming media of today, other people's stories help us feel less alone. It's our nature to eagerly jump into the lives of people we'll never meet or don't even exist. Have you ever watched a movie or read a book that made you want to do things differently? Think about the last movie you told your friends about. Did you laugh, cry, jump in fear, or burst with joy? If you did, what you experienced vicariously felt real enough to create a lasting impression. You established a relationship with the characters and their fears, hopes, and triumphs. You connected and got a better idea of who you really are.

Our subconscious doesn't care if what we watch or read happened to someone else or to us. We feel it on a visceral level. Stories are real to our imaginations, and what we imagine is real to us on some level. In fact, we would not be able to create anything new without our ability to believe in what we cannot see. Without imagination, we could not hope for something better. And our ability to hope may be our greatest human power, for without it, there is no room for faith.

When you *listen* closely to your heart, how you feel about what other people do teaches you what you really think and feel. It's up to you to listen, to look, and to realize. It's not simple or easy, but it's the only way you are going to remember who you really are.

At times, it's natural to think you are alone and helpless. We all do. Things happen to you that you would never ask for. People want things from you that your heart doesn't want to give. It seems crazy to think that everything that happens to you is for a reason — until the day something happens to someone else that makes you feel differently than *you* felt before.

CHAPTER 1

Dear Journal

My journey started when I was four years old. My favorite imaginary friend was a young girl named Zoryia. She lived in a world filled with unicorns, fairies, bunnies, and good friends. I was an only child who had already lived in three countries with caring, busy grandparents and sometimes my mother. When I was sad, I made up Zoryia stories in my head that made me feel better. She had powers and I was always by her side. It was the perfect relationship.

When I was six, I moved to Florida with my mother and her new husband. To escape the confusion of his obsession with me, and my fear of him, I pretended *I was Zoryia*, though I didn't tell anyone. I hid my journal under my bed and dreamed I was the girl with glowing skin who flew with birds and eagles, rode across green meadows on the back of "Andor," a powerful and very tall white horse with a long flowing mane.

By age nine, I wrote about what happened to me, as if it happened to her, in hidden journals. What kept me going was hidden in the powers and allies I gave to Zoryia. Her life was going to be happy one day. I had hopes for Zoryia. I had faith in her future. When other people were around and I couldn't write because I didn't want her to be discovered, I dove into other stories.

Where the Red Fern Grows by Wilson Rawls was my first chapter book and to this day my favorite. As I grew older, my curiosity led me to all kinds of books about adventure, drama, love, and mythology. *Wuthering Heights* by Emily Brontë and *The Iliad* by Homer led me to other worlds. Danielle Steel romances and John Grisham titles were closer to home but just as exciting and I admit, a little easier to understand.

At twelve, I wrote about Zoryia as a serious hobby and left my journals in the open. If anyone asked me about them, I planned to say that I wanted to write stories. People loved fantasy and science-fiction books and movies and I thought this explanation would keep me from being discovered. While there were hard scenes of sexual molestation, betrayal, rejection, and rape, there were also scenes of fun and adventure, a beautiful girl with a white horse, and magical people and creatures with thrilling powers. In a few years, there were scenes of romance and true love. It was the perfect ruse. No one ever asked.

The stories I wrote about Zoryia were my attempt to live a better life. I created her strengths and gifts, then pulled them through the portal of my mind into my world. Over the years, she became more like me and I became more like her. In a sense, I pulled a rabbit out of a hat and climbed through a window to follow it down a mysterious hole. Anywhere that rabbit went was going to be better than where I was — as long as I wrote the stories.

I am Sydney DeVold. The relationships I write about tell my story. Zoryia's relationships tell our story. Who can know for sure which stories, if not both, are true?

CHAPTER 2

Promises

My greatest relationships were often hard to live through. Some were exciting, some quite wonderful. As a young girl, I escaped the hardest ones by imagining that I lived in another world filled with magical people and creatures who made bad things better, who took me flying, and told me things that made sense. My imaginary world had to make sense because the one I was living in was inexplicable.

Juliana and Mateo were part-time commercial models and full-time students at the University of Lausanne in Switzerland.

He was half Swiss, half El Salvadorian, she was half American, half Costa Rican. He fell in love with her good looks, she with his. I was born three years later. Before I was two, Juliana decided that Mateo was an unfaithful husband and she could no longer be his wife.

I was two years old when, during their divorce, I moved to Panama City, Panama, with Juliana's parents, the Witos. To be clear, my grandparents' last name was not Wito. My attempt as a toddler to pronounce the Spanish words for grandmother abuelita and grandfather abuelito became the family endearments "Wita" and "Wito." This was not an uncommon practice in Latin homes. My Wito was an American diplomat on his way to a new assignment in Panama. My Wita was the niece of a former, highly respected Costa Rican president.

Juliana and I had ridden in the backseat of Wito's new 1976 white Ford coupe from Washington, D.C. to an apartment in Panama. I thought this place was our new home and my father would live here, too. Juliana didn't tell me this. I just expected it, until the day Juliana said goodbye to me. She hugged me a long time and said she would see me soon. I didn't understand why I couldn't go with her.

I remember standing in the entrance foyer. She closed the front door behind her. I thought I would never see her again. As a two-year old, I did the only thing I could to make her come back. I screamed, ran to the door, and threw myself at it. Nothing happened. I threw myself on the floor and hit my head on the cold tile. I screamed and screamed. Nothing happened. I turned over on my back. Wito stood over me.

He smiled. I wanted my mother back.

He rubbed his hands together, smiling. He looked up at Wita. I turned my head to look at her too. My head hurt but I kept screaming, though not as hard. She stood in front of the stove with a long wooden spoon in her hand. Morning light streamed in around her from the kitchen window. She lifted the spoon up and shook it in the air at me. "Jou are going tu hurt jourself. Estop it, estop it now!"

Wito pulled me up into his arms and held me. He took me into the kitchen. Wita did not reach for me. Wito said, "Now dear, she is confused and so little. Give her some time. I'll take her to the patio and read her a book. Why don't you bring her some juice? She likes juice." Wita answered, "Okey, jes, I'll du dat. Jou are rright. ¡Pobrecita!"

They say young children will adapt to their circumstances. I think children of all ages just figure things out the best they can and deal with it. The Witos told me Juliana was coming back. When I talked to her on the phone, Juliana promised to come back for me. I didn't know what promises were. I was living with the Witos.

I figured out that letting the Witos take care of me was okay. When I wasn't crying, we had fun. In the mornings, Wito carried me to day-school on his shoulders. It was hot every day and his forehead dripped with sweat. His shirt, what he called a guayabera, was dry when we left the apartment and wet when he kissed me goodbye at the school door.

Wita had maids to help and they were nice to me. I played on the blue shag rugs. I learned to stop pulling the shoots trailing all the way to our patio floor from Wita's fern baskets. They hung from the balcony above us. She didn't like it when I did that. I figured it out.

The Witos read to me and kissed me goodnight. I remember crying for my mother in bed when they turned out the light. After a while I stopped.

My two-year old experience was like a recurring dream, until the day, as a young adult, I spoke to the Witos about this event. I remembered everything told here. Wita gasped and asked, "How du you rremember how as it was? How can ju possibly rremember the apartemento and the colores? Y my prized ferns that touched the floor?" I was shocked by her questions and realized in that moment that my memories, at times, could be photographic.

What I didn't understand was where my mother was. Juliana had moved into the Witos' house in Atlanta to find herself. What she found was a job with IBM and Peter Tappen Fairchild.

She was his secretary. He was a technical engineer. They married when I was four. Peter was my first stepfather and Juliana adored him. In some ways he was like my father, Mateo. Smart and ambitious. In other ways, Peter was nothing like him.

A year later, the Witos flew me to Atlanta to live in a new home with Juliana and Peter, and my new stepbrother, Brandon. He was four years older than I. I was happy to play Princess Leia to his Luke Skywalker.

After school, Brandon would run into the house looking for me. It usually went something like this:

Brandon: "Let's go outside and build a fort. We have to get ready for the battlefront. Grab your light-saber and I'll get R2D2!"

Me, grabbing my wooden broomstick with aluminum foil carefully wrapped around the end: "The Force is with us, Luke!"

Juliana: "Be careful with poison ivy and stay out of the kudzu, you never know what's in there!"

Brandon: "We will; 3-CPO is waiting for us!"

Juliana, with a tilt to her head and a hand to her forehead: "What, who, 3 what?"

Brandon, slamming the screen down shut behind him: "Oh, why don't you just watch the movie?"

When I was six years old, IBM moved us to Boca Raton, Florida, and we settled into a nice new home with Spanish tile floors, big windows and a private pool. That's when Peter began his courtship with me. His approach was to take my innocence, but never my virginity. Peter groomed me to be his mistress, making sure I would cooperate and never tell Juliana. I learned later that he had also groomed his adopted daughter, Amy, from a previous marriage with some successes and some failures. By the time we moved to Florida, Peter was well into his plan to turn me into his greatest masterpiece.

The Witos taught me how to swim in Panama. I was at heart a fish. Peter decided he would teach me how to dive in our pool. He coaxed me to lean forward and go in headfirst as he waited in the deep end. I didn't want him to teach me and I said so, loud enough for Juliana to hear.

Juliana yelled from inside the kitchen window watching us, "Peter, don't push her. She'll get it."

He ignored us both. "Headfirst and put your arms above your head. The water is deep, and I'll be next to you. If you want to be on the swim team, you have to learn how to dive in. Put your chin to your chest and lean in." I didn't know what a swim team was.

Brandon squealed in the background, "It's easy, Sydney. I could dive when I was five. You can jump a little when you lean in. That helps."

Not wanting Brandon to laugh at me, I said to Peter, "Okay, I'll go in," in a small, timid voice. "But don't touch me. I can do it myself." I didn't want him to grab between my legs like he did the last time we were in the pool.

Peter responded loud enough for Juliana to hear, "I know, honey, I just want to show you how. You can do it."

He slapped the water, probably getting tired of treading. "Oh, come on. If you do this for me, I'll buy you and Brandon a double Popsicle to share from the ice cream truck."

I did the best I could. My stomach and face hit the water at the same time. I swam past him toward the ladder, trying to keep my legs together. Peter grabbed my bathing suit bottom, squeezed my butt, and pushed me forward.

He got out of the pool when Juliana told him he had a phone call. I practiced diving with Brandon's help and got it on the fourth try. When Peter came back, I showed him.

"I knew you could do it," he smiled. Julianna clapped and whistled from the window. That afternoon, Brandon and I each enjoyed an popsicles.

Peter knew what I liked and gave it to me when I played along. I had figured things out and dealt with them the best I could. Peter promised that if I told Juliana or anyone, I would not get anymore treats, such as ice cream or stuffed animals. I knew what promises were by then and I believed him. Anything Juliana did that he didn't like turned into holes in the walls, broken mirrors, and thrown vases or candle sticks. If Juliana wasn't home when he made a mess, he made me clean it up.

By the time I was nine, Peter lost his job with IBM. Soon after, we moved to Denver, Colorado, for Peter's new job with Honeywell. By then, Juliana and I were completely dependent on his world. I survived by learning how to be the perfect chameleon. I had to be more than pretty, I had to be happy, polite, helpful, athletic, and most of all, compliant. I kept my intelligence to myself. I kept my journals and stories about Zoryia hidden back then. By that time, Peter had made it clear to me that my mother's life depended on me being silent about his affections for me. As long as I could be the perfect girl, as long as I could keep him happy, we would all be okay.

When I gave Peter what he wanted — touches inside my panties or his, letting him watch me take a bath, looking at pornography and telling him how it made me feel, he gave me what I wanted — Juliana's safety, family ski trips and vacations. I wasn't proud of it; I just didn't know what else to do.

When I was twelve, Honeywell promoted Peter to a management position in Darmstadt, Germany. From there Honeywell moved us to Lausanne, Switzerland. Strange but true — that was the city where I was born.

Juliana was not aware of Peter's relationship with me. How could she be? She was in a deep relationship with her own needs. I loved my mother and I resented her. How could I not?

CHAPTER 3

It finally came out

Whether alone or with Juliana, somewhere between the U.S., Switzerland, Germany, El Salvador and Costa Rica, I had learned to fly with style and confidence. When flying alone, I talked with friendly passengers and flight attendants and told anyone who would listen about the wonderful life I desperately needed them to think I was living. When there was no one to talk to in the air or on the ground, I pulled out my journal and wrote about Zoryia.

I was always somewhere between a take-off and a landing. I didn't know exactly what was real or in my own mind. To me, Zoryia was real. Skiing down mountains was real. Being on the school volleyball team was real. Dancing with my friends was real. Any athletic activity was real. If I wasn't in motion, I was just on a long layover — or stuck in a holding pattern.

Life had no certainties for me. I needed some ground beneath me, even if it was through Zoryia. So, I gave Zoryia a place that was uniquely her own. She needed it. The escape that airplanes provided me were not a part of her reality.

Zoryia reached Thalia's old shack as daylight ended. Her mother's family still held property that sat 12 strides beyond the small hill that lay between the barn and the winding creek that defined the neighbor's border. She looked back, caught her breath and pulled back the vines that covered the half-broken wooden door of her sanctuary, and shimmied through. She sat on the rug pulled from her mother's discards and placed in her special hiding place. One short candle and a box of matches sat on a rusted stove. She hugged her knees tight and rocked back and forth.

In my fourteenth summer, Juliana sent me to stay with the Witos in Atlanta, where Wito had retired from his diplomatic career. Things were getting difficult in Germany between her and Peter, and based on what she told them, the Witos agreed an extended visit would be good for me.

Wita was petite and rather handsome in a feminine way, with a strong jaw, flashing brown eyes, and always perfect hair. She had a lot of opinions and used them to get her way. "Jou look nice," meant she approved, "Can't jou du someding," if she didn't. Wita was my model for Zoryia's grandmother, Isadora, a big name that sounded like a royal woman with plenty of spirit and friends wanting to keep her happy.

Wito was tall and slim and smelled like peppermint. He once told me, with a shine in his blue eyes, "My cheekbones and white hair were gifts from my grandparents. They left Eastern Europe just before the 'Great War,'" he grinned. "You come from a long line of people who knew how to dream and make those dreams come true." I loved it. Wito was my model for Zoryia's grandfather, Laertes, a name a heroic warrior could bear with pride.

To my way of thinking, the Witos looked good together and they never argued. At least I never heard them raise their voices. At times they were rather romantic, at times they didn't speak to one another. I always knew who was going to win their silent arguments. Usually, Wito was just practicing his diplomatic arts.

I thought of the Witos as my other parents, my sanctuary. What I didn't know was that to their way of thinking, they had already raised their children and were too old to raise another teenager.

Even though Juliana and Peter were far away in Germany, I knew my summer was just another layover. I was expected back before September, but I was too old to live with Peter. I couldn't be the perfect child anymore. I had to stay in Atlanta, but I couldn't tell anyone why. I wanted to live with my father, Mateo in El Salvador. But I couldn't. I was broken and needed attention, any kind of attention.

So that summer I did the usual things teenagers do when they can't tell the truth. I played the game called, "I'll show you how much I don't need you!" The game goes something like this — I agreed to do what they asked but didn't. I wore a whore's outfit to a costume party. I snuck out of my room at night and got caught sneaking back in smelling of smoke and beer. I got a fake tattoo and told them it was real. I came home with the left side of my head closely shaved in true skater style. The hair on the top and right side of my head was bright orange.

Wita looked at me and said, "¡Ay no! Why du jou du dis dings?" She raised her open hands to the side of her head then quickly chopped them down to her side, one of her favorite gestures of frustration. "¡Ay no!" gesturing again, "What am I going to du wit jou? Jou luk so oghly!"

I didn't like hurting her and was afraid I might go too far, but sometimes I couldn't stop myself. I didn't want them to throw me back across the ocean. It almost happened on a Saturday evening in late August. I was in front of the house, sitting on the sidewalk with two older teenage boys. As long as she could see me, Wita tolerated our conversation. When the sun had almost set, she told me to come inside. I said okay but stayed outside with my friends because we were having fun. When I couldn't see Wita at the front window, one of them let me have a few puffs of his cigarette.

Just at dark, Wita came outside, grabbed my arm and pulled me to my feet. She said two sentences in her best commanding, aristocratic Latina whisper, loud enough for my friends – but not the neighbors. "Jou are going back to jour moderr. We don't know wat to du wit jou anymorre."

Without knowing it, she had sentenced me to hell. If she had yelled at me, I would have won the game. Instead, she won the game with two whispered sentences. I stomped up the stairs to my room and slammed the door to hide my shame. I needed to be with Zoryia. She was the best kind of therapy for me because while I could never write about Peter directly, I could let my deepest anger, broken heart, and highest hopes flow through Zoryia's world with my raw and often beautiful imagination.

Zoryia and Andor stood at the top of the hill looking down into the beautiful valley she called "Freedom Land." The valley lay between the sheer rock face of two mountains, protected from the harsh ocean weather that constantly blew in from the north. In the center of the center, stood a gigantic tree that always, no matter what the season, boasted a bouquet of huge gold, red, orange, and brown leaves. Thalia, Zoryia's mother, had told her to never cross the shallow creek into the valley. As many times as she had gazed into that beautiful land, she had never seen anyone or for that matter, any animals, not even a bird.

"Sydney, come down for dinner," Wito called up the stairs. "I mean it now. Your lasagna is getting cold." I put my pen down. My stomach hurt.

I slipped my journal under my pillow and took a deep breath. "Wito is going to hate my hair."

I walked into the kitchen with my head up, trying to be brave. I couldn't eat much. I wanted to throw up. Wito didn't mention my hair — why should he? Wita had made her decision. After dinner, Wito asked me to call my mother. I pushed the long side of my skater hair behind my ear. He noticed that my hand was shaking. I could tell because his left eyebrow shot up.

"I will," I replied softly. "But you need to ask her about Peter." Wito stared at me. "What's wrong, Sydney? You need to tell us what's wrong with you."

I started crying in long, low whimpers because I couldn't scream. "Peter plays games with me and I don't want to play them anymore, I can't. If you make me go back, I won't have a choice."

"Wat du jou mean, play games, wat kind of games?"

"Well," I whined in a high pitch sob. I knew it was coming out now and I couldn't stop it.

I took deep breaths and clinched my stomach, trying to not throw up. "He ... tells me to do stuff and if I do, he gives me things."

"Stuff? What kind of game involves stuff?" asked Wito, moving his chair closer to me.

"¡Ay, no!," Wita rasped and gestured. "I dink I know wat jou arr trying to tell us! Please, Dios mio, don't let it be true!" Wita held her face between her hands and shook her head back and forth.

I lowered my head, looked at my feet and whispered, "Yes, Wita. It's true. Please don't ask me about the games. Peter is going to kill Mom if I tell you."

"I knew it! I didn't like when jou used to sit on his lap. It gave me da pimple bumps on my skin. Everry time!" Gesturing, she added, "¡Ay no!"

"I'm not sure I understand, exactly," Wito said slowly.

Wita reached across the edge of the table and slapped his shoulder. "Wat don't jou underrstand? He is, jou know, what du jou call it...? ¡Un hijo de Puta!"

"Yes, dear, he is a son of a bitch!" Wito reiterated.

I continued, "I told my mother what he was doing with me. She was shocked and called Peter into the room and asked him. He didn't deny anything and with a cocky attitude he asked, 'So what are *you* going to do about it?' and the next thing I remember is packing a bag and getting on a plane to come here."

Wito dropped his forehead in the palms of his hands. A moment later, he looked up at me with concern and love in his eyes. Patting my hand, he said, "Wita, call her now, I don't care what time it is. Get on the phone in the living room. I'll speak from here."

I held my breath.

"¿Alo? Arr jou there? Oh, gud. I have Wito on da keechen phone." I could hear Wita clearly.

"Juliana?" Wito said, then listened to her while I listened to the thumping in my chest and the blood in my temples.

"That is good to hear, Juliana. But we have something important to talk about. Are you alone?"

Moments go by while he listens. "Okay, good."

"Sydney is no gud. We must talk to jou about this game ding wit Peter."

I couldn't hear what Juliana said, but I watched Wito list his free elbow to the table and rub his hand over his brow back and forth, trying to be heard during the conversation between his daughter and his wife.

Finally, able to interrupt, Wito said, "Juliana, Sydney has been behaving strangely. We didn't understand why she was trying to get negative attention. We told her that if she didn't behave properly, we would have to send her back to you before the end of her summer vacation. She informed us that she was afraid of

Peter and why. She never wants to go back. We don't know all the details, for she is clearly not ready to divulge this delicate information. What can you tell us?" Using formal language was Wito's way of staying in control.

Again, silence in the room, pounding in my head.

"I want to hear what she is saying," I whispered to Wito, leaning in to the receiver to hear.

"Okay," he whispered back and tilted the receiver toward me. Together we held it between us.

"I caught Peter in Sydney's bedroom one night," Juliana said. Her voice trembled. "It was when she was about six. We were living in Boca Raton then. He liked to put her to bed, but that night it was taking a long time. I thought maybe she didn't feel well. I found him sitting on her bed. Sydney's panties were down around her ankles and Peter was rubbing between her legs. I yelled at him to stop. He told me he was just helping her relax so she could go to sleep."

"What did you do"? Wito demanded. I could tell he was upset. I wasn't used to hearing him upset.

"At first I didn't know what to do. I was stunned. He didn't deny it, I felt sick to my stomach. The only thing I could think of was to get her away from him. I picked her up and put her in the car. I drove around because I didn't know what to say. I finally just told her that what he did was wrong. I told her that it was not her fault and she didn't do anything wrong, but she could never let him touch her private parts ever again. She seemed to understand, and we went back home."

"And jou sleep in his bed again? ¡Carajo! I wood have called da policia in dat moment. He is a horrible man, un hijo de puta."

Juliana responded, "Mom, he said that rubbing his daughter in this way used to help her get to sleep. He promised he would

16

never touch Sydney that way again. I didn't have any reason to think he was lying."

"Well, he is a puta lierr." Wita's voice cracked between her sobs. "And Sydney said dat he made herr play dese games and he has threatened to kill jou if she told anyone all these jears. ¡Ay no!"

Juliana could barely continue, "I thought he had stopped. I didn't know anything was still going on. Sydney never, ever said anything about it until . . ." Juliana paused, "until we agreed she should spend the summer with you."

"Wat? Wat do jou mean? I don't underrstand?" Wita questioned.

"Did you expect her to be fine with everything by just pretending nothing happened?" Wito asked.

"I just didn't know how else to handle this problem. I told Peter that he needed professional help. I knew she would be safe with you until I figured things out."

"Is Peter getting help?" Wito asked in a stern voice.

"We haven't found the right person yet," Juliana answered in a small voice.

"What is Sydney supposed to do at the end of the summer?" Wito demanded

"Can you have her stay and go to school there? I think that would be best solution for now," Juliana replied.

"Jou need to leave el hijo de puta now and be with jour daughter. I don't underrstand! Wat is wrong wit jou?" Wita exclaimed.

"I don't know what to do. I have to go," Juliana mumbled quietly as if she couldn't swallow.

That was it. I slumped over and put my cheek on their kitchen table. It was cool and my face was hot. I was exhausted and just wanted to be alone.

Wito pulled the phone away and looked at me.

The Witos hung up, not waiting for her goodbye. I sat up and covered my face.

"Please look at me Sydney," he asked softly. I put my hands down and looked at him.

Wito's blue eyes were rimmed in red. He sighed slowly, then nodded. "We'll get you some help, someone you can talk to who knows about these things." His voice was deeper and more tender than I had ever heard before.

"Jes we will," agreed Wita as she walked into the kitchen. She wrapped me in her arms, and I laid my head on her chest. In a moment, when we had both calmed, she lifted my face, brushed back wet strands from my forehead, wiped my tears and kissed my cheek.

"Jou know, we will just plan on having a gud time in Costa Rica for our familia's vacation in Decemberr. Jou will meet my familia and for two weeks, jou can du all da dings jou like to du and forget all about dis."

I smiled a little to let her think I was listening.

"We arre going to see the Santos familia. Jou know my niece Carmen is married to their son Mario. They have a big ranch wit a pool, a lake and a boat. When we go to the beach, jou can ride horses, go surfing, hike up volcanoes, ride helicópteros ... jou will see."

The weeks that followed was much easier for the Witos in one respect. I did everything they asked because I felt I had been heard. The truth was out. I didn't know what was going to happen, but I didn't have to hold the secret any longer.

Wita was busy making vacation plans and I was busy blending into a new school that fall. I went to their country club, swam in the pool with "respectable" friends, played a little tennis, ate lunch in the restaurant, and alone in my room at night, I wrote a happy Zoryia story.

Zoryia dumped her wash basin and ran forty strides to the barn. She lifted the rope to unlatch the doors and pull them open. Her nose crinkled from the smell. She covered her nose with her left hand and walked over to Lucia, the family cow, standing in the corner near the back door.

She grabbed the rope around Lucia's neck and led her to the milking stall. She picked up the old metal bucket and placed it under Lucia, then turned and retrieved the wooden milking stool and sat down. She patted Lucia's fat stomach. "Good morning Lucia, I hope you have much milk to give me today."

CHAPTER 4

Need to Breathe

At fourteen years old, I was an experienced international flyer. I had never been afraid of flying. Landing for the first time at the International Airport in San Jose was different. It lies in the Central Valley, a flat patch of earth ringed by sulfuric volcanoes and steep, jungle-blanketed mountains. Landing was like sliding down a corkscrew. We spiraled down sharp and quick and so did my stomach.

I sat in the window seat on the side leaning into the spiral. I closed my eyes and tried to feel the plane around me. I thought of it as a giant silver bird making graceful downward loops. That didn't help much so I did what I naturally do when I'm upset. Get someone's attention.

"Mom, when are we going to land? My stomach hurts."

Juliana looked at me, nodded, and smiled a little. She had landed here several times before. Her smile made me feel better. It was a sweet moment.

"We'll be down in a few minutes. Look, can you see the ground?" she asked trying to distract me.

I was pissed that Peter was even on our plane. I couldn't believe he was going with us. This was supposed to be a chance for me to have fun. The madman had found a way to be included.

I guessed Wita let him come because of her eternal need for everything to look perfect. Wito usually let her have her way, but this time I wondered why he allowed it. I found out why on the beach at Playa Escondida.

At the exact moment I felt the 747 shift its nose downward for descent, Peter got up to go to the bathroom. In a few minutes, our plane would drop out of the clouds and find its runway.

I turned and looked at my mother directly for the first time in the flight. She was in the middle seat reading. "Do you think they all know?" I asked, trying to keep my anger to myself.

"Know what, Sydney?" My mother's soft hazel eyes narrowed as she turned and looked at me. Her eyes were pretty, but not as big as mine, I liked to think. I looked at her long, straight brown hair. It framed her face as it fell behind her shoulders. It was nice, but not as thick and dark as mine.

I knew I'd have to pretend everything was perfect. But I wanted to know what I should expect from Wita's family.

"Do they know what Peter has been doing to me?"

"Of course not, sweetie! Who would tell them?" Mom gasped. The alarm on her face seemed real. I wasn't so sure. Wito had told my mother's brother, Henry and his wife, Dawn. Henry was a doctor and Wito had hoped he could help me. I was terrified. My secret could no longer be mine.

She turned away from me to look down the aisle for his return.

"You know it breaks my heart you felt that you couldn't tell me for all those years. How else could I have known he was lying to me?" she asked.

I wondered how she could not have known, or even asked. Mom didn't say it was Peter's actions that broke her heart. Her heart was broken because I couldn't tell her about it. What mattered most to her was her need to be supported by a man, and that broke my heart. I had kept silent to protect her from the madman she had married.

Not seeing Peter on his way back, Juliana turned toward me again and took my hands. Her eyes were tearing. All I could do was wonder why hadn't she paid more attention? Why hadn't she cared enough to find out? Didn't she realize that I had been too young to know that I couldn't tell her, and Peter threatened to take everything away and possibly kill her? His rage, even over little things, was uncontrollable at times. She was an adult. Surely, she could figure it out.

Trying not to cry, I changed the subject. "I really want them to like me," I forced my best smile. That was something I could do on cue.

"They will love you, Sydney," she replied and lightly brushed the back of her hand across my right cheek. "There is just too much about you to love for you to worry about anything."

I closed my eyes and said, "Thanks, Mom. I'm sure we'll have a great time." Then I sat up straight, eyes wide open. "Does Peter know that I told the Witos?"

"No. He's been working a lot. But don't worry, you'll be safe in Costa Rica and then you can go back to Atlanta. You don't need to worry about anything."

The fasten seatbelts sign dinged just as Peter plopped into his seat. "We're almost there Sydney!" he said, folding his tall, skinny body into the aisle seat and clicking his seat belt.

He looks stupid, I thought, watching him through the corner of my eye. I was always wary of what he was doing whenever he was around. He tried to smooth his wiry brown hair into place, but it kept sticking out. *He is stupid*, I agreed with myself. Mom just looked at her book.

I closed my eyes. I felt sweaty and wiped my forehead with the napkin I was still holding from breakfast on the plane.

Peter decided this would be a good time to act like a concerned stepfather. He leaned over my mother and put his hand on my thigh just above my knee, right in the open. I sat up straight, forgot about my stomach and stared down at his hand. I couldn't believe it. All I could see were long, bony fingers and the thick, bumpy veins on the back of his hand.

I pushed his hand away. *It's over*, I told myself. *And he's about to find out.*

I crossed my right leg over my left tightly and turned away from him. I didn't look at Juliana either. I didn't even care what she was thinking. Through my window I could see blue ocean, green cliffs rising from the water, and the tops of forests running through the city just beyond the valley. I focused on how it would feel as soon as the wheels hit the ground.

It was the roughest landing I had ever experienced. The pilots got us through wind shears that took us up and down, up and down until we got low enough to touch the ground. We bumped over two huge potholes and rolled around another one before we finally approached the gate. The passengers applauded. Something shifted in me during that landing. I wasn't afraid of Peter anymore.

I heard the voice of an attendant welcoming the passengers to San Jose.

"Damas y caballeros, bienvenidos a San Jose, Costa Rica. La hora es onze y treinta y Quarto de la mañana y tiempo bueno con veinte y siete grados celcios. Porfavor mantenganse en sus asientos con su cinturones bien aporcados hasta que el capitán a quitado el signial de aprochura y hemos parado completamente.

"Ladies and gentlemen, welcome to San Jose, Costa Rica. The current time is eleven thirty-four a.m. and twenty-seven degrees Celsius. Please remain seated until the captain has turned off the fasten seatbelt sign and we have come to a complete stop."

All I could hear was the sound of seatbelts clicking open. I stuffed my napkin into the pocket of magazines in front of me. I grabbed the cold metal flap of my seatbelt, pulled it up, and stood up to a high crouch under the overhead bins. I turned to look at Peter looking at me with that expression on his face. I knew he wanted to criticize me so he could "punish" me later. This time, I stared right back at him. There was nothing he could do to hurt me, or Juliana, anymore.

Juliana put her hand on his arm. He must have realized they were closely surrounded by strangers because he didn't say anything. I looked down the aisle for the exit. The plane came to a stop, the seatbelt sign turned off with a ding and the cabin lights flickered on.

Passengers filled the aisle and pulled their carry-ons from the overhead bins. I counted ten rows between me and the exit. Juliana and Peter gathered their things. A flight attendant stood in front of the exit door, grabbed the large red lever with both hands and pulled hard to the right. I heard the suction release and the pop when the door opened.

Finally, I thought. "I've got to get out!" I complained to Juliana. I had to get out of that cramped space and breathe fresh air. I needed to breathe air that Peter had not shared.

And then I smelled it — warm, sulfuric air. It was stronger than I had ever smelled before in Central America. It was exciting. This was a new place. No one else in the family knew. I could be myself here. I could be anyone I wanted to be.

We cleared Customs, got our bags, and walked outside. We pushed through crowds of people standing behind a long, low concrete barrier looking for loved ones. It was hot and took a while to get past the other departing passengers and persistent peddlers trying to sell local juices, cut pineapples, souvenir trinkets, and taxi rides. Peter was busy keeping us and our bags together.

I filled my lungs with the late-morning steamy air, thick with the smell of sulfur. It wasn't exactly pleasant, but it smelled like freedom to me. We finally pushed through to the curb. I turned in a circle and saw the ring of huge, green volcanoes that formed the valley in which we landed. They were less intimidating from the air. While Juliana looked for her relatives, I looked at the streams of smoke leaking from the tops of those deep green volcanic mountains. Their heat promised much.

"Zoryia will like it here," I smiled. "Tonight, I will make sure she has a bird's eye view of my newest adventure."

CHAPTER 5

The Perfect Family

Juliana spotted her cousin Mario and his wife Carmen. They all waved and smiled. This was my cue to be a perfect member of our perfect little family. The full count of Wita's family reunion-vacationers that flew in from other parts of the world was about forty. We all stayed with various cousins and uncles who lived in or near San Jose. Every activity and meal had been well-planned by the senior members of Wita's family for almost a year, and it was going to be an event worthy of the Santos social status, no matter what.

Our drive to Mario's home bothered me almost as much as the plane landing. The roads in Costa Rica have more potholes than pavement because the asphalt is constantly being washed away by rain, at least eight months each year.

I figured Juliana could tell I was upset about the traveling conditions because I kept grabbing the door, the window, arm rest, or whatever I could hold onto.

"The famous potholes of Costa Rica!" she laughed, trying to make it seem less torturous than it was.

"They never get it right," said Peter. "The only way to repair a road is to strip the erosion out, level it again, and pave it with fresh tar. Here they just fill in the potholes and pour another layer on top. If the Santos' family would actually spend the government's money, they could repair the roads correctly...."

Mario slightly turned his head to Peter in the backseat and said in clear English, "You are absolutely right. However, the government doesn't pay for the roads to be maintained properly. We know how it is done."

I wanted Peter to shut up and stop acting like he knew everything. He was messing up my escape to Wita's promised paradise — someplace different and new where I could forget he even existed.

Carmen, perhaps sensing my irritation, interrupted, "Do you know that we own a helicopter? Don't you want to go for a ride, Sydney?"

"Oh, I didn't know. That sounds like a blast!" I replied, picking up on her direction.

We were about to spend two weeks with family members I had met only as a child. If I could be part of that family, if they could care about me as much as I cared about them liking me, then maybe I could fit in. In spite of Wita's hopes for me, to gain admittance here, appearing perfect was the game I had to play to win. I knew how to play that game at home. Winning here was another matter.

I was the oldest grandchild and ready to be a good chameleon. Wita needed us to look like a perfect family unit. I knew how to look pretty, be sweet and helpful, and no matter what, say only what her family wanted to hear. I wasn't sure who knew what, and I was happy to keep it that way. I was going to fit in and enjoy myself because this was my escape. Peter be damned!

Mario's house was much like my father's — hidden behind long streets, high guarded walls and servants. When we arrived, I kissed and greeted Wita's family members who had gathered to welcome us. The maids, dressed in white cotton aprons, served coffee, sandwiches and fruit in the central courtyard.

I didn't feel like talking, so I just listened. I was excited to be there, but Peter was there too, acting as if he was a successful businessman on holiday. Wita's family talked with him as if he was as he pretended to be.

"So, what are we going to do tomorrow?" Juliana asked Carmen.

"First, we are going to the town Wita grew up in. Her brother still lives there, and he can't wait to see everyone. You know, the town of Alajuela."

Juliana exclaimed, "Oh yes. I remember. And please tell me we are going to have paella!"

"Of course," Mario added, walking over to the group of ladies talking in the kitchen, sipping on his drink. "Your cousin Victor makes the best paella. He's very careful to use only the freshest ingredients."

Juliana asked, "Does he still make it over a fire in the front yard in a homemade skillet?"

"How did he hand-make that? I hope it doesn't leach any toxins," said Peter, trying to keep the attention on himself.

Juliana rolled her eyes and asked him to go freshen up. When he left the kitchen, Carmen said, rolling her eyes as well, "He is so American."

"I know. He's just trying to look out for us. You know, he is an engineer," Juliana said smiling, but when I looked at her, her eyes were not smiling.

At that moment, Carmen's nanny led baby Roberta into the room, just woken up from her nap.

"Ah, mi niña," said Carmen. "Look how beautiful she is!"

Baby Roberta was a bit chubby in my opinion, but very cute. She gave me a big smile. That was my out.

After I played with Roberta for a while, I ate a snack and told Juliana I wanted to rest in my room. I would join them at dinner.

Hearing my excuse, Peter said, "Teenagers," and returned to his attentive crowd. Juliana looked at me but didn't say anything.

In the bedroom I would share with another cousin who had not yet arrived, I unpacked a few things. All I wanted to do was be with Zoryia. I pulled out my journal and settled on one of the twin beds.

Zoryia woke up in a jolt and inhaled sharply. "Why am I smelling rotten eggs?" she wondered wrinkling her nose in disgust. "I have never smelled such a smell in the cottage before.

It was a dream," she realized and at that moment the smell was gone. She checked her sheets. They were dry. She smiled and stretched and remembered her strange dream. People sat in rows of chairs in a metal tube and from the sky, they glided to the ground in circles like a giant bird. A voice rang out loud, but she saw no one speaking. Bells chimed by themselves, small lanterns glowed without fire.

"Hmm, such a dream," she shook her head a little to clear the image.

I never made it to dinner. When I woke up, my cousin Julia was asleep in the other twin bed. In the dark, I found my way to the kitchen. A sandwich and a glass of orange juice were waiting for me on the counter. Nothing on this vacation so far tasted quite as good.

CHAPTER 6

Proving Me

The next morning, we drove to Wita's brother's house in Alajuela. Victor made a huge pot of paella over a fire in the front yard, just as promised. That's when I decided we would put on a little song-and-dance show for the grownups. I wrote a play about what we had learned while exploring the volcanos, got the kids to rehearse it, and constructed some simple costumes with paper, string, glue, and crayons Diego's wife gave me. We performed my variety show after supper. My creation was a huge success. I loved the applause and laughter. I loved being told how smart I was, and talented. I especially loved not being told that I was pretty.

By noon each day in Costa Rica, the steam and sulfur lifted away, and the air became dryer and more pleasant. Our family group spent four days exploring volcanoes and their lakes, slashing our way through the tamer jungles, wading in natural springs, and taking helicopter rides over the ocean. Whatever we were doing, I jumped in, had fun, and helped where I could. I never minded feeding and changing the babies and watching them when asked. I wanted to make it fun for them, too.

On the sixth day we visited Rio Quarto, a cattle ranch outside of San Jose, situated between four rivers. It was owned by the Fulco family. The patriarch, Otto, had two sons and a daughter.

Otto inherited his land and money from his family and while, as I learned later, he never had to work to enjoy the riches produced by the workers on his land, he used his money to buy power and influence in the government to become minister of exterior commerce. The Fulcos had several homes in Costa Rica. The ranch was as much their private vacation home as it was a working concern.

Caravanning the group to Rio Quarto took almost two hours. It wasn't very far from the city, but we had to go slowly over roads that were so eroded they almost crumbled beneath our tires. As we climbed up the mountain, I wanted to say what I thought about the situation, but Peter was in the car. I stayed quiet.

As a young girl, my father had told me over and over, "You are going to be among some very important people and politicians. You need to learn now that if you have anything to say, it had better be something good. I won't let you embarrass me by talking bad about people." He pointed his finger at my nose and said, "You may think you know something, but you don't. And once you've said what you think, you can't ever take it back."

I knew that if I actually ever expressed a negative opinion to anyone, my father would find out and punish me later. The odd thing was that everyone else in his family criticized everyone else in the world, all the time, as if it were a sport that needed practicing.

Working our way up the mountain, we passed strawberry fields and coffee plantations, major crops for this area due to the elevation. A little farther up we drove through "the Switzerland of Central America" an area that resembled the mountains of Europe. Higher still was more jungle. I remember seeing waterfalls. Some had rainbows floating over them. At one point we stopped to take pictures. We made as small a group as we could so the camera could capture us against the splendid background.

When I look at that picture today, I see my arms around my favorite cousin Roberto, and slip back into the scene. There I feel connected, liked, included, a part of. Innocent and grounded, unaware of the changes about to take place in my life and my opening, hope — filled heart.

The higher we got, the more I worried about the steep cliffs above and below us. There were no caution signs. I was beginning to wonder if this particular trip was going to be worth the danger to our group. Despite the wild world of beauty around us, I kept thinking that one good rockslide would wipe out our entire family. Finally, we managed to get through a pothole we couldn't drive around and leveled out on more solid ground. We passed through a little town and took a left on a muddy road that led to the entrance of Rio Quarto.

The entrance was humble and showed no evidence of what lay a hundred yards behind it. We pulled up to a blue house with white trim and a colonial structure that seemed out of place at first. I wondered why they had built a wooden house in this area. Surely it would suffer from jungle rot. It was very rustic but seemed sturdy and in good shape. A stone walkway led to the front steps and branched in front of the wrap-around porch to

the pool at the side of the house. Kitchen windows were to the right side of the first floor. I never imagined that I was going to live here for a brief time.

That day, the air was warm with ribbons of cooler breezes flowing through the trees and we had much to do. Some of us rode horses or went on tractor-pulled hayrides, while others played in the pool or hiked into the jungle to hunt for wild boar. Those who wanted to water ski packed up several trucks and headed to what the Fulco family called their lagoon. The small lake was completely surrounded by steep mountains with no shoreline except at the mouth, the only point of access. The lagoon was filled with very cold, dark water and the edges were covered in vines that reached up or grew down from the dense vegetation.

Getting to the lagoon was a very slow bumpy ride through-not over-a dugout trench road. The truck I was in got stuck at one point and we had to walk the rest of the way, lugging the coolers and chairs. When I finally looked up, it seemed to me as if a giant had punched a hole through the mountains until he got to water. I was told that some Americans had visited the lagoon years before and tried to reach the bottom but couldn't. No one knew for sure what formed it. Some thought it was formed by a pre-historic glacier.

The lagoon was the perfect size to go around and ski in circles. There were no other boats to compete with. I was preoccupied about what was in that dark water. The male members of the Fulco family said the water was quite safe, but I wasn't buying it. I was an accomplished slalom skier, and I wanted to be me and do what I wanted to do just once on this vacation. Part of me knew this would be my opportunity to show off and gain approval from Wita's family for my skills and daring. The problem was that I simply did not want to put my body in that water.

Hearing the high-pitched screams of the spider monkeys and the calls of the Toucans in the trees all around didn't help either. This was a rain forest and as usual, there were huge, hairy, disgusting bugs wherever there was open dirt. I could hear my aunts shriek when bugs landed on them, making it difficult to relax in the chairs they had positioned on the ground near the trucks at the mouth of the lagoon.

My younger cousins and I wanted to get on the boat, but there was no dock. We summoned our courage and climbed over boulders and walked through black mud and gnarled vegetation until we got close enough to the small power boat to climb in.

That's when and where I met Tomas. It was our first introduction. He had been busy getting the boat ready and filled with gas. To me, Tomas was clearly a man in his early twenties and I certainly didn't look at him romantically. While he had good facial characteristics, I was disturbed by the scars and sore red acne bumps that covered his face and neck. It was a disfiguring disease that reached almost to his chest. I immediately felt sorry for him.

There was no way I was going to kiss his cheeks in the customary form of greeting. He could sense my attitude and good naturedly assumed a little attitude toward me, with every right. I was judging him and his face based on something he couldn't control. Tomas was used to getting that kind of reaction and had developed a silly, almost goofy child-like personality as a way to help people feel comfortable with him. He made me feel quite comfortable very quickly.

We pulled skiers and took the young cousins for rides. When a skier fell, Tomas would say something funny to the rest of us on the boat. His jokes weren't really mean, they were kind of silly and made us laugh.

I remember Tomas made me feel welcome and accepted. He seemed to be a nice guy who was happy to pull people around the lake for hours under the hot sun. It didn't take long before I stopped seeing his scarred face and just enjoyed his personality.

Then it was my turn. Tomas didn't know that when I visited my father during summers, I skied almost every weekend at Lake Coatepeque.

I looked at the water and must have made a face. Tomas said, "Don't be a *pendeja*," which means asshole or bitch in El Salvador. I said, "Who do you think you are calling me a *pendeja*?" feeling quite disrespected. He realized the word meant something different to me and explained that in Costa Rica, calling someone a *pendeja* was like calling them a "scaredy-cat." It was his way of challenging me to get in that water.

Everything in me said "don't do it." It was very cold and dark water and I was afraid it would suck me down into its bottomless mysterious world of vines and creatures. The problem was that I really wanted to show everyone, especially Juliana, who had never seen me ski, just how good I really was.

So, I devised a quick strategy. I would put the slalom ski on in the boat. Then take the rope and slide into the water. I told Tomas. "The moment I get in the water, I want you to go full throttle."

"How fast do you want me to go?" he asked.

I replied, "Between 30-32 miles per hour. But don't worry about getting the rope straight; just gun it until I get up."

Tomas nodded but looked at me as if he wanted to ask a question. I ignored his look and made sure we had the same hand motions for faster, slower, stop, and go. I sat on the side of the boat, grabbed the rope and handle and slid into the lake. He watched me lean back as little as possible and position my ski.

I yelled "Go go, go, shit, go!"

He pushed the throttle forward and we moved fast. There was no time for the lag in the rope to straighten and pull me out of the water gently. A jarring force tore at my arms, but I held on. I was out of the water and I wasn't going to fall, was absolutely not going to fall for any reason. Tomas kept looking back at me, his mouth wide open. I pointed ahead and he did a quick turn as we had gotten too close to the edge. The corner of that turn was so close I could see the vines under the surface of the lake.

I was back in my world, the real world, doing what I do best. I knew everyone was watching as I maneuvered across the water, back and forth behind the boat, making sure there was big spray where I had been. We went around the lake again and again. I did what tricks I could perform without the risk of falling in.

When I was tired and done, I pulled myself along the rope to get as close as I could to the boat without getting hurt by the motor and yelled to Tomas to cut the engine. I sank and pulled even closer and took the ski off, all the while trying to keep my hands and feet as high as possible above the water. By the time I was finally in the boat — probably the fastest scramble ever witnessed by those monkeys — I knew I had proven myself and would never do that again. That evening, Tomas told me later that I was a really good skier. His praise was almost worth the price of getting into that dark abyss.

Back on the boat with the ordeal successfully completed, I could see that Tomas was tired and ready to get off the boat.

"Do you want to ski?" I asked.

"Sure," he replied. "But my Dad is on the shore." We both turned to look at Otto, who was paying no attention to our lagoon activities.

"I can pull you," I told him. "I do it all the time when I'm at my father's in El Salvador." I didn't tell him that I was used to driving all kinds of boats and often pulled my father and his friends.

Tomas seemed almost convinced, then explained, "You have to be really careful in this lake because of the vines. And it's smaller than lakes you've pulled in, so you have to make quicker turns than you're used to."

Actually, it was a simple little speedboat for the small lake, but he was very tentative. To build his trust, I said, "Before you get in the water, I'll show you that I can do it." I drove him around and demonstrated that I knew how to go fast and slow, back up and turn. I showed Tomas where I would take him around the lake. If it wasn't for the bugs near the lake's edge where we stopped, his mouth would have stayed open. He had never known any high-society girl to be that self-assured and independent. No girl had ever thought about what he wanted or offered to pull him; much less be able to do it. I think what most caught his attention was that I had put myself in his position.

I pulled Tomas around the lagoon six or seven times. He was an expert skier. When he was done, he took off his vest, yelled something in my direction, and dove down in the water. I sat there, not moving. I was not going in after him. He popped up to the surface and laughed and clowned around in the water to show us there was nothing to worry about. From the boat the cousins and I were happy to watch him play and we clapped for him. Having made his point, Tomas swam back to the boat and climbed in. We returned to a bug — tired family eager to go back to the ranch.

Dinner was a grand buffet in a rustic environment. There were torches to light the grounds and keep the bugs at bay. Music played as huge chunks of meat roasted over a fire pit.

We ate spread out in the house and around the yard. A couple of times that evening I caught Tomas looking at me and I smiled back, feeling only appreciation for his generosity and the beginnings of friendship. After drinks and dessert and agreements to meet again at the Fulco's home in Grecia, our group started the journey down those treacherous roads, this time in the dense, dark fog of late-night Costa Rica. I was too tired to worry much about staying alive. I couldn't fall asleep because of all the jarring and sliding, but it was easier to trust the driver when I couldn't see the primitive world we moved through just outside my car door.

The next day we visited the Fulcos at their secondary home in Grecia near San Jose. Like most homes in the area, it was surrounded by a high stucco wall. Guards kept watch and servants kept to the background. The house was near an old volcano that reminded everyone it was still alive by emitting the kind of sulfur that ate through silver. In that area, pewter was becoming the new standard in serving pieces.

Tomas's parents, Melia and Otto, greeted everyone warmly and busily hosted my extended family. We spent the afternoon talking and singing, and my Aunt Thelma, a former flamenco dancer, taught us some of her special footwork. Otto worked the barbeque while Tomas made sure no one was thirsty. My young cousins played around the pool but declined to swim because it didn't have a heater.

Tomas played with us and his particular attention to me made me feel important, without expectations, or so I thought. That was a new experience. It felt good. Really good. I had read about it in novels and seen it in movies but had never felt it before. Maybe I had undiscovered powers, like Zoryia.

After lunch, I took a glass of soda and wandered into the family game room at the back of the house. It had floor-to-ceiling dark-stained shelves along two walls filled with old-looking books and artful treasures from their travels around Europe and South America. I kicked off my shoes, stretched out on the long, over-stuffed black leather couch and admired the piano, dart board, and pool table. I had played and won many games on the pool table in the Wito's Atlanta basement.

I'll see if some of the cousins want to play with me, I thought just a fraction of a second before Tomas came up behind the couch, leaned over and asked, face upside down, "Do you know how to play pool?"

"HA," I laughed. I jumped up, grabbed a pool stick and made the first break. Again, I had caused Tomas's mouth to fall open in amazement. I loved it. Reactions like that were so rare with my family.

"Wow," said Tomas. He got right into the game and as good as I thought I was — he was certainly better. We played several rounds and I was able to win one of them.

Before it got dark, everyone found their way to the back yard and took photographs and videos to document the gathering. The pool challenge had built my confidence, evidenced by my hair flipping and flirty smile captured by Uncle Henry's videotape. It had been a good day. It would be a good day for Zoryia as well. She was getting older, too.

CHAPTER 7

End of Innocence

That evening, as we said goodbye to the Fulco family, Tomas offered to show me San Jose on nights when the family had nothing else planned. He lived in their primary residence, a compound of three spacious apartments in the city, surrounded by a thick and guarded high wall. I thought he was just a friendly guy looking for something to do. I knew I looked older than fourteen and was comfortable with friends who were older than I. I agreed to accompany him. Juliana and the Witos were pleased for me to go out with Tomas because he was part of our extended family. We went out several nights dining and dancing with his friends. I felt like an adult. He took my hand when we crossed the street and when we danced, he was always a gentleman. When it was time to leave Grecia, Tomas said goodbye, kissed my hand and said quietly that he hoped to see me again soon. I looked over at the Witos. They smiled at us.

As Wita had hoped, this trip was helping me to relax. I was an athletic hero to my younger cousins, a reflection of youth for my aunts, and more than just pretty to my uncles. I had enjoyed the flirtations of a young man and felt admired and welcomed by Juliana's family. My orange hair had almost grown out; only a few dappled tips remained. I was opening up and eager for more. Peter was there, but he was pretending to be Juliana's perfect husband and my perfect stepfather. And San Jose was a long way away from my father's cold stares and the confusing impossibility of meeting his expectations.

The final days of our family vacation were spent in the Santos' family compound, a series of attached apartments at Playa Escondida. It was a sparkling private bay surrounded by a lush green background of mountains in one direction and huge rocks in the other. Beyond the rocks at a distance I could see the main port and town of Punta Arena. The first days weren't too cold or too hot. The families relaxed on the beach, played games, and swam in the clear water. The sand was black, all volcanic, making all the other colors that normally decorate a beach stand out like mysterious gems. The water was like a pond, we could swim far out, but never recognize what ocean creature was swimming below us. I loved it. Helicopter and boat rides, fishing, and snorkeling kept us entertained. Each night there was a cookout or picnic served by the Santos' staff in their courtyard.

On the second evening, after taking a shower and getting dressed for the cookout, I went to Julia's room. She was two years younger but smart and sweet and I liked her. We talked for a while when I spotted a cute pair of white shorts on her chair. Her father, Pedro, was wealthy and she had expensive clothes.

"Can I borrow your shorts?" I asked.

Julia looked at me, smiled and said "Sure. They'll look good on you."

I took off my jeans, put the shorts on, and thought nothing more of it. I was happy the family was together.

This was what families do, I thought.

I was surrounded by cousins and people who seemed to have a really good time together. No one was being stuffy or disapproving. It was the happiest vacation I had ever had up to that point. Looking back, I can see why the hardest moments in life can seem harsher when the previous moments are the most pleasant of your life. I didn't have the luxury of such perspective on that night.

During early evening as the sun was setting and the torches were being lit, we gathered for dinner. Pedro, a small man with a receding hairline and large nose, looked at me, then down at my shorts as I walked past him to the buffet. He almost knocked over one of my youngest cousins as he marched over to Julia, sitting on the courtyard wall looking at the water.

"Why is Sydney wearing your shorts?" he bellowed with his arms extended, shoulders and hands up, as if he was about to slap her. Everyone who heard him stopped talking, looked at me and then the shorts. That was about half of the group.

Julia turned her head around and shrank back as she replied, watching Pedro's hands, "It's okay. I let her borrow them."

I didn't want Julia to get in trouble. I put my plate down and walked over to them quickly. Pedro's small black eyes were wide open and excited. His round face was redder than usual and his brows, which barely had any space between them anyway, were one angry scowl. I swear the man was shaking.

"I'm not going to get them dirty," I said defending Julia. "Teenagers share clothes, it no big deal. I'll take care of them. I'm not a seven-year old."

"I'm not worried about you getting them dirty, I don't want a dirty person wearing them," he said lowering his voice and looking around.

"What do you mean?" I asked, truly not understanding him. "I took a shower."

That's when Pedro leaned into my face and killed all of my newborn feelings of belonging.

Speaking slowly, he grunted with a snarl in his throat, "I don't mean *that* kind of dirty."

I had been through so many things with Peter that no child should ever experience, but they were hidden. Pedro's intentions were different. He wanted to kill my spirit, make me less of a threat to other men, and he knew just how to do it.

Pedro aimed his blow at my guilt. It didn't matter that I was a child. I was a dirty girl. It was all my fault. I had let Peter threaten and manipulate me. From the age of six, I had kept the secret. (To protect Juliana, not Peter). Now everyone knew about it and blamed me. Nothing would ever be said or done about Peter.

He was a man and would never be held accountable.

I wasn't a hero, a reflection, or more than pretty to anyone. I was the dirty girl they were forced to tolerate for Wita's sake. Pedro didn't embarrass me. He reached inside my just — opened heart and slammed the door shut. His action was a kind of murder. My relationship with Wita's family was over. I saw that with the purity of eyes just relieved of all hope. Wita's family was as contemptuous and resentful of me as my father's family — and they didn't even know about Peter.

Everyone pretended. Every kind word and caring gesture I had known was fake. Nothing was real to me anymore.

I went upstairs, took off the shorts and put them on the floor next to Julia's bed. Pedro had the servants wash them immediately. The hall bathroom was the only place I could be alone and cry, and I cried hard. Part of me had died. I wanted the rest to die, too. For the first time when I was upset, I didn't want anyone's attention. I just needed to be with Zoryia. I went back to my room and pulled out my journal, but the words wouldn't come. I had nothing to write. I felt worse than alone. I was nothing.

The only thing I could do was to pull everything back inside and become as numb to the world as I could. We weren't going to Atlanta for another few days and I couldn't even hold my head up. I had to figure out my approach. I had to find a way to keep anyone from noticing that I had died. The family was unchanged.

And I would never be who I might have been — had I never borrowed those shorts.

In the morning, perhaps the ocean sensed my mood — I had certainly thrown enough anger and despair into the atmosphere. The waves were high and slammed into the bay. Some of us were brave enough to swim anyway.

I just wanted to go out, away from them. Peter came up to me as I headed into the boiling surf. He took my hand and we waded out together. I had no energy to resist, and really didn't care. The waves hit us hard. Peter put his arms around my waist and held me close. Again, I didn't care what others were thinking or saying, I just didn't care. I turned around to see how far out we were when I noticed my Uncle Henry was filming us.

"Just part of the illusion," I reminded myself and again felt nothing.

Ski boats were sent out to bring in the weaker swimmers. I didn't feel the need to be rescued. In Peter's arms, I had never felt more physically safe — or as emotionally dead.

I knew that I was going to make him stop. Peter would never taunt, touch, or reward me again. My compliance was no longer for sale. The residual *mind fuck* that lived within me would be my challenge to overcome. But faced with what was waiting for me on that shore, riding those rough waves with the abuser, was all I had ever known. I was done and it just didn't matter.

Juliana and Peter flew back to Switzerland. I flew back to Atlanta.

Years later in Atlanta, when my own children were little, my husband, and I watched the San Jose vacation video with Juliana in our family room. The end of the video was of Peter and me in the rough ocean holding hands. When your stomach can't handle that falling out of the sky, sliding-down-a-corkscrew feeling, you need to find a way to feel better. I got up out of my seat shaking my head and started to walk away. My husband grabbed my hand warmly. I paused and said, "I don't want to watch anymore and I'm taking the kids to bed."

When I returned, the video was over and Juliana asked, "How abused could you have been if you were out there having fun with Peter? We had some great moments."

I looked at her and realized she would never understand her part in it all. I nodded and smiled a little. It was not a sweet moment.

CHAPTER 8

Caught in a Net

After my hopes to be accepted by Wita's family were lost in San Jose, in Atlanta, the Witos were kind and patient, but I realized they were getting older and dealing with my deeply personal trauma was not good for any of us.

Spring break was in mid-April, just before my 15th birthday. I was exhausted from hiding, even if it was just in my mind. For my birthday, I just wanted to be with people who knew the truth and didn't hate me for it. I said nothing more, but Mom seemed relieved to let me go with Uncle Henry and his family to Panama City Beach, Florida, for the week. She had made plans of their own.

We left Atlanta Saturday morning and drove seven hours, including stops along the way, to the waterfront condo Henry had rented. Every hour on the road was an hour closer to the soft white sand we would be walking on. I knew how warm that beach was going to feel beneath my feet. I could already hear the little crunching noise it would make with each step. The water would be greenish blue with constant low waves, perfect for body surfing, floating, and swimming out to the nearest sand bar. I listened to *Straight Up* by Paula Abdul with my headphones. I imagined us lying on the long blue cushions typical of rented beach lounge chairs, building funny sandcastles with my little cousins Maddox and Zach, snorkeling above the crabs and fish, and seeing who could find the best shells to take home. They were just the right age for these simple things, and they would love doing them with me. We were going to have a great time as a family. Henry and Dawn would understand when I wanted to be alone, or hopefully, make some new friends.

The second Henry pulled into the condo parking spot, Zach and Maddox scrambled to get out of the car. As the oldest and their guest, I let the kids go first and ran behind them down the planked walkway, past the pool, and over the grassy area that led to the beach. We didn't walk down the final steps to the sand, we jumped down two or three steps at a time whooping and shouting. I was practically screaming with excitement, "We're here, we're here!"

People on the beach were packing up and heading toward their condos. It was time to clean-up for dinner. We had just arrived and were heading toward the waves. We dropped our flip-flops on the sand and ran into the water as far as we could go and not get our shorts wet. Nothing in a long time had felt nearly as good to me, as we walked on the wet packed sand, right where the waves play tag with the shore. Slushing through washes of shallow, foaming water, I kept an eye on Maddox and Zach trotting ahead of me. I was in heaven, literally. I breathed in the sunset colors and the sound of seagulls squawking for their supper. The gulf air was salty sweet and brushed across me, streaming my hair toward the dunes. Nothing, absolutely nothing, disappointed.

It was hard to turn back, but it was getting dark and I didn't want Henry and Dawn to worry. We took the lobby elevator to the third floor, walked down the open corridor and found our condo.

Henry was on the balcony taking chicken off a small gas grill. Dawn had set the table and placed a foiled-wrapped baked potato and a dinner roll on each plate. A tossed salad filled a large bowl in the middle. It all looked so festive on the red checkered plastic cloth she had thrown over the balcony picnic table.

"Perfect timing," said Henry. His ruddy skin was more reddened from the heat of the grill. "He didn't want to have to come after you," said Dawn, faking a laugh and taking a long drink of white wine from a tea glass. I noticed the wine bottle was almost empty and a full one sat beside it.

"Can I have a glass?" I asked politely, knowing she would give it to me without pause — once she was a few glasses in. Dawn poured a half a glass of white wine and handed it to me. Henry watched but said nothing. He knew I drank wine with dinner at home if Juliana was having some.

To the right of our balcony, the sky grew more golden as the sun found its way into the water. I sensed that great new adventures were possible for Zoryia and me. The kids told Henry and Dawn about our adventures on the beach. I smiled and nodded my head, letting them run the show. Maddox pulled some shells out of his pocket and put them neatly beside his plate. Henry examined them and commented on each one as if he were an authority.

After dinner, I helped with the dishes and excused myself from watching the new *Honey I Shrunk the Kids* videotape they had brought from home and already popped into the condo's VCR.

I went to my room and locked the door. Not that I was afraid of anyone watching me here, it was just instinct. My room was the smallest, but it was on the beach side. I silently thanked Henry and Dawn for that consideration. The window screens were locked, and we were on the third floor, so I decided it would be safe to turn the little handle and crank my windows wide open. I had been too excited about going to the beach to sleep much the night before. The bed was soft, the linens fresh and clean. I listened to the waves for only a moment, then woke up and smiled at the sunshine streaming across my bed. I felt my backside and it was dry! I knew I was getting better and decided to start a happy Zoryia adventure later today. Maybe on the beach. We deserved it.

The family was in the middle of eating eggs, fruit, and toast when I joined them in the small dining room. "Coffee or milk, Sydney?" Dawn asked when I sat down. "Coffee, please," I replied with a big smile.

"Well, you seem happy today," Henry chuckled, happy that I was fitting in and not acting like a defiant teenager one minute and withdrawn the next, as I had been before my secret life in hell became family knowledge.

"I am happy. Really happy, Uncle Henry. I want you both to know how much I appreciate being here with you. It's perfect and just what I needed," I said, leaning over to give him a hug. I turned to Dawn and said, "And I want to show you my appreciation by cleaning up the kitchen so you guys can go enjoy the beach."

Dawn grinned and with a little lift in her shoulders said, "Well, I did want to go for a walk before the sun gets too strong. And I'll get the lounge chairs and swim with the kids. You come down when you are ready."

My cousins pushed back from the table with a shout "Yay!" and ran to get their bathing suits on.

"I will, I said. "I feel like writing on the beach today, and maybe see if I can play volleyball if anyone shows up at the net."

"Okay!" Henry and Dawn said at the same time, smirking at each other as if they shared a secret. "We'll call your mom tonight when we get back from Captain Anderson's," said Dawn.

My face must have dropped because Captain Anderson's was not my favorite place to eat in Panama City, but they liked it, so I shrugged with a small smile. *After all*, I thought. *We have plenty of time to go to my favorite restaurant later this week.*

Henry patted my hand and said, in his best patient doctor's tone, "You don't have to go with us if you don't want. There's still some grilled chicken in the fridge. And you have some spending money, right? You could walk down to The Pavilion and get something there. I left a key for you by the door."

Pleased by his confidence in me, I replied, "Oh, okay, thanks!"

I cleaned the kitchen as quickly as I could, then changed into my favorite bikini. With my beach bag packed, I turned off the lights, grabbed my key, stepped into the corridor and locked the door behind me. "This was my day and I could spend it any way I wanted!"

Henry and my cousins had set up beach camp in front of the condo about four yards from the water. I plopped my bag on the empty lounge chair next to them but pulled it a few feet away from the umbrella. I wasn't ready for shade. Henry grinned and tossed me a bottle of sunscreen and a can of Coke. I fixed my towel, sat down, and took a few sips. I thought about writing. *No, not yet*, I looked around. *I want to remember all of this.*

People streamed around us carrying coolers, blankets and loud boom-boxes. They walked the edge of the water, going somewhere, or nowhere, in both directions. Some walked briskly for exercise, others walked slowly, pausing to gaze at the water. Some played Frisbee, others practiced their boogie-board skills. Fat, thin, muscular, pregnant, old, young — I watched them all. *Some women shouldn't wear bikinis*, I laughed to myself, "*and most of these men need to cover up more!*

Henry panned the people with his huge, expensive video camera. He and I laughed at some of the sights at the same time, so I knew he was thinking what I was thinking. At 10:00 a.m.sharp, music blasted the beach from huge speakers above the hotel pool area. *This place was made for everyone to have a good time*, I thought. *God created the beach; people created the entertainment.* I laughed at my very mature realization and made a mental note to include it in Zoryia's adventures. No one played at the volleyball net behind us, but it was early, and I wanted to get some sun before showing off my varsity skills. But first, I pulled the disposable *FunSaver* Kodak out of my bag and took some shots to show Juliana.

That morning, only a few clouds shaded the sun, but it wasn't too hot. I rode waves near the shore with my cousins and showed them how to use the snorkels and masks their parents had brought. We made three sandcastles and stuck small shell pieces on them for decoration. Maddox dug moats and Zach filled them with sea water. I finished each one with a dusting of dry white sand for sparkle and pushed pieces of grass into their highest points for flags. I took a picture of each castle and the kids covered in sand for Juliana. It was my idea to name the castles Nervinia, Jestaville and Opolosa, the fantasy lands each of us secretly ruled. My cousins loved that idea. I decided it was time for another Coke and went back to my chair. Maddox and Zach decided it was time to get back in the water.

Dawn stayed at the beach for another hour, swam a bit, and then went back up to the condo. "I need to make lunch," she said when I protested. "I want all of you to come in before noon. The sun is too strong, even for you, missy," she said pointing to me. "You can come back later."

After lunch, she and Henry took my cousins to the Panama City strip to ride the rollercoaster, eat cotton candy and play arcade games. I went back to the beach to get a deeper tan. I also wanted to meet some of the older guys we had passed coming down the walkway as we headed up to the condo. Two of them had looked at me and smiled. One of them was carrying a volleyball and a beach bag. The other was carrying a cooler in each hand. I thought he was very cute.

Back at the beach alone, I turned my chair to watch the game. There were six guys and two girls, and they all seemed to be friends. Trying not to be obvious, I took a few photos of the game.

They don't want me to join them, I thought. *But they don't know how well I can play.* I realized it was a conceited thought and decided to just enjoy watching the game for now. *Maybe later I can find a way to get invited*, I thought watching "cute guy."

Five points in, cute guy made an impressive spike to score. Both teams applauded and shouted in appreciation and, caught up in the moment, I whooped out loud and threw my fist in the air in a triumphant gesture. It's just what I do when I get excited about winning a hard point. Cute guy said something to his friends, and they stopped to take a break. Feeling a little embarrassed, I got up and walked toward the water to go for a swim, but cute guy was jogging toward me, so I waited.

He stopped right in front of me with his hands on his hips. "You want to play with us?" He was a head taller than me with lots of muscles. I noticed he was breathing a little hard and his chest glistened with manly sweat. In that moment, I thought he was the best thing I had ever seen. And he had noticed me!

"Yeah," I replied, secretly thrilled. "That sounds like fun."

"Can you really play? Or should we go easy on you?" He smiled, tossing his long dirty blond bangs to one side as he looked up and down my body. I didn't like the way that made me feel. *Maybe he's just judging how good a shape I'm in*, I hoped.

"Of course," I said, trying to sound cool and confident, but not stuck up. "I've played since I was a child, and I'm on my school's varsity team." That, I thought, would make him think I'm closer to his age.

"I'm Sydney," I said extending my hand.

"I'm Brad," he smiled taking my hand. I liked his nice smile and perfect white teeth. He pulled me beside him, paused and smiled at me again. We turned and ran to the net.

His friends finished their beers, decided teams with me included, and started playing. I showed them I wasn't afraid to serve or cover the net. My team won. Brad's team lost. I was happy with that outcome because if I had been on his team and we lost, he would think I had caused it.

We started playing again. I stopped looking at Brad or thinking about him. I was playing volleyball and my team was going to win. Three games and four beer breaks later, whichever team I played on won. *Maybe*, I thought, *because I wasn't drinking beer*. Thankfully, they had included a jug of water in one of the coolers.

After the third game, I sat down on the long pine log on a nearby dune that served as seating for spectators. Brad sat down next to me and plopped his cooler by his feet. "Thanks for asking me to play. That was fun," I said. He put his arm around my shoulders and pulled me in for a hug. His arms were strong.

"I knew you'd be good luck," he said, leaving an arm around my shoulders while he took a long drink from his beer. I laughed and looked away from him. I wasn't sure how I felt about his arm around me and I didn't like the way he smelled, but I was excited that he seemed to like me, so I didn't say anything.

Brad told me that he and his friends were sophomores at the University of Maryland. I knew I'd never see him again when we went back to Atlanta. And I didn't want him to know I was only almost fifteen. This was my fun day at the beach. No one needed to know anything about it. But I didn't want Henry to come looking for me. He laughed and pointed when his friends started playing another game without us.

Around five o'clock, they started packing up. When Brad didn't move to help, they shouted for us to "Come on!"

"It's getting late," I said pointing to the waves. "The tide is going out and I promised to help my aunt make dinner." It was a lie, but I thought it made me seem smart and responsible.

"Okay," Brad shouted back. I stood up and his arm fell away. For some reason I felt relieved.

"Hey, Sydney?" Brad asked, cocking his head in that way again.

"Yeah?" I replied, turning to see him standing so close to me we could have kissed. I shivered. I wasn't comfortable with this kind of attention. He ran the palm of his hand down my left arm and took my hand. "You're trembling," he leaned in to my ear and spoke softly.

I looked down and took a step back. "I'm just tired and the wind is getting stronger."

He dropped my hand and said, "Sure, you need to go. But there is going to be a bonfire on the beach near the Pavilion at ten o'clock tonight. Do you want to come with me?"

I thought for a minute. Henry said I could do what I wanted for dinner tonight, but the bonfire at another beach would keep me out late.

"That would be fun," I said, smiling at him. I could see him again and we wouldn't be alone.

"I just need to make sure it's okay with my aunt and uncle. I think they wanted me to babysit tonight." *Good one*, I thought! Now he really thinks you aren't old enough to hang out with them. Brad fished another beer from his cooler, popped the top off with his thumb, and downed it in one long drink. I watched his neck muscles move the beer down his throat. Even his throat was fascinating.

"Suit yourself," he said, swaying a little off balance. "Go on now," he gestured with the bottle. He reminded me of a drunk commanding his dog to get home.

"Okay, see you later," I said. My feelings were crushed by his manner, but I tried to sound happy and upbeat. I ran back to my chair, pulled my bathing suit cover on, grabbed my bag and walked as fast as I could up the beach and up the walkway. I didn't look back at him. I just wanted to go in, take a shower, and see what I could wear to the bonfire. If Henry and Dawn were still in the condo, I could go eat with them at Captain Anderson's and talk them into letting me go for a little while.

When I got to the condo parking lot, I thought about using the elevator, but decided it would be faster to run up the outside stairwell. The lights weren't on just yet, it was getting dark, but I could still see in the twilight. I hesitated but was too excited about Brad's invitation and started sprinting up the stairs.

I made it up the first two flights when I heard Brad call, "Wait a minute," to me from below. I stopped and turned to see him climbing up the stairs. I was surprised but glad that he had followed me.

He must really like me, I thought, waiting for him to catch up. I smiled and said, "Hi," when he reached the step below me.

Without a word, Brad grabbed my shoulders and kissed me really hard on the mouth. Shocked, I tried to pull away, but he grabbed the back of my hair with one hand and pushed me against the stair wall with his body. I pushed back against his chest, wondering what was going on. He knocked my hands away and kissed me again hard. He reached down into my bikini bottom and grabbed me. He pushed a finger into my vagina. It hurt. Peter had done that to me too.

"You are so wet," he gasped. "I know you want me," he snarled. "You want me to fuck you, you little cunt!"

"Stop it! Don't! Let me go!" I screamed as loud as I could, praying someone would hear. I hit his arms and kicked his legs to get away. He said nothing but pulled his free hand up and slapped my face. Shocked, I stopped struggling. He took that moment to throw me down and himself on top of me. The back of my head hit the edge of a stair and I couldn't move. I couldn't breathe. I could only feel him holding me down.

Brad pulled my bikini bottom down and off one leg then pulled his trunks down fast while lying on top of me. I tried to scream, but this time nothing came out. That's when I felt him pushing hard to get inside me. When he did, I could feel the skin on my back ripping against the concrete and his penis ripping apart my insides. It hurt and it burned. My head hurt. My back hurt. Everything hurt. I could not believe this was actually happening. I closed my eyes. I wanted it to be over. He pounded inside me until he was done. No one came to help.

He got up and was gone. I was in too much pain and shock to cry. I had to get up but was shaking too much to control my arms and legs. I heard a car pull up in the parking lot and people laughing. I grabbed my things and crawled to the next landing and curled up in a ball in a corner. If anyone found me, I would say that I had slipped and hurt myself. I hugged my knees and cried silently until I stopped shaking enough to look up. The stairwell lights were on. I got up and quietly found the condo door and let myself in, grateful no one was there. I was alone.

I took my bag to the bathroom and got in the shower. All the cuts on my head, back and legs stung as the water washed my blood down the drain. I washed crusted blood from between my thighs. My body shook and shook. I washed my bathing suit and cover. I turned the hot water up until I could barely stand it. When it ran cold, I stepped carefully out of the shower, wrapped a towel around me and made sure there were no signs in the bathroom of what had happened. I went to my room, locked the door, got in the bed with the wet towel and fell asleep. During the night, I heard someone trying to turn my doorknob.

The next morning, I had a hard time getting out of bed. I was sore and stiff in every part of my body. I dressed in the sweatpants and long-sleeve T-shirt Juliana insisted I bring to keep from getting sunburned. The family was eating breakfast.

"There you are, Sydney," Uncle Henry said. The concern in his voice was clear to me. "I tried to offer you some banana-cream pie from dinner last night, but you didn't answer." I just stood there trying to keep my trembling under control. *He can't know!*

"Are you all right?" Dawn asked. My cousins were watching TV in the living room. Everything seemed normal enough.

"I must have eaten something at the Pavilion that upset my stomach," I mumbled, wanting to just disappear.

"Why don't you go sit on the couch and I'll get you some ginger ale and saltines. That will be good for your stomach," said Dawn. "Hey guys, go put your suits on and let Sydney have the couch."

My cousins jumped up and ran to their room to change. "Can we rent boogie boards today?" they asked. "Sydney can show us how to ride them."

"Not today," said Henry. "Maybe tomorrow when she's feeling better."

Dawn handed me the soda and crackers. "Please put it on the table," I said, rubbing my stomach, scared that she would see my hands shaking.

"I'll check on you in an hour," said Henry, putting two Tylenol on the table next to the glass. "Take these if you need them."

I was glad Henry seemed concerned about what I needed and most importantly, had no idea what had happened.

I stayed in bed all day. I hurt. Between my legs, my back, my head, legs, arms, even my hands were sore. The Tylenol did not help at all. I kept wondering why I didn't use the elevator. It was my first thought, but why did I go up the stairs? I knew it wasn't as safe. Why didn't I fight harder? Why did I let it happen? Why didn't I use the elevator?

There was nothing left of me or in me, only the privacy of my room and the sound of waves just outside my window. Funny, until that moment, I had not heard the ocean since the volleyball game. I opened both windows as wide as I could to let the sound and sweet salty breeze fill me up with something clean and beautiful. I sat at my small desk, watched the sky, listened to the ocean and waited for sunset.

With the back of my hand I wiped my tears, then dropped my head, turning my face to the window. My own touch brought my mother into the room. It was her habit to comfort me by brushing the back of her hand gently down my cheek. A seagull squawked nearby. A strong, late-afternoon breeze rustled the open pages of my journal on the desk where I left it yesterday morning. The purple ribbon bookmark lifted with it, and its round crystal pendant, still hanging over the edge of my desk, twirled a little. I moved my left palm in front of the crystal to catch the rainbow colors on my hand. I knew Zoryia was waiting for me and I needed her comfort now.

"I don't have that kind of power," Zoryia protested, pulling against the vines.

"Yes, you do. You are more powerful than this mandragon. Stop resisting and start thinking about what you want. And with that thought she stopped fighting against the vines. "I want to be free. I am free. I am free to go. I want to go home. I am going home. I am running up the hill to Andor, safe and free."

I got through the week, playing up my stomach flu. I didn't have to go to the beach. I hid my bruises under a wrap at the private condo pool. No one knew. My skills at assuming the colors of my surroundings were highly honed and at play.

Later that summer I decided to move to San Salvador to live with my father. I had lived with him and his new family several times before and was well aware of what I had to do — who I had to be.

CHAPTER 9

Influence of the Rose

Regardless of who raises you, the man who released his sperm into your biological mother shapes and influences the quality of your life. His DNA is half of your DNA. His preferences and the choices he made impact you whether you are aware of it or deny it. Who you are as a person, your mind, heart, and especially your self-esteem, is influenced by this man to some degree. There is no escape from the fact that he existed. He had a huge impact on your mother. You were born. Even if you were born from artificial insemination or adopted by wonderful, loving parents, his presence or absence affects your existence today.

Such is the first half of the nature/nurture equation of human existence. How well you were nurtured is the second half of the equation. It is extremely complex. Who you are now, and who you want to become, springs from the depths of your own unique equation. We share this amazing complexity with every human being who lived before, lives today, our children, and the children yet to be born.

While we may live with a loving biological mother and father, a father's influence on us can be elusive. Whether we are his son or daughter, or he is the authority figure in the family or not, there is a very specific place in our hearts that needs what only this man can give. Beyond nature, we need his nurturing. We need connection with him and a very basic sense that he approves of us being alive.

Without it, we have no choice. We become dependent on others to give it to us. Our mothers and other family members can be an extremely important part of our equation, but unless they are very stable, secure in their own lives and generously dedicated to our nurturance, no matter how well meaning, they will not be able to fill this void. While they may love us, family members can be immersed in their own concerns and confused about what it is that we really need. In some cases, like mine, how we appear is more important than how we really are. If the world thinks we are happy and successful, then we get to survive. Reality was the enemy to my family.

For a young woman scared to tell the truth about the reality of her life, there was nothing for me to do but wear the colors of my family. When I told them the truth about Peter and was sent to a therapist for counseling, I painted pictures of rainbows, butterflies, and smiling family members. Ten years of sexual molestation, and being raped by a stranger, was more than I could handle. I needed to leave. I needed to have fun. I needed my father. He agreed that I could stay with his family and go to school in El Salvador. I was elated.

But the love I needed from him was not his to give. My father wanted wealth and power. In the end it cost him everything.

Zoryia had the power to glow. As a good chameleon, I had the power to choose the colors of the moment. It would have to be enough.

On the plane to El Salvador, I sank into the seat and again, I wanted to cry. No, I wanted to scream! But I was too tired to do either. I closed my eyes as we leveled out above 20,000 feet. The ding of the intercom sounded twice. I sighed, pushed the button and leaned my seat the full one inch back. The man behind me grunted. I have invaded his five inches of space. Well, he could deal with it.

I turned to my left and loosened my seatbelt to feel less constrained. The older lady with kind brown eyes who sat next to me smiled. We seemed to share the same thought about the man behind me. I rolled my eyes and she winked back.

The lady reached down and pulled her knitting out of her carry-on. The yarn was a soft rose pink. My thoughts stopped. I looked at the color, not understanding. I saw that she was knitting an afghan or small blanket. I had been surrounded by that color before. But where? It felt good. I closed my eyes . . . .

I was in my grandmother's bathroom in El Salvador. Titita, my father's mother, was washing my hair. My stomach hurt and I wanted her to tell me my father loved me.

I looked at the yarn again and sat back, immersed in warm water in a rose pink tub surrounded by rose pink tiles, a pink toilet and matching sink.

I was ten years old, visiting my father during the summer. Helga, my stepmother, was pregnant and I was scared my father would love the new baby more than me. If he found out about Peter, he would never love me again. This was my last chance to make him happy. If he had any reason to like his new baby better, he would send me back to Juliana and Peter forever.

I saw my father on weekends. When he walked through the door, he kissed Helga and Eugenia, my baby half-sister, on the cheek. Then my father asked Helga what I had been up to and if he was satisfied with her answer, he kissed my cheek. If he wasn't, he would just look at me and tell me what I needed to do better, or how I should obey Helga. I always tried to be good, so very good. On this night they were going to a party. When I had asked if I could spend the week with his mother, Titita, he agreed it was a good idea.

I remembered how nice my father and Helga smelled when they left for the party. When we got to Titita's house, my driver walked me to her front door. She opened it before we could knock. Just seeing her made me happy. She stepped out, hugged me and took me inside. Titita was tall and full bodied — very graceful. She was dressed in a blue skirt, white cotton blouse and white slippers. Dark tendrils of hair flowed around the white ribbon that held the rest of her hair above her shoulders.

I had spent afternoons in town with her at her men's tailor shop. But this was the first time I would be alone with her in the house where my father grew up. It was a much smaller house than where he lived with his second family. It didn't have guards on the roof. But it was in a pretty neighborhood and lots of other kids ran around and played in the school yard, across the street.

She let me dance around the living room and library and touch the desk, dishes, pictures, books and lamps of my father's world when he was my age. I chattered on in English about everything I could think of and asked her about everything. Titita did her best to answer my questions. I pretended to be hungry when her cook announced that dinner was ready. But I was too excited to be hungry.

After dinner, she ran a bath for me in her bathroom. Everything in that bathroom was pink. I sat down in the warm water and soaked. I was in heaven. A dish of pink bath pearls on the side of the tub captured my attention. I took two of them in my hand to see if they were soap. They were soft and smelled like roses. When I squished them together, rose oil squirted out. I wanted to smell like this for my father when I got home so I rubbed the oil on my skin. I squished more into the water and the rest into my hair. I had to make sure I would smell good for days. I wanted to smell better than they smelled going to the party.

I slipped down into the water and let the oil cover me all over. This could make him love me. Maybe Helga could even like me. What could smell better?

Titita called from outside the door. "It's time for bed now, Sydney. Come on out."

I tried to stand up but I couldn't. I was too slippery to get out of the tub. Titita opened the door and looked at me. She didn't fuss, in fact she laughed. I loved her laugh.

"I'm too soapy," I said quietly, looking down at the drain, not sure how to ask for help.

"Oh, muñequita," she laughed as she helped me stand up. "What have you done to your hair?"

I smiled and shrugged, pointing to the dish. "These smells good. I want my hair to smell good for Father so he will love me."

Ay no!" said Titita raising her palms to cheeks. I watched her eyebrows lift as high as I thought they could go. She leaned over and touched my oily head. "You know your father loves you."

"He does?" I asked, wanting more.

"Of course, he does. He's your father. But we will never be able to get this out of your hair!"

I stood still not knowing what to say. I did not expect such a reaction from her. "But Titita, it smells so good. Father likes girls who smell good."

She bent down and held my face between her hands. Her dark eyes smiled at me but not her lips. I thought that was funny and I felt a little better because I knew I wasn't in trouble with my grandmother.

"Well," she said looking toward the pink bathroom cabinet. "I will try to get it out with some shampoo from America. We'll wash your hair every day until the roses are gone!" We both laughed.

Titita pulled the stopper out then ran fresh warm water. She left the bathroom and came back with a pitcher. As she gathered water from the spout and poured it over my hair, she gently massaged the American shampoo into my scalp.

"Muñequita, sometimes it's okay to try new things. But didn't you think using all the soap pearls was too much?"

"I just wanted to smell good for father." Titita rinsed my hair, lathered it up again, and said nothing.

On the fourth rinse, she lifted my chin, looked into my eyes, and said gently, "Don't you know that your father loves you no matter how you smell?"

"Okay," I nodded with a shy smile.

"Muñequita, what's wrong?" she asked.

"He has another daughter now," I shrugged, looking at the water running toward the drain.

"That's true, Sydney," she replied quietly. "But you are still his first born daughter."

I said nothing and continued to look at the drain. Titita gave me a final rinse. "Come out now. It will be okay."

I smiled and hugged my grandmother as she wrapped a towel around me. Not realizing at the time, I had never felt so safe in my life.

In my pajamas with a towel around my head, Titita led me to my bed and pulled back the covers. When I settled in, she sat next to me and held my hands.

"Muñequita, you should never feel like your father doesn't love you as much as Eugenia. You are his precious Sydney. I know he loves you. He talks about you so much!"

"He does?" I asked and giggled.

"Yes, you are very special to him," she sighed.

"Do you know why I have green stones in most of my jewelry?" she asked. "They are called emeralds. That is my birthstone. Your birthstone is the diamond, a precious gem. Every gem is very valuable because they are so hard to find.

"Are emeralds the green stones in your rings and necklaces?" I asked.

"Yes. One day, I'll leave each of my grandchildren an emerald for you to remember where your strength comes from. I just want you to be happy and to be yourself. Let's not worry about your father anymore. You are here to have fun and if you want, you can come help me in my shop."

"Yes, Titita," I solemnly agreed. "I didn't mean to make you mad."

"I am not mad at you. But you can be a daring young thing. And I love that about you!" Titita laughed and kissed my cheek. It felt good to be loved by her.

The airplane bumped and swayed as it found its way to the ground. It was, for a moment, more distant than my memory of Titita. I was always safe with her. I missed her and didn't want to go home then or now. When she died a couple of years later, I cried because Juliana and I could not go to her funeral.

I turned to the lady next to me and said, "That's a nice color." She nodded and said, "Why, thank you dear. I like it too." Titita's wisdom and love was the closest thing I had to Zoryia's mentor

— Rangi. *Maybe that's where he came from*, I thought, as I prepared to depart the plane.

It was a difficult decision to live with my father again. I could never tell him about Peter. I would have to be the perfect chameleon, again, and keep my feelings to myself. Juliana had told him about Peter. He just accused her of wanting more money from him. He had to deny it all because accepting the ugly truth would embarrass him, disrupt his place in society, and I would no longer be allowed in his world at all. I was learning — whether I realized it or not — that fitting in, rather than standing out, worked better for me.

Throughout that summer I kept my truth to myself and behaved as required. I did enjoy swimming and playing tennis at the club during the week and driving the boats and skiing at the lake house on weekends. My father came up on Saturdays by helicopter, making sure his appearance was noted by the neighbors. At the lake house, when he wasn't working, my father and Helga entertained their friends. That gave me the chance, while under the watch of my father's always standing guards, to party with the neighborhood kids down by the lake.

In the fall, I returned to the American School in El Salvador I had attended when I was younger. I reconnected with a few friends and focused on sports. I was strong and healthy from summer activities and physical challenges were my outlet, especially volleyball. I met Erik through volleyball. He was a year ahead and had been watching me. Erik brought me my favorite beverage after a game and continued bringing me what I needed and wanted through the year. He listened to me and made me feel important, cherished, and loved. He bought me little gifts he knew I would love. I told him everything about my past: Peter, Mom, and all about my Father and his family. I even told him how I had been raped on a condo staircase in Panama City, Florida, by a drunk college boy the previous summer. I had never told anyone about that, but Erik wanted to know everything about me. He was my best friend, confidant, and at that time, the love of my life.

At my father's house, I thought being a good girl would keep me in good stead. I was wrong. My stepmother Helga treated me like a guest she had to tolerate, not as a part of their family. My father traveled frequently and when he was home, he was involved with Helga and their two young daughters. He only had time for me when Helga gave him a reason to correct my behavior. I suspected she was threatened by me and my father's previous life. I didn't understand why my father was unwilling to be a father to me, unless it was to keep the peace with Helga.

Living in a cold and abrasive house was not the sanctuary I needed. Erik made the year bearable, but my father did not let me date him. I learned how to get past the guards and dogs when I wanted to, but one spring night, my father caught me sneaking back to the house after having dinner with Erik. I was grounded to my room for the rest of the school year and could only see Erik briefly between classes.

I decided to go back to Switzerland. I missed Juliana. Erik and I stayed in touch. Things would never be the same between us, but we were still in love. It hurt, it was unfair, and there wasn't anything we could do about it. Sweet sorrow, indeed.

Tomas had kept in touch with Juliana and me and repeatedly invited me to visit his family's home. As spring break approached. I told her over and over that I needed to get away and have some fun. She agreed to let me go to Costa Rica by myself. It would be better for me than hanging around the house for two weeks with Peter and no school. The Fulcos agreed to pick me up at the airport and take care of me until my return flight.

My big adventure didn't exactly turn out that way. Looking back now, with five children of my own, I cannot understand how a loving mother could allow a 16-year-old girl to fly halfway across the world, by herself, to visit with a 24-year-old man, even if she is staying with his family. And how could this mother continue to live with a man who had sexually abused her daughter for ten years and simply claimed that he had stopped?

CHAPTER 10

Spring Break in Costa Rica

I opened my eyes, stretched my arms and legs and rolled to my left side. The light from my windows was bright. For a moment, I hazily watched the shadows on my wall dance as tree shadows waved in a soft wind. As I woke up, I realized that today I will be flying from Switzerland all the way to Costa Rica on my own. While I had done a lot of international flying, I had never gone that far by myself. I knew the routine and I told myself everything was going to be just fine. I was 16 years old now and it was my big adventure. I was going to have fun,

Voices downstairs and the smell of bacon got me out of bed. Mom was making breakfast. I moved barefooted between my room and the bathroom. In our house, the heating system was in the floor. The carpet and tile were always warm even when the outside was covered in snow. It felt wonderful. But I was about to spend two weeks in a world where it was hot, wild animals roamed, and waterfalls splashed against large boulders and tiny ferns. I couldn't wait!

Showered and dressed in the carefully selected blue jeans, white shirt, and sweater I had finally decided on last night, I brushed my hair back until it parted on the left, not the middle, so people wouldn't think I was only Latino. Then I put on makeup, having mastered the ability to accentuate my eyes without getting too heavy with the eyeliner and shadow. Based on the reactions of my family and friends, I was doing a pretty good job.

Peter knocked on my door. I heard "Sydney," in Peter's friendliest voice. "I just want to say goodbye. Will you open up?"

For some reason I looked at the pictures of Erik stuck in the grooves between my dresser mirror and its frame. Another jab hit my stomach and swallowed. The back of my throat felt sore. I wished I was going to see Erik instead of Tomas. I wished Peter would drop dead.

As the good girl I was trying to be for Juliana's sake, I opened the door a crack and looked up at Peter. He leaned forward, smiled, and pushed the door open. I stepped backward into the room, keeping his 6-foot 3-inch, wiry red-haired body in front of me. "This is a big day for you," he said with a grin that I knew was fake. He didn't want me to leave, but he played the concerned stepfather role as best he could.

"I know," was all I said in reply with a sugary sweet smile on my face, just like his.

"You'll be going through three Customs at different airports. Do you have everything together, in one place in your carry-on bag?"

"I do," I said, pointing to my backpack, then putting my hands on my hips to keep as much space around me as I could.

"That's good," he said. "I don't want to have to worry about you getting detained." His eyes narrowed and I almost laughed out loud. Thinking about me being detained probably delighted him.

"I won't," I said, still smiling.

"Promise me you won't talk to any strangers, only the Customs Officials. You don't have to talk to anyone on the plane either, unless you want something from the stewardess," said Peter.

"Got it," I replied.

"Just have a good time, but behave like a lady. The Fulcos are being very nice to let you visit so don't get into any trouble."

"Right," I replied, no longer smiling. Peter was my trouble. And my father's unwillingness to love me like his other daughters.

I turned my head to look at Erik's pictures. "Anything else?"

"It's finally warmed up enough so I'm going to get out of your way and go ride my bike." Peter had stopped smiling too, but for an entirely different reason.

I said, "Okay, and looked at the open door. Instead of turning to walk out, Peter crossed the distance between us in one long step, wrapped his arms around me and hugged me tighter than any stepfather should. I pushed against him and said, "Goodbye."

He kissed my cheek, let go, smiled again, nodded, turned, and left my room. I slammed the door shut behind him, turned the old-fashioned metal key in the lock, and pulled it out of the hole. This key, at least, I could control. I wiped his kiss away with the towel I had used to dry my hair and let out a deep breath, not realizing I had been holding it.

My freedom starts now, I thought and put the last items in my luggage. All I had thought about for weeks was what I needed to wear to look grown-up and make a good impression on Tomas and the Fulco family. We would be going to restaurants and clubs in the city, visiting their friends, and whatever we decided to do at Rio Quarto. I wanted to look good, no matter what.

"Five minutes to breakfast, Sydney!" Mom called upstairs. Her voice and the smell of pancakes made me feel loved and cared for. It's hard to find Bisquick in Switzerland, but she always had a little stash for special occasions. I fluffed and smoothed my comforter and arranged my pillows just right, wanting to make her proud that I left my room in good order. With a last look around the room, I zipped my bags. In two trips I carried them all down the stairs and stacked them neatly in the front hallway.

I walked into the kitchen, almost too excited to eat. Mom gave me a plate, and we stood in the long, narrow kitchen and leaned against the countertop. We giggled and talked about my future adventures in Costa Rica and ate our American pancakes with Log Cabin maple syrup.

From the kitchen I could see the black upright Steinway Mom played when she was in the mood. I played it too sometimes, when I was alone. Neither of us talked about Peter.

As we packed her black Mercedes, I had an overwhelming sense that this castle, this cute Swiss chalet as I thought of it — was about to crumble. Despite the cleanliness and organization anyone could see from the outside, this small niche of paradise in Switzerland that seemed calm and perfect was going to crumble. It couldn't stand forever because it was nothing but a lie. Sometimes I just knew things I couldn't explain.

I was glad Mom was taking me to the airport. I was glad Peter had put on his boots and cowboy hat and tied up his pant legs and stuffed them into his long tube socks to go for a ride on his bike and enjoy the new fresh spring air. Why shouldn't he? Why should he be inconvenienced?

For now, it didn't matter. I was going to be an independent adult for the next 18 hours. I would make my own decisions. I would speak to strangers if I wanted to. I would handle Customs. I would get a window seat in the front of the plane. It was quieter in front and had a better view.

We pulled into the drop-off lane at the Geneva airport. "Remember everything we talked about, Sydney. Keep your money and your passport with you. And don't be afraid to ask the stewardess if you need something. Call me when you get there and don't talk to strangers. I love you."

"I know, I love you too. Thank you for letting me go," I said and gave her a big hug and kiss. *Thank you for letting me get out of here,* I thought.

We stacked my bags on the curb and a sky cap put them on a cart for me. I waved goodbye to Mom and pushed through to Customs. Without a hitch I made it to my gate and waited. I was assigned one of the first seats in the plane, right where I wanted to be. When we lifted off I felt another jab in my stomach but this time it was pure excitement. My adventure had begun and no one could bother me now. I felt something I had never really felt before and certainly not to this degree. I was in control and it was delicious. Though no one is really in control on an airplane, I was in control of me. I sat my seat back and watched out the window as we climbed. The stewardess brought dinner and I ate hungrily, not caring very much that it was airline food. We watched a movie and I was content in that little world in the sky. When the movie was over, I worried for a few minutes about what we would be doing in Costa Rica, but as it got darker and the cabin grew quiet, I fell asleep.

The next morning, the stewardess leaned over the young mother and child sitting next to me and touched my shoulder. I blinked from the light coming through the window and sat up straight. "Do you want eggs Benedict or French toast?" she asked with a French accent that I admired. "I see that you are alone. Do you need anything? Do you need help getting through Customs in Amsterdam?"

"No, thanks," I replied in English. "I can do it myself," I replied, smiling, trying to be firm but polite. "And I'd like French toast, I hate eggs Benedict. And orange juice, please." I was all by myself and I could be anyone to anybody.

When the tires hit the ground in Amsterdam, I gathered my things, freshened my face and hair, and as soon as the doors opened, was the first to proceed down the narrow corridor to the next leg of my journey. *I'm a young lady and I should have some coffee*, I thought. I felt like I could do anything in the world.

The coffee served at the tiny stand inside the gate where I waited was strong and their croissants were soft and buttery. The man standing next to me in line seemed to be in his late 40's and I thought he was handsome in his designer suit and tie. Just to start a conversation I asked if he was going to Costa Rica. We talked as we moved forward in the skyway and I was thrilled when he sat next to me on the plane, again, a window seat right in front.

"Well, if we are sitting together, I should introduce myself," I said extending my hand. "I'm Sydney."

"I'm Chris," he replied with a warm and firm handshake that lasted just long enough. It was the best handshake I ever had.

We talked about a lot of things, mostly about what my father did. I'm pretty sure he suspected that half of what I was saying was a lie, but I didn't care. It was going to be a long trip to Curaçao, and I wanted to have fun. So, I created what I thought would be a person of interest to this man. What I liked most about him was that he paid attention to me. No wonder I talked about my father.

We watched a movie, ate lunch and dinner, and ultimately breakfast. This time I choose Huevos Rancheros. It was disgusting. The eggs were rubbery from being frozen and the sauce was too spicy. I didn't make a fuss, as I wanted to seem mature to my companion. By the time we landed in Curaçao, I was hoping that he had not caught on to my lies. Then I relaxed because I knew we would never see each other again. I said goodbye to him at the gate and wished him luck with his business meeting in Curaçao. I walked quickly down the short terminal to catch my next and final flight to Costa Rica. It was a short flight and I was able to relax a bit before we landed. I went directly to the airport bathroom, stuffed my sweater into my carry-on bag, brushed my teeth, and made the long walk down the hallway to get my luggage and go through Customs. I remembered how the carousels in the San Jose airport were rickety and banged up and how some people's luggage tended to disappear. I was happy to see that my luggage had made it. I was disappointed that my companion was not there to help me.

A young Customs officer with greased black hair processed my papers, shook my hand briefly and said, "Welcome to Costa Rica." I said, "Gracias," in perfect Spanish and pushed my cart through the doors.

I coughed from the hot sulfuric air and remembered the smell and the weight of the air from my first visit to Costa Rica. But I focused on managing my cart as I weaved through the crowd, filled with the same people going the wrong way — vendors selling the same trinkets, food, and pamphlets of tour packages. I tried to ignore their assertive smiles and pleas to buy.

Taxi drivers dispersed themselves upstream and looked with their trained eyes for well-dressed passengers that paused in their steps or seemed hesitant to press forward. I moved as fast as I could toward the street looking for the Fulcos, but I wasn't moving fast enough to avoid two taxi drivers, each insisting that I ride with him. I didn't look at them directly, wanting to discourage their attention. I shook my head no and waved them away. Where were they?

I made it to the center of the curb and saw Tomas. He was waving his arms over his head across the street, laughing like a little boy. My cheeks got hot. I was glad that he was happy to see me. I waved back, but in that instant, I almost cried from worry. How can I keep him happy for two weeks? Did he know about Peter by now? Did his family?

CHAPTER 11

The Taste of Tongue

It was early afternoon in Costa Rica and the sun was on my face. There was nothing I could do but give him a big hug as we kissed one another's cheek. I was glad to be with him and this time I didn't care about the scars on his face. He was alone with the truck and I must have looked puzzled. "I had to bring the truck," he said. "There wasn't enough room for everyone so they're making dinner and waiting for us at home."

"What is for dinner?" I asked, feeling better at the thought of a home-cooked meal.

"My favorite," he replied. "Cow tongue." Fortunately, everything my father had taught me about being diplomatic and polite around important people no matter what, flooded my head. This was going to be one of those times. I didn't dare say what I was really thinking.

The hour-long drive from the airport to Grecia gave us time to catch up and talk about the two years since we had seen each other. I remembered how comfortable I had been with him as an older friend and forgot all about appearing to be a sophisticated international traveler. I told him things about living with my father in El Salvador. I talked about the Witos and about how crazy Mom was, in a fun way. Of course, he defended her because she had allowed me to come visit him. Tomas turned off the main road onto an eroded gravel dirt road.

"Not much longer, right?" I asked, remembering the route.

"That's right," Tomas replied, happy that I recognized the way. Within minutes we were driving through the country. I noticed how green everything was here. Colors popped out at me from the trees and lower vegetation. When we approached my favorite waterfall, where our families had taken pictures two years ago, I asked him to slow down. I wanted to watch the water flow into its rock-filled basin. The glimmers of a rainbow above the falling water reminded me of Colorado. I watched the falls as we passed and turned to try and remember it all. Tomas was silent until we lost the view behind us.

"It's all much prettier than I remember," I said quietly.

"So are you," he replied in a low voice. I smiled and blushed. I said, "Thank you," to my friend and looked away. His approval felt good. Tomas patted my knee. His touch felt reassuring, like friendship.

"Sydney," Tomas said in a solemn voice. I looked at him and replied, "Yes," in an equally solemn voice with a playful nudge with my elbow.

"Are you ready to have some fun?" he asked quietly. "Your mother said you needed to have fun and forget about school for a while."

I laughed a little at this and said, "Why, what do you have planned for us to do?" I was relieved that there were plans and not entirely up to me to find ways to keep him happy.

"You will see, my dear," Tomas replied, trying to seem reserved, then laughed out loud. "We are going to entertain you, my lady!"

"Really?" I replied excitedly. "What are we doing, and don't tell me you can't tell me."

He didn't reply for at least a minute as he focused on navigating the potholes. In that short time, I dared to hope that it was all going to be okay. The Fulcos liked me and wanted to make me happy.

"You'll find out," he said as the road smoothed out near Grecia.

"It had better be good," I laughed and smiled my best flirty smile at him. He smiled back and batted his eyes as if to say, "I can flirt, too."

In sight of the gates to Grecia he reached for my hand. I didn't resist. The long winding driveway was warmly familiar, lined with huge overhanging trees, a lovely canopy. The Fulcos had made a lot of improvements to the property. The driveway was paved, a guest house was being built, and new landscaping was everywhere.

We pulled into the front parking yard. Melia and Otto, the maids, gardeners, and cooks, stopped what they were doing and came out to the truck to greet us. I felt a soft pain in the back of my throat, swallowed and blinked. I did not want to cry unexpected tears. Tomas got out of the car, came around and opened my door. He extended his hand and helped me step onto the ground, as if I were a lady from a foreign land. His attention and this colorful group of people welcoming me to their home was exactly what I needed.

Melia, a petite woman with short reddish-brown hair, had the bluest of blue eyes. She was about my mother's age, but I remembered how her smooth, milky-white skin made her seem younger. A perfect widow's peak crowned her forehead and a tightly wound bun sat at the nape of her neck. At that moment she was smiling at me as if she knew something special was about to happen. I gave her a big warm hug and thanked her for having me in her home. I liked the perfume she was wearing — just enough to notice, not enough to call attention to. I didn't realize it at the time, but this was the Fulco way of demonstrating their wealth and refinement. Everything was tastefully done, and friends were always welcome.

Otto was taller than I by a head, stocky and muscular. His skin was dark and ruddy, and his salt-and-pepper hair was neatly parted to the side. His face was hard-lined however, with a strong German nose. If he wasn't smiling, he looked like he might be pissed off. His favorite conversational approach was to interview you as if you were applying for a job and, if it suited him, poke fun at your answers. Otto asked about my flights and the weather and how things were going in school in Switzerland and what I was going to do with my life. He got right into it, looking at me with dark, probing eyes. As a young guest in his home I was quite pleased to have his attention.

The house was completely open. There was no air conditioning, but a cool breeze ran through it every day. I heard thunder in the distance and knew that an afternoon storm was approaching. It rained every day for eight months out of the year in that part of the country. We were very close to the rain forest. As we talked, the thunder came closer and I could see lightning over the volcano. It was very dramatic, I thought. The air pressure grew with the mustiness of rainfall. I loved it.

One of the maids wearing a white work dress showed me to my room as Melia and the cooks finished preparing lunch. I put my things away in an elegant wood dresser and ran my hand down the fresh linens on the high queen-sized bed. Melia had put fresh flowers in my room, a few votive candles on the table by the side window, and candies in dishes lined with doilies. She had given me things she thought would help me feel at home. I was impressed. Mom puts out the best things we have for guests, but not quite to this extent.

Tomas called me for lunch, and I joined the family in the dining room. His brothers and sisters had arrived with their families and the two cousins I had met two years ago. I bent down to hug Di-ana's two little girls. They had grown so much. Their oldest daughter looked a lot like me and Di-ana's husband made a comment about it. I couldn't wait to get through the hello's, as I was starving. Tomas sat me next to him. A simple salad was served made of lettuce and cucumbers from Melia's garden that she tended, not her servants. The salad dressing was also homemade, a creamy dill with vinegar. I liked it so much I wanted to pick up the bowl and drink the rest of it. But I knew better.

Watching the servant retreat with the salad bowls to the kitchen, I worried about what was coming next. For a moment nothing happened other than Anita spilling her milk on the tablecloth. Her mother cleaned it up with her own napkin and poured her another, smaller glass. There was no yelling about how stupid she was. There was no upset, no look from Dino that said, "Just you wait."

The door to the kitchen swung open. A male servant, *he must be the cook*, I thought, placed a huge pot of something long and thin covered in red sauce in front of Otto. *Right out of the cow's mouth*, I thought. Tomas winked at me and smiled reassuringly. Somehow, he had felt my concern.

Otto cut the meat in small circular pieces while I watched intently. He walked around the table to serve me first, as their guest, and plopped a couple of pieces gently in the middle of my plate with a little bit of red splatter. I didn't think about the tablecloth. I took a long drink of water and reminded myself that I was going to eat all of it. I smiled and nodded in gratitude to Otto as he turned and proceeded to serve this delicacy to his delighted family.

Just as I hoped there would be more to choose from, bread, rice and my favorite, French green beans, were served by servants following in line behind the cook. I decided to start with the green beans first and keep the rice and bread for chasers. With two forkfuls of green beans eaten, and with courage bolstered by my great hunger, I carefully cut into a circle of tongue, closed my eyes and remembered as a child having to make myself eat something I absolutely did not want to eat. I started to take a small bite when Peter's voice screamed, "Eat the peas!"

I saw myself at eight years old, sitting at the kitchen table in the house in Woodstock, Georgia. I had eaten everything else on my plate except the peas. These peas were small, round, and green. The peas would taste like how old things smelled. Like things that had been old before I was born. I knew because I had been forced to eat them before.

I also knew that I had to eat the peas, or he was going to do something to make me. I looked at Mom with burning eyes. I wasn't going to cry because that always made things worse. I just wanted Mom's help in this situation. She was there. It wasn't like when only Peter was there. But Mom did nothing. She didn't see that Peter had a smirk on his face. I saw it and knew that if I didn't eat the peas, I would have to give Peter what he wanted at bedtime as punishment, and he wouldn't do anything nice for me.

I put one little pea in my mouth and my face drew up in disgust. I couldn't help it. Peter jabbed me with a fork on my forearm near my elbow and said, "Don't be a smartass." Mom just looked at him. Peter's son, Brandon, just looked at his plate.

Then I put a full fork of peas in my mouth. It would be better to eat them than to do what Peter really wanted. Every pea made me gag as they sat in my mouth. Pure steamed peas, no flavor or spices. Just old smelly peas. I swallowed looking at him. Hated him. I drank some water to make them go down. He kept looking at me with that smirk. I put more peas on my fork and swallowed.

One minute was all that it took for the peas to fly out of my stomach and land all over the table. And not just the peas. My whole dinner came up. That's when I got the reaction I wanted from Mom. I would never have to eat any food I didn't want to eat again.

That night was the first time I tasted Peter.

I shuddered and looked up, remembering I was in Costa Rica. The entire family was looking at me with expectation. *Everyone here is nice*, I thought. *They aren't trying to make me do anything.* I decided the adult thing to do was to try and enjoy the tongue. My father's voice insisted, "Do what you have to do to be polite. I won't have you embarrassing me in front of these people."

I took a bite.

It tasted a lot like a stew Mom made in the crock pot. Not so bad after all. And it's not tough, I realized with happy wonderment. I turned to smile at Tomas as I chewed to show him that I liked it. Actually, I liked the strong flavor of the red sauce. The tongue didn't have much taste of its own. I ate what I had been served and asked for more. "It's really good," I said with some surprise. Otto smiled and nodded at Tomas. Melia, clearly pleased, offered to teach me how to cook tongue. She had no idea I wasn't interested in learning how to cook anything. But I had passed an important test. I figured it was a guest-of-Costa Rica culture thing.

I wished my father could see me so grown up.

When dinner was over the family migrated to the outside porch. Servants brought coffee and dessert as everyone continued talking and catching up. An hour later when the clouds cleared, Otto issued the family's traditional challenge. The men changed into their tennis clothes and trotted down to the courts below the patio.

We, the ladies, followed and drank cocktails, watched, cheered, and harassed the men in friendly fashion as they completed three sets. The men teased and challenged each other without getting angry. It was all in fun. "This is how it's done here," I reflected happily. The sun fell slowly behind the distant mountains.

Without realizing it, I had begun to allow small feelings of finally belonging somewhere to circle around my heart. *I'm a young adult here*, I thought. *I am an equal.*

No one made a comment, or seemed to care, as I sipped two Pina Coladas. I didn't have a clue what was really going on. I was too grateful.

When the match, played under the court lights, was over, Tomas walked me to my bedroom. "Get as much sleep as you can, Sydney. You're going to need it for tomorrow." I was too tired to try and pry it out of him. "It's going to be a great day," he assured me. "I'll see you in the morning." He wrapped one arm around my shoulders, gave me a hug and kiss on the forehead, and walked to his room.

As I got into bed, I remembered my promise to call my mother. I rushed into the hallway and caught Melia going to her room. "I'm so sorry," I said. "Is it all right if I call my mother? I was supposed to call her when I got here."

Melia's face lit up and said, "Of course, Sydney. I should have insisted on it when you first got here. Please apologize to your mother for me."

Juliana answered in her best understanding mode. It was two o'clock in her morning.

"I knew Tomas would call me if anything was wrong," she said. I told her briefly about my flights, the tongue, and Tomas' mysterious plans. She insisted that she had no idea what it could be, but told me to enjoy myself, be a lady, and to call her in the next few days.

Something felt odd too when I hung up the phone. Maybe it was my easy, unconcerned conversation with my mother, or Tomas' mysterious assurances that bothered me. Something was up and I didn't know what to think. But everything had been so much fun I told myself not to worry. This was my vacation and I was going to have a good time.

I walked back to my room a bit confused and shut the door behind me. I started to get into bed but saw that the drapes were still open. I closed them and carefully checked the room for peepholes. Finding nothing, and actually feeling rather grown up, I pulled out my journal. It was time for Zoryia to feel grown-up, too.

"I would like a flask of your finest wine, kind sir. What is your price?" Zoryia asked the seller.

"One small flask is four doskets."

"How much for a large flask? I have a long journey ahead of me," she responded.

He replied uncertainly, looking at her closely. "You are alone?"

"I didn't say that," she replied with confidence, realizing he questioned her age.

"Very well, then, a large flask is double."

"I will you give you six and a half doskets at the most, sir," she said standing as tall as she could.

He eyed her up and down taking his time to get a good look at her. "I will give it to you for seven doskets, if you tell me what you put on your skin to make it glow like that."

"If I tell you, you will give it to me for six dockets," she smiled coyly and swayed back and forth.

"Huh, you drive a hard bargain, young maiden. Tell me your secret first."

"I will tell you the truth sir, put the wine on the table and I'll put my coin beside it and I will tell you."

He nodded, turned, selected a large flask from the shelf behind him and smartly dropped it on the table between them.

"Can you change a silver mullon?" she asked, keeping her gaze on his eyes.

He grunted, "Eh," and reached below the table for change. She put her silver mullon on the table. He picked it up with one hand and laid the change down in its stead.

"Perfect," she smiled as she picked up her flask and her change. "Now, I will tell you how I make my skin glow as agreed."

The seller stood there in anticipation of a secret that could make him some profit.

"Andor," she called to him. "Come here."

The moment Andor was by her side, she grabbed his reins and turned back to the seller.

"There is no secret potion, I was born this way," she said almost laughing. "And that's the truth."

I turned off the lights and waited for my eyes to adjust to the darkness. I walked to the window, lifted a curtain enough to peer out. I saw only the faint lights of the compound. No shadows, nothing moving. I took a deep breath for courage and closed the drapes tightly. I got into bed with some confidence that no one was going to watch me sleep.

CHAPTER 12

Fitting In

A light rap at my door woke me up. I pulled on my robe, ran my fingers through my hair, and opened the door. Tomas, in his pajamas, looked at me with a sly smile. *He's up to something,* I thought.

"Good morning," I yawned and smiled. "Did I oversleep? What's going on?" I asked the last question to see what I could get out of him.

"Nothing much," he replied. "It's time for breakfast. Oh, and we're going to celebrate your birthday on Friday, here at Grecia." He waited for my reaction. I just stood there, hoping for more information.

"It's a small party with our family and some friends. Not a big deal. We've already made most of the arrangements, but I thought you should know."

Yes! I thought. *I knew it!* My smile grew wider.

"We'll need to help my mother and pick some things up for the party. Is that okay?"

"Absolutely! We should help anyway we can," I said.

"But today," he said, "we are just going to have fun. Would you like to go to our country club in San Jose?"

"Yes, I would, that sounds good," I replied, trying to be cool.

"We can play tennis and you can meet some of my friends who are coming to the party."

"I'd like that," I replied.

"Good," said Tomas. His eyes were bright. "When you are ready, come have some breakfast."

I looked past him down the hall. The family was headed to the terrace in their pajamas.

"Can I wear this?" I asked.

"Certainly," he replied.

"Give me a few minutes," I said. "I need to brush my teeth."

"Take your time," said Tomas. "We'll see you on the terrace."

I put on my house shoes, crossed the hall to the bathroom and closed the door. When I came out I walked straight to the terrace.

I stopped in the doorway, eager to join them at the table but I didn't know where to sit. Melia waved me to the empty place across from her and next to Tomas. I was secretly pleased to hear that the subject under discussion was my party. Melia was going over the final plans in hushed tones with Dino's wife. She looked up and winked at me but did not include me in the conversation.

The family's relaxed start to the day was disarming for me at first, then after a few minutes I began to enjoy the comfortable, happy chatter.

Everything is so easy here, I thought, relaxing in my chair, taking in the laid-back atmosphere that was morning at Grecia.

A servant placed a cup of hot black coffee in front of me and I took a sip. Without milk or sugar, it was more delicious than any coffee I had tasted before. Tomas' brother Mario explained that the coffee was grown in the back of the Grecia compound. The servants roasted the beans every morning while the family was still sleeping. It was as fresh as coffee could possibly be, and to me, it tasted like heaven.

As I sipped, I lifted my face to a light, cool breeze and watched the soft morning sun shining through the trees. There were no clouds. It was a lovely place to be and I wanted the morning to last all day.

Otto came to the terrace and sat at the head of the table near the door. He was dressed to go to the family plantation, in a white T-shirt, khaki shorts, and boots. With Otto in place, the servants brought steaming platters of eggs, rice and beans, sausages, tamales and peppers, as well as fruit, breads, cheeses, and various kinds of salsas and preserves to the table. I loved how in Costa Rica, breakfast was a feast.

Otto put some red and green coffee beans on the table and told me to try some. I looked at him as if it might be one of his tricks. He repeated in a less directive voice, "Try it." I took two and put them in my mouth. The beans were bitter. Otto said, "Those are from the same coffee beans you are drinking."

I spit the beans into a napkin as gracefully as I could, trying to hide my grimace. Then I asked, "They are bitter, how can they taste so good as coffee?"

Otto explained intently, "It's a long process. Our coffee beans are grown, harvested, and roasted very carefully. It's an art, actually and most people don't know or care how their coffee is really made."

I nodded to let him know I was listening as intently as he was speaking.

"If you roast and brew them just right, only the flavor fills the water and the bitterness stays in the beans. And so, you know, Melia is part of the Avila family, one of the most successful exporters of premium coffee beans in all of Costa Rica!"

I replied, "Oh, I didn't realize that," and smiled sweetly at Melia.

"But no matter their quality," Otto said, "unless you roast them on the same day that you drink it, you are drinking coffee made from old beans."

As the Minister of Exterior Commerce, Otto facilitated the production and exportation of all Costa Rican produce. I saw that Otto was as proud of his responsibilities and authority as my father was of his. *They could be friends*, I thought, then remembered why that could never happen. The Fulcos were tied to Mom's family.

While they talked about coffee, Melia decided that enough party plans had been made and it was time to spill the beans, so to speak. She wanted to see my face light up.

"Sydney, we want to celebrate your 16th birthday because you are a woman now in our tradition. It's important that your coming-of-age is noted and celebrated with the right people." She paused for effect, then continued before I could say anything.

"My family is coming. They are eager to meet you. The Nuinta family is coming, they own part of Imperial Beer. I think you went to school with the youngest brother who lives in San Salvador. The Vegas and Taquinas families are coming. And the Guerrera family. They are important local coffee and sugar plantation owners."

I thought carefully about what all this meant, and what it would mean to my father if I had the opportunity to tell him.

"Oh my gosh, Melia. I don't know what to say except thank you. I appreciate it very much. I'm sure it will be a lot of fun for everyone!" I was confused and impressed that they were doing all of this for me. Something about it worried me in the pit of my stomach. At the same time, I hoped for the best. *This is what a real family does, and for some reason, they are treating me like one of them.* For the rest of the hour-long breakfast, all I could think about were the outfits I had brought, and which would make look the most grown-up for this party.

Otto excused himself to go to work. Everyone else went to get dressed. Tomas told me to dress for tennis and bring something to change into for the afternoon. The servants cleaned up after us.

I took a quick shower, crossed back to my room, shut the door and locked it. Then realized that in my excitement about the party, I had not checked the bathroom walls for peepholes. "It's okay," I assured myself. "I looked last night."

I put on the short, pleated white tennis skirt and white polo shirt I had packed. I was going to be sweating so I pulled my hair into a ponytail and applied some light makeup. My immaculate white tennis shoes and socks perfected my look. I packed a day bag with sandals, my best khaki pants and a gauzy linen blouse trimmed with turquoise beads. It wasn't my favorite, but I wanted to look feminine for Tomas' friends. With everything in place, including diamond stud earrings and a matching tennis bracelet, I joined Tomas in the family room.

He jumped up to greet me. "You look beautiful," he said, looking me up and down and grinning so openly it made me blush.

He took my bags and led the way to the parking yard. Tomas opened the passenger door of the family jeep for me. Sometimes I enjoyed this kind of treatment, especially when going out at night because it made me feel special. At that moment, however, I secretly hoped he wouldn't keep it up on a daily basis. It didn't feel like they were just being friends.

As we drove, Tomas said, "You're going to enjoy the club. My friends will love you. You met the founders of the club two years ago. They want to play double's with us. And don't worry," he said patting my knee, "Mom enjoys putting on parties. It makes her happy."

I smiled nervously at him, unsure of what was going on, but hoping this could be my best day yet.

Tomas drove faster than I was used to, causing the bumps and holes in the road to jostle us rather roughly. I braced myself with the arm rest and the side of the door but said nothing.

"I'm sorry," said Tomas seeing my discomfort. "We just need to hurry to get to the tennis courts to beat the afternoon rain."

We pulled into the parking lot at The Costa Rican Tennis Club. The Fulcos had been members for more than twenty years and were well known by the membership and staff. Attendants greeted us and took our bags to the changing rooms near the tennis courts. We grabbed our rackets and trotted behind them. His friends, Jon and Patty Williamson, were waiting at their reserved court.

With quick hellos, stretches, and a coin toss, the doubles match was on. We won one set. The Williamson's took the match. Tomas was excited to see that I was a good player. He asked how I was at golf. "I don't play golf," I said plainly, not wanting to encourage him.

After the game, Jon, a stockbroker whose family held 100 acres of land near the club, pulled Tomas aside as they were leaving the men's changing rooms. They spoke quietly and glanced sideways at me several times. I knew they were talking about me. When Jon slapped Tomas's shoulder and they shook hands, I had a feeling they were plotting something about me, and my stomach fluttered. I didn't know if it was a good surprise or not.

The club's cafe was the perfect place to meet for appetizers and drinks. Full dress wasn't required, and it looked out over the courts and swimming pool. As if on cue, a light rain started to fall. The topic of conversation was my party and the guest list. I listened carefully for clues as to what to expect — and what they expected from me. I had attended similar parties at my father's house but knew this party would be different. It was in my honor and I was going to be seen as an adult. I needed Tomas' friends and family's approval because Melia would surely tell the Witos all about my visit.

The windows near our table grew dark as the rain grew heavier. Within minutes a torrent of rain and wind pounded the side of the building and lasted for at least an hour.

I thought, *I could never live here with all this rain. Even when it stops, it smells musty. And it's always foggy at night and messes up my hair.* This part of life in Costa Rica I did not love.

We left the club around four o'clock. The afternoon rain was over and the sun was shining behind a thin layer of clouds. I watched the water evaporating off the pavement as we drove toward Grecia. Tomas told me we were going to have an early dinner at a very special restaurant. I expected we would stop in the village near the compound and was surprised when he pulled off the road onto a muddy track that led to El Tucan, a secluded restaurant frequented by the local people.

I was impressed before he helped me out of the car. "It's made out of palm leaves!" I exclaimed.

El Tucán was actually a very large hut in a clearing surrounded by palm trees. The hut was covered with palm leaves held in place with lashed branches and thick sticks. There were no doors or walls, as it was completely open. The floor was packed dirt and dry, protected by the thick layers of leaves that extended beyond the first set of tables.

Tomas showed me around. He explained with delight that all of the tables and the bar had been hewn from the trunks of old large trees. They had been carefully polished to look as if they were made from the same tree.

I was surprised to see real toucans sitting on stick branches placed in the palm leaves overhead.

"This place is crazy beautiful," I said admiring the birds looking back at us.

Tomas replied, "Yes, and they serve the best meat I've ever eaten. Not toucan meat," he assured me.

I interrupted him with a little punch to his shoulder, saying, "Thanks for that!"

Tomas laughed and continued, "There's entertainment too, and it's about to start."

The only other patrons were at the bar, as it was early for dinner. I picked a table near the center of the hut and sat down.

All the toucans immediately began squawking.

"Oh, my God, they are so loud," I shouted to be heard over the high-pitched sound coming at them from all directions. I covered my ears with my hands.

"It's okay," Tomas said taking my hands from my head and looking directly at me so I could understand. "We just have to throw food at them to shut them up. Trust me," he winked.

He went to the bar and ordered for us. The food was served in five minutes and Tomas showed me how to throw scraps to the birds. It wasn't as messy as I thought it would be because the birds caught and ate every morsel in the air. *No wonder*, I thought. *Everything is delicious.*

As soon as we finished eating, we headed back to Grecia. The sun was setting just as we arrived. Servants met us at the car and took our bags to our rooms.

Melia was annoyed that we had already eaten, but she softened when I told her about the day and how much I enjoyed eating at El Tucán .

Otto joined us and we talked for another hour, enjoying a dessert of fresh fruit and cheese on the terrace. When the conversation began to slow, I wrapped an arm around Tomas' waist and said, "Thank you for a wonderful day. I'll never forget it."

Tomas hugged me back and asked if I wanted to watch *Footloose*, his favorite movie, and proudly showed me his Beta Max machine. It was all I could do to keep from laughing at the machine. *This wealthy powerful family still uses a Beta Max?* I wondered. *And Footloose is his favorite movie?"* Fortunately, I kept my thoughts to myself. It was a big contrast between the family's sophistication and their cultural lack of current technology. In a way it was comforting.

I was too tired to watch a movie and by now, fully suspected that Tomas was interested in me romantically and that his family was in on his intentions. I didn't feel secure enough to sit in a dark room with him when his family had gone to bed.

"Maybe another night," I said. "I guess I'm just worn out from all that tennis, and I'm still a little jet-lagged."

Tomas smiled, gave me a hug and kissed my cheek, this time near my mouth. "Of course, it's been tiring for you. Get some rest. And I think you played really well this morning." His compliment made me feel better about declining the movie invitation.

I washed my face then went to my bedroom, closed and locked the door, made sure the curtains were closed, and put on my pajamas. I worried about offending Tomas. *Maybe I should have agreed to watch the movie. After all, he has taken time away from work to be with me.*

Then I thought that, in itself, was a little much if they were just friends. He wouldn't do that for a guy friend. But maybe he would. I didn't know enough about their customs to be sure. I did know enough to know that he was being too attentive. He opened my doors, carried my things when there were no servants around, and listened to every word I said, as if what I said was important. I liked his attention very much but wasn't sure how I felt about him beyond friendship. Snuggling on the couch was not something I was ready for. I certainly didn't want to lead him on. Our families were connected, but I didn't know how to deal with what I didn't understand.

I decided that I had done the right thing and we had plenty of time to figure it all out. Sleep came quickly that night, but in the early hours of the morning, I kept waking up, feeling as if there was something I needed to do, to say, but didn't know what.

CHAPTER 13

Like a Family

On Thursday, Tomas took me back to Rio Quarto to show me the pineapple farm. The road was as steep and choppy as I remembered. The landscape reminded me again of the foothills of Switzerland with its rolling hills and fog. "Little Switzerland is the perfect English nickname for Costa Rica," I mentioned, having heard that reference many times. "I think you are right, my lady," Tomas replied with a laugh.

The higher elevations were cool and various degrees of mistiness decorated the green blush of rolling hills and plateaus we drove through and the plantations we passed. He explained that some crops, like coffee and strawberries, need cool weather to thrive.

We drove onto the plantation and Tomas took the truck up a path and parked at the top of a hill. He helped me onto the top of the truck to look over the vast fields of pineapples. It seemed endless.

"It's a sea of pineapples," I exclaimed. "They grow over the horizon!"

Tomas told me he was very proud of how he had developed the whole plantation. He called himself an agricultural engineer. I appreciated now, what that meant to him. Before, when he talked about pineapples, I had listened politely but had no frame of reference other than eating them.

He explained the entire planting, growing, harvesting, and shipping process to me while we sat on top of the truck. I gave him my full attention as I really wanted to know. He drove us to the plant facility and introduced me to the head engineer. Then we walked to a section where women with hats and gloves inspected the pineapples and placed the acceptable ones on conveyor belts. Those pineapples, he explained, would be sprayed with insecticide, dipped in wax, stored in refrigerated containers, and shipped to America.

There were strict rules for shipping to the U.S. Each pineapple had to be a certain height and color, and the crowns had to be straight up and down. Inferior pineapples were either thrown away or sold to local produce companies and grocery stores. Only perfect pineapples were allowed to be shipped.

Tomas had contracts with several major American distributors, arranged by his father. At that time, when Americans ate pineapples from Costa Rica, chances were they were eating Tomas' pineapples.

After the tour, we drove to the plantation house at Rio Quarto. Everything was exactly as I remembered. Nothing had changed. At first, I was disappointed that there wasn't enough time to ski in the lake but laughed when I remembered how scared I was of that water. There was enough time to eat a late lunch prepared by the servants. While we ate, Tomas asked a plantation worker to bring me a stalk of sugar cane. He shucked it for me and demonstrated how to suck out its sweet nectar.

It was getting late and we didn't want to upset Melia again, so we rushed back to Grecia for dinner. It was foggy, but Tomas had grown up driving those roads and got us home in time.

For two days, Tomas showed me parts of San Jose that tourists didn't know about. He took me to small parties at his friends' homes. He seemed to have friends everywhere we went, especially at the clubs he took me to at night, after dinner with the family. He proudly introduced me to everyone we met, and often the topic of conversation was my birthday party and how much fun it was going to be.

The evening before the party, preparations were almost finished. Otto dove into the backyard pool to change the colors of the lights to match the flowers to be placed on all the tables. Servants and vendors moved around the house, cleaning and cooking. I didn't know what to say to anyone involved, so I thanked everyone I ran into and said, "Thank you. I'm sure it will be a lot of fun!" I was impressed and excited that they were doing all of this for me, and a little concerned about living up to what they expected.

At the same time I wanted to feel at home. This is what a real family does, and for some reason, they are treating me like one of them.

CHAPTER 14

My Party

The next day, I helped Melia finish arranging the flowers and decorations. At lunch, she encouraged me to eat something, but I wasn't hungry. I wasn't sure if I was too excited or worried about being perfect, but food was not something I could face.

Finally, the sun began to set. Every detail was in place, Melia told me to go ahead and get ready for the evening. Guests would be arriving soon. "It's time?" I asked. Melia grinned and assured me by grabbing my hands in hers, "It surely is."

Showered and back in my room, I rolled my hair in big electric curlers and applied makeup a little heavier than usual, trying to look older. Carefully, I dressed in black satin cocktail pants that looked like a skirt and a strapless tube top. I tied a black sash at my waste to make it look like one garment. High fashion at the time.

Black high platform heels, Cartier watch, onyx dangling earrings, and an emerald and diamond ring I had inherited from my father's mother, Titita, almost satisfied my attempt to look classy. Then the last most important part — I unrolled my hair and brushed it to fall in long, sexy waves.

"It's good to be fashionably late," I thought. "I have to look perfect." While getting ready, I could hear the sounds of guests arriving outside my door. Twice, servants knocked politely, asking me to come out.

Finally, Tomas knocked on me door. "Sydney, it's time. People are waiting."

I opened the door. Tomas looked taller than ever in his black tuxedo. He beamed when he saw me standing in the doorway — his face a little red.

I took his arm. He escorted me down the hall, excited to present me to his guests. I didn't realize it, but as far as Tomas was concerned, I was his. Tomas had already claimed me to his friends.

The party became a cloud of music, lights, food, distinguished guests, and Fulco friends. I drank and danced, with Tomas at first, then his friends and the older male guests until I couldn't feel my feet. I flirted with them all and didn't care. I was beyond myself — accepted, included, approved of. Tomas smiled at me whenever I looked at him. Everyone liked me and wanted my attention. I rode my emotions like a surfer rides waves of challenge and joy. I had no idea that what they admired had nothing to do with who I really was.

Between dances, I accepted the small gifts offered to me that were in truth, tokens of regard for the Fulco family. I received bracelets, purses, hair clips, and beautiful trinkets from the fine families of Costa Rica. I smiled and thanked each person warmly as I opened their gifts. They didn't know me, but they came to Grecia with something to give. I wanted the night to last forever.

An hour after dinner the older crowd began to thin. Melia and Otto passed through the great room and said goodnight to each cluster of guests. With only the young crowd remaining around us, she whispered in my ear, "We are going to bed. Don't worry about the noise. It won't bother us."

We kept the party going, drinking, dancing, and having fun. The servants continued serving and cleaning up where they could. The DJ kept playing.

The moments that passed before 4:00 a.m. were divine. I was happy in the company of sophisticated, worldly people and not at all tired. On some level I knew it couldn't last and I would have to go to bed. But I was going to wake up and remember these moments over and over again.

At 4:00 a.m., I was sitting on the top of a couch in the family room, talking with friends gathered around me. Tomas came up from behind and wrapped his arms around me. I relaxed into him and laid my head back on his shoulder. I knew I was surrendering to what he wanted, and at that moment, it felt right. We swayed to a romantic ballad the DJ was playing.

The moments that followed took me a long time to comprehend. In those moments, lives were changed forever.

Mario, a friend who had left the house minutes earlier, rushed back through the front door. His eyes were wide and he was confused, not sure what to say or how to say it.

Tomas left me and ran to the door, catching Mario by the shoulders and sitting him down in a foyer chair. "What's wrong, Mario?" he asked firmly.

Mario, holding his head with shaking, blood spattered hands, could only say quietly, "No," "No," "No."

"What?" shouted Tomas. "What happened?"

The DJ stopped playing. Everyone turned to see Mario and the blood on his clothes and hands.

"I was following them. There was a car accident," Mario finally spoke. "She was hurt really bad."

"Who was hurt, are you hurt, what happened?" asked Tomas, quickly becoming unnerved.

"It's Annabel. She went through the windshield. Her head went through the glass. The ambulance is taking her to the hospital."

"What do you mean?" ask Tomas. "Who was driving? Was she driving?"

Mario shook his head and looked around, trying to catch his breath. He looked up and said, "It was Diego." Diego, I learned later, was her former boyfriend.

"That son of a bitch, I'm going to kill him!" shouted Tomas. "What were they doing together? Diego knew he was drunk. He told me he was drunk and was going to sleep here. How could he put her in that situation? Why would she go with him?"

Mario shrugged his shoulders and covered his face with his hands, not believing what he had seen.

Otto appeared in the hallway, pulling his robe around him, and looked at Tomas. He pushed his son back a step and said, "You are not helping the situation." He took Mario by the shoulders and said, "Mario, calm down, man. Get hold of yourself. Now tell me what happened."

Mario, speaking in short breaths, explained that Diego had crashed into a tree near the hospital and that Annabel had gone through the windshield. There was blood and glass everywhere. Annabel was going to the hospital, but he didn't know about Diego. The guests put down their drinks and gathered around the foyer.

In a sudden realization, Mario cried out, "I've got to be with her." With too many drinks himself, and in shock, Mario ran out the door and got into his car. Tomas and Otto tried to stop him. Mario sped away. Hearing the squeal of his tires, we all followed after him, a drunken group of very upset people. We heard a crashing boom and the crack of a huge mango tree at the end of the driveway. Mario had missed the turn.

Hearing the news and the chaos outside, the servants still working, cried almost in unison, "A Dios mío," and stayed where they were, not sure what to do.

Tomas and Otto ran to Mario's car, and carefully pulled him out. Tomas drove him to the hospital. All of the frantic guests left the property. It was a big commotion. I was too scared to move.

Hours later, having done what he could do to help, Tomas returned home. He went to his parent's room to let them know that Mario would be okay, and there was nothing the family could do for Annabel or Diego except pray.

At the end of the best night of my life, Tomas found me sitting alone in the family room, crying. I blamed myself for everything. "It's my fault," I kept saying. "I'm so sorry."

Tomas sat down next to me and held me gently, protectively, as if assuring a child. He spoke slowly, "None of this was your fault, Sydney. Annabel, Diego, and Mario are being taken care of and everything will be all right in a few days. You'll see."

"No, it won't. If Annabel went through the windshield, I don't think she will ever be the same," I sobbed as I wiped my eyes with a mascara-soaked tissue. "She had such a beautiful smile. Will her smile be the same, Tomas, will she be all right?"

"You didn't make her get into that car," said Tomas. "She made that decision. You didn't make Diego drink; he made that decision. It's not your fault."

I leaned into his chest and welcomed his comforting touch, which is all that he offered.

When all talking about it was done and exhaustion set in, we finally went to bed as the first timid rays of sunrise began to glow outside our windows.

The next morning, I didn't want to get out of bed. Tomas rapped on my door lightly and said in a husky voice, "Breakfast is ready on the patio."

I got out of bed and walked to the door without opening it. "Thanks, but I'm not hungry."

Tomas replied, "Well, how about a cup of coffee?"

"Coffee sounds good. I'll be there in a few minutes," I replied quietly.

When I got to the patio, Otto looked at me and suggested that instead of going to the beach as planned, we should stay at home in case anyone needed their help. Melia rubbed her temples and said, "I can't believe this happened."

In the silence that followed, I asked if it would be okay for me to sit in the orchid garden and write in my journal.

"As long as you don't bring sadness there. You have to speak love and lightness to the orchids, or they will die," replied Melia. "Bring happiness to them. If you can't, you should sit in the gazebo by the pool."

I smiled a little to show I understood her passion for the orchids. Melia touched my hand, then grabbed her napkin and wiped her cheeks.

I wanted my Mom to be with me now. She was far away, but in my heart, I could feel closer to her through Zoryia. That's where I would go, and we would remember our mothers. "I'll be in the gazebo," I replied.

CHAPTER 15

Beats

We spent the next three days at Playa Hermosa Beach with a small group of Tomas' friends. Our first dinner was on the beach beside a small bonfire. We sat on a long picnic table the servants had brought down from an apartment patio. Tomas raised his glass to Annabel, who was still recovering in the hospital. The group responded with hearty get-well wishes. I enjoyed being with them, and we did have fun, and yet I noticed there were many moments of quiet that fell among us.

While with his friends, Tomas was polite and appreciative. Whenever we were alone, he was more familiar with me than I wanted him to be. I didn't mind kissing him but kept busy blocking his hand from my blouse and thighs. He always backed off and said something like, "It's okay. You know that you are a beautiful young woman. As a gentleman, I respect your wishes. If you are not ready for real love, I will wait."

Two nights before I was to fly back to Atlanta, we returned to Grecia. On the last night, Tomas said he had a surprise for me and was taking me to an especially beautiful overlook of San Jose. "It will make you feel better about Annabel," he promised the night before, waiting for my appreciation of his effort. I just shrugged with a smile. Melia hugged us both when we walked

105

out the door. Otto simply waved and said, "Have a good time. Bring her home safe."

With somber goodbyes and vows to get together again soon, we left our friends around 2:00 a.m. I could feel Tomas' excitement about going to the overlook. I didn't want to disappoint him, but I was tired and pointed out that it would take a few hours to get home to Grecia. He smiled at me like I was a scared child, "It's a short drive to our family's apartments in San Jose. If we need to, we can spend the night there. My parents will understand." My stomach fluttered like a scared child. But I decided I wasn't a child and ignored it. At Tomas's insistence that I would love it, I agreed to go. I thought that I could use a beautiful view of the city. I expected him to be the gentleman he had always been in his family's driveway.

We drove up a winding steep road for a while until we got to a clearing. It was dark but he knew the way. We pulled into a clearing that could easily hold several cars some distance from the overlook. We were alone. I thought it was lovely and it was cold, but I asked if we could get out of the car and look over.

"No, it's too cold for you. Let's stay here and look at the city," he replied softly as he wrapped his arms around me. We sat there looking for a few minutes. "It is beautiful," I said, trying to show appreciation.

Tomas lowered his head and spoke with a deep voice I had not heard before. "Like you," he said. "Beautiful."

He leaned over, grabbed the back of my head and kissed me. I kissed him back and did not pull away immediately, just as we had kissed in his parent's driveway. He rubbed his hand on my breasts with an intensity we had not negotiated before. This was not what I wanted; I tried to pull back and push his hand away. His hand moved under my blouse. I could not pull my head away. I was locked against him, wanting nothing more than to be free and to breathe my own breaths.

He pulled his head back and asked, as if he was hurt and needed me to make him feel better, "Don't you want to be with me? Don't you love me?" Before I could answer, he kissed me harder and didn't let me pull away. Then, he grabbed the handle on the side of my seat and pushed me back. He climbed over the stick shift and said, "Just trust me. Can you do that? I want to show you how much I love you and help you understand that we are meant to be together."

It was dark and I couldn't see his face. He rubbed his cheek against my cheek and said as if I had agreed, "You know you are mine. Everyone knows it. Especially you. Stop teasing me. We are far past that now." I understood his words and grew cold, knowing what he wanted. I felt his roughness on my face, and it was hot.

I screamed as loud as I could and still seemed, I hoped, polite. "No! No, Tomas, I don't want to!" He heard only his own need, and despite my defiance, I knew what he wanted. I had known it all my life.

Desperately needing to move and get away, and unable to do either, was not new to me. Like a doe in the woods smelling a hunter nearby, my only defense took over — stay completely still.

Why am I here again? Am I stupid? Why am I so stupid? What did I do? How do I make it stop?

Eyes closed; I searched my heart to find a way to make it stop. I whimpered. Screamed again, and again, but made no sound either of us heard. No light, no movement. All was still. I wanted to live. Suffocated. I wanted light. I needed light to see and make it stop.

Tomas pulled my skirt up, reached between my legs and squeezed. He moaned. I stiffened. He struggled to pull down my pantyhose and unbuckle his pants. I could not breathe. I whimpered again and screamed silently against his heaviness and sweat dripping on my face.

Still trying to get my pantyhose down, Tomas cried, "Sydney, I love you. Let me have you and you will love me!"

I heard his words; his voice was husky. Suddenly, I was aware of tiny gaps in the space between us, beats of movement, sounds in fragments of time. I focused on the gaps. Getting through the beats. It was something I could do.

Beat.

I heard a loud thump. Then another, then two more. Car doors slammed shut. I saw a flash of shadows behind my eyes. I saw red, then opened them to a bright white light in my face. It hurt my eyes. I blinked fast to see what was happening. Tomas stopped moving. "Holy shit," rasped my ears. What happened next were beats of memory recalled from another time.

Beat.

The car door opened, and the cold air was wonderful. The interruption would stop Tomas!

His weight lifted off me and men yelled. They were angry. They were there to help. I screamed "help me" without making a sound. It was more a prayer than a scream.

Beat.

I tried to see who was there to save me. Rough hands pulled me out of the car and stood me up. Strong arms held my arms from behind. These are hostile men, I realized. One man yelled at Tomas, "Give me all your money." One man hit Tomas in the face. Another pushed him in front of truck lights across the clearing. One man held him from behind while the other grabbed his wallet from the pants hanging at his knees.

Beat.

This was worse than just moments ago. I didn't want Tomas to die. I wanted to see my Mom again.

Beat.

Men kept shouting and pushed me next to Tomas. All I could see were shadows of feet. Their faces stayed above the headlights. My heels sunk into wet ground. Arms wrenched away my jewelry and ripped open my blouse. Angry feet kicked my shoes away.

Beat.

I looked down for my shoes and saw how close we were to the edge of the overlook. It was a long way down.

Beat.

Angry men pulled me to the edge and grabbed between my legs, right where Tomas had grabbed me. Ready for more, they laughed, and one man shouted to the others, "We can throw her over when we're done." Locked in by rough hands and panties between my feet, I could not run away.

Beat.

"Mother-fucker," the man by the truck lights said slowly, deeply, in clear Spanish. "This guy's name is Tomas Fulco." I looked at a form of a man holding Tomas's wallet in the truck light. Tomas' head was down. The other guys laughed, not letting go — not moving away from the edge.

Beat.

"Let's get out of here now. We want no trouble with them. It's not worth it." The men holding me shouted, "no," they had earned me. The guy at the truck punched Tomas in the stomach and shouted, "Shut up, you asshole. Keep this to yourself or we will find your girlfriend."

Beat.

I felt hands let go. I watched scared men run to their trucks. I heard doors slam and motors race. Taillights moved away from us and disappeared. I dropped to my knees and crawled away from the edge. Tomas and I were alone. I didn't know how to feel. We were both alive and I was not raped. I could not stop shivering.

Beat.

Tomas pulled his coat over me and led me to the car. We were going to stay at his apartment and drove there in silence. At the apartment he put ice on his face and asked me if I was okay.

"Call the police," I begged, handing him the phone, my hands shaking too hard to dial. I already knew he would not. "You need to report this, call your parents, get us help!"

Tomas took the phone from my hands and tried to hold me. I did not let him. "Sydney, I'm sorry but we can't tell anyone about this. We were not supposed to be up there. You understand, don't you?"

I looked at him, but with all the screaming inside, I couldn't hear him. I went to his parent's bathroom and took a very hot shower. I managed to wrap a towel around me and lie down on their bed. Tomas covered me with a blanket. My body shook. I did not sleep.

The next morning, Tomas acted as if keeping his secret was something any other woman would do, if it meant keeping his attention. Handing me a cup of coffee, he said, "You will keep all this a secret, of course."

"I can't do that," I said as steadily as I could manage. "I can't keep a secret like that."

"But you have to," his plea turned into that of a small boy child begging not to be spanked. "This has to be our secret. I need you to trust that I will take care of it myself."

I didn't respond. I dressed in his sister's clothes and stuffed mine in a grocery bag. We drove back to Grecia as if nothing happened. He told his mother that he had been hit in the face on the dance floor.

Melia look doubtful and kissed his cheek softly. She turned to me, "Are you all right Sydney?"

I kept my trembling hands in my coat pocket. She couldn't see my bruises so nothing else needed to be explained. I nodded, "It was a long night. May I get some sleep?"

"Of course," Melia replied sounding concerned. "Both of you, off to bed. We will get you ready for your flight to Lausanne before we leave." Tomas's brother had invited all of us to dinner. I would be home tonight.

I woke with a rap on my door. Servants came in to pack my clothes. I showered and changed into my jeans and sweater. I never saw my clothes from the night before again.

Tomas sat next to me at dinner, but never spoke to me directly. I was nauseated and cold and could not hide my hands. The shaking was unstoppable. Otto asked me if I was ill. "She's probably just still upset about the accident," said Tomas, smiling and with a warm touch, reached for my right hand. I pulled it away. Food was placed in front of us. I couldn't smell anything.

Beat.

I came to in the back seat of a car. My head was in Tomas's lap. He was stroking my hair. "Everything will be okay," he kept saying. We were going really fast. I realized it was the bumping over potholes that woke me up. I kept my eyes closed.

Beat.

Pressure on my sternum woke me up again. An authoritative voice asked if I knew my name. I said nothing. The doctor said I must be in shock. Melia's voice was there. She said there had been an accident at my birthday party. It must have been too much for me to handle.

Beat.

Between dry heaves over a plastic barf pan, I heard Tomas talking to Mom on the phone. He said that I was fine but needed to postpone my flight. Mom did not ask to speak to me. Two days later I was on my way home. The truth held hostage in the heart of the man I would marry was, for a time, safe.

Beat.

CHAPTER 16

Ping Pong Anyone?

When I returned to Lausanne, I was exhausted, confused, and hiding another terrible secret. But I was worried about Juliana and stayed home more to protect her from Peter's anger, until the day he took a knife and scared us both. I gave her my ultimatum. We had to leave.

In two months, we moved to an apartment in Atlanta and Juliana got a job with Coca-Cola as an executive secretary. I finished the year in a private school and hated every minute of it. It was academically challenging, the students kept to their groups, and again I was the new girl trying to fit in.

Once that difficult school year finally ended, I asked to live with my father again. Juliana and my father agreed and I left. Secretly, I felt that she was relieved and happy to give her time and energy to a new man. I didn't trust him and was uncomfortable around him. He claimed to be a police officer but I saw a chameleon like me, hiding something important to get what he wanted.

When I arrived in El Salvador, I was thrilled to see my father waiting for me instead of his chauffeur. I concentrated on remembering the way home instead of feeling bad that he didn't ask me about my trip, my past year, or anything that had to do with me. We climbed the San Salvador Volcano, drove through the Masferred Roundabout and up the very steep Calle Escalon. I knew we were almost there when we drove past his country club, Club Campéstre, and finally turned left onto Maximo Jerez Street. I hoped that we would talk once tucked away into his home.

In the late 1980's, there were few real neighborhoods. The long row of high stucco walls we drove past reminded me that there was a war going on between the poor and the rich. Something I had not even seen in previous visits — like not noticing the wallpaper in your grandmothers' dining room. It's there but has nothing to do with you.

Most of the walls surrounding the homes had solid rod-iron gates. Some of the smaller houses had decorative gates onlookers could see through. The fortunate people of El Salvador lived or worked behind one of these walls. My father's wall was nine feet high, two feet thick, and ran about eighty feet along the street. The top was embedded with broken glass and electrified barbed wire that dared anyone to cross it. That school year, my junior year in high school, I would scale it on a regular basis.

As we approached his home, I saw two guards standing on the roof with machine guns. I sat up as our driver hit a button below the car dashboard. The gate opened and we pulled in. I noticed two other guards standing in front of the servants' quarters and stared at the machine guns slung over their shoulders. At this point in the war, my father's guards were always standing.

We parked in front of the flower garden. Helga's gardeners had kept it in symmetrical tropical perfection since my last visit. I rolled down the window to breathe in its familiar, magical smell. It was a wall of colors, dirt, sun, mustiness, and the scent of corn tortillas. My stomach reminded me that like the garden, I could be uprooted and must show my best, most acceptable colors if I wanted to live here.

It was all familiar and I knew it could be fun living here. Was this what Zoryia would feel when she got to her father's home

113

where she had never been? I smiled to myself. That was entirely up to me.

Two of my father's house servants came out to greet us and take my bags. My father walked away from the car and said without turning toward me, "The servants will settle you in the guest quarters. I will see you at dinner."

I remembered the guest quarters. They connected to the right side of the main house through a long hallway and faced the covered driveway. While the rooms were nicely decorated to please their guests, there would be more than a physical distance between my room and my father's home. I was to be his guest, living under Helga's rules with my two younger half-sisters, Eugenia and Inez. Both girls were polite to me, but as I remembered, had a tendency to blame me to keep out of trouble. Whenever I protested to my father, I was without evidence, guilty of lying. Zoryia and I had a lot of work to do.

I followed the servants down the long walkway through the middle of the garden toward the guest entrance. To the left at the front patio and beyond to the fenced yard, were seven black Rottweiler guard dogs cooling themselves in patches of shade. I felt their frustration, how they waited for night to fall so they could be free to roam around the grounds. All seven dogs turned to look at me. Only the one named Cindy was allowed to be in the house at night — an inside protector. She wagged her tail for me, briefly, then turned away.

Nothing much had changed since my last summer vacation. Beyond the dogs' gate to the left, was the entrance to the servants' quarters. It was a separate building with two rooms with four sets of bunk beds for eight maids, and a large room the gardener and guards shared that also served as a simple living space with a shower and sink. The roof extended over an open common area with a washer and dryer for our finer clothes, and a table where the servants and guards ate. There were two shallow washbasins and a well where the maids would throw water on a wad of clothes, rub them vigorously against the basin sides, then drop them in the second basin where other maids would rinse and hang them up to dry.

Beyond the common area against the outside wall of the servants' quarters was a door that led to a room called the Bodega. It was a walk-in pantry that held all the food imported from America. Helga kept it locked tight. No one was allowed to eat that food without her permission. Even their daughters had to explain what they wanted and why. If our requests met with Helga's approval, we were rewarded. If not, we went without.

Next to the Bodega was a large kitchen where the maids cooked and gathered. Outside the kitchen was a long, narrow vegetable garden. The kitchen was isolated from the breakfast area and dining room by a heavy wooden swinging door with a small window. The door was kept shut to prevent the family from being bothered with noise coming from the kitchen. And though it was kept clean and in repair, the kitchen wasn't decorated or updated with modern equipment because family and guests never bothered to go in there. In my father's world, plastic red cabinets, a worn stove, and burned counter tops were good enough for the maids. "They aren't educated and don't care about taking care of fine things," he told me the last time I was here. I didn't like his answer.

The head houseman opened the guest quarters with a key and escorted me into the living area. He dropped the two large bags carried from the car and left. Isabel, who always tended to me during my previous visits, followed in with my two smaller bags. I turned, happy to recognize her voice and gave her a hug. She hugged me back, smiled, and asked, "Do you want me to unpack for you?" I replied, "Si, gracias, I would love your help," I replied.

"Very well, Miss Sydney. We are glad that you are here. Let us know at any time that you need something. Dinner will be served in the dining room at 6:00 p.m."

I relaxed at her kindness and for a moment, felt more at home.

We tucked and hung my things away in the closet that spanned that entire wall with huge, dark wooden shutter doors. I walked out to the living area and looked across the courtyard to the backyard of my father's house. I felt alone and unwelcomed. I was a guest, not a cherished family member. I studied the floor-to-ceiling windows that spanned across the living and dining area, framed by tall glass doors that opened to a covered terrace paved with creamy marble tiles.

Early every morning, the maids opened those doors to make the terrace part of the main living area. At this moment, the sun was moving down and golden splashes hit the man-made waterfall in the backyard. The water fell into a bubbling rock pond filled with live fish and turtles. No one played on the half-basketball court next to it.

Surrounded by tropical plants, this yard was a playground. At night, colored spotlights lit everything up. My father's house was not a mansion, but it was an impressive environment for entertaining guests. The bedrooms could not be seen from the outside. They were hidden around a covered, open-aired garden courtyard in the center of the house.

My guest room was not air-conditioned. But it had a wall of windows I could open and a ceiling fan. This would work well for me in the near future. It was almost 5:00 p.m. and I went inside the air-conditioned family room to call my mother to let her know I was here and safe. She didn't answer so I left a message, trying to sound excited and happy. These were the colors she needed right now. Our goodbye at the airport had been rushed, filled with last-minute updates on her plans.

Showered and dressed in a black pantsuit I hoped Helga would like, I decided to wear no makeup or jewelry that night. I didn't want to give anyone something to criticize.

Dinner with my father, Helga, and my sisters were polite. The conversation was about plans for Eugenia's birthday party. It was going to be an afternoon cookout at the lake house, with musicians and a magician. There would be boat rides and skiing, and dancing for the adults. Eugenia also wanted a sleepover for all of her friends.

No one asked me about what had happened or why I was here. Immediately after we ate dessert, my father went to his study. I said I was tired and needed to sleep. Helga nodded approval. I tried to call my mother again but could not get an outside line. I went back to my room and started to write her a letter but decided to write it the next day. With the outer door deadbolt locked and the chain in its receptacle, I checked the windows to make sure they were locked and covered. Satisfied that no one could see me or get in, I put on my pajamas and tried to write about Zoryia but was too tired. I told myself I had plenty of time and turned on the television in my bedroom.

The next day my father came home early and had the maids summon me to his study. I walked quickly and knocked lightly at the door as I came in. He sat behind his desk, hands palms down on either side of a newspaper. I stood there smiling, excited that he had called.

"Tell me the truth, Sydney," he commanded sternly, without preamble. I was startled by his tone and wondered what I had done wrong. He paused and looked up at me with narrowed eyes.

"Did Peter do things to you?" he asked. "Things he should not have done?" In one heartbeat, fear shot through my stomach and I felt a terrible need to scream "YES!" and tell him everything. I wanted him to get up, come to me with warm, open arms and hold me. I wanted him to say that he was going to kill Peter.

This was not my father caring about me. This was not anything like I had imagined or dreamed of. This was Mateo demanding that my world had nothing to do with his. Even Wito's truth was not real here. I sat in a chair and held on as I sank into a dark empty space where, beyond survival, I did not exist.

What he needed was everything. What I needed wasn't even a consideration. Legally and publicly, he had to provide me shelter and school until I was of age — as long as I followed his rules. As long as I could wear my father's colors to his satisfaction, I could be a small part of his world. If I spoke the truth, I would be on my way back to Atlanta — a dirty girl unacceptable to his society. So, I did the only thing I could while Pedro's words stabbed my heart. I shrugged and look at my feet.

He slapped his desk sharply with both hands. "That's what I thought. Juliana wants more money out of me. Can you believe she said that about you?"

I couldn't speak. If I stayed silent, that meant my mother was a liar. If I said it was true, his family would see me as a dirty girl. I couldn't live through another "white shorts."

As long as I said nothing, I would not be sent away tonight. I looked at the clock on the wall and whispered, "I need to get dressed for the club." He went back to reading his paper. When I left the room, he said nothing. I knew the matter was over. He had what he needed.

If I wanted to live in his world, my world had to remain secret. The only control I had over anything in his world was how well I could wear his colors. I walked back to my room. My fantasy of having a loving father that could save me was over. I was alone in his world. I needed to write about Zoryia but couldn't think.

He was so mean. Life was so mean to me to make him my father. I hated him, hated him hard. It was his fault. Everything was his fault. Peter was his fault and both of them got me to cover it up and I let them get away with it. Like I let them all get away with it. I could have told him every detail, made him listen to the ugly facts about his daughter. But I didn't.

I threw myself on the royal blue silk sheets Isabel had just turned down. Fuck it. I'm taking advantage of his world. His money. His society, chauffeurs, country club, beach house, lake house, boats, helicopters, jets ... I'll make my own friends. "I will have fun!" I cried out loud, then laughed.

On Fridays, Helga would take us to their house at Coatepeque Lake. "That is a great place to have fun," I squealed. "And tomorrow is Friday!"

The next morning it was raining hard and Mateo announced at breakfast that he would drive us to the lake house for the weekend himself, in his bullet-proof Land Cruiser because the weather would prevent him from flying in on Saturday. I snickered. He did so love to make a grand entrance to the lake community. Too bad his helicopter would not be able to help him make an impression.

We started our journey on the road going up the volcano. I listened to my sisters and made funny comments I thought they would like. It worked for a while. I was part of the family, or at least a welcome visitor in their eyes. About half-way up, an old rusty red truck weaved back and forth in front of us. The back of the truck read "To ota." My sisters laughed because they couldn't figure out where the "y" was. Mateo tried several times to pass the truck on the bumpy, eroded road, but the driver kept weaving in front of him.

Finally, we got to a wide enough clearing at the base of a hill for him to pass him safely. As we passed, my father pointed at the driver and started laughing. Everyone turned to look at him and realized why he had been weaving so hard. The truck's windshield was missing, and the wipers were moving back and forth. The driver was trying his best to see through the rain hitting his face. He was blinking and blinking and kept turning his face from the rain but could not because he had to see ahead. I thought he had left the wipers on to help knock away some of the rain from his face. But the wipers were vibrating so much from the wind, the whole scene seemed completely ridiculous to Mateo and my sisters. I watched him laugh until the tears streamed from the corners of his eyes. It was the first time I had ever seen him be so openly human, even at the expense of that poor man.

That night, the servants, who had arrived the day before with food and supplies, barbequed on the lake-house porch. We watched a movie, and my sisters played games with neighborhood friends. About 10:00 p.m., the rain stopped and a group of teenagers I had met before stopped by our house. I was glad to see them. We talked for a while outside, near the house to be seen, then slipped away and smoked cigarettes on the lower dock, below the sunbathing platform next to Mateo's boat house. It was past the helicopter landing pad and far enough from the house where no one could see us.

As long as any of my father's family members were outdoors, the guards had to stand with machine guns and grenades and watch over us. At two o'clock in the morning, the guards made me go inside and tell the others to go home. We pushed our cigarette butts into a hole in the grass and covered it with fallen coconuts. Mateo's guards were always standing, always watching, always focused on protecting his assets.

The lake itself was formed by the volcano. Legends and myths about it were woven into stories the neighborhood children would scare themselves with at night. "There is a whole town at the bottom, but so deep no one can go down far enough to see it." "Whirlpools in the middle of lake have swallowed boats. That's why we can't drive a boat straight through to the other side." Sharing and listening to imaginative stories was one of my favorite things to do. It helped pass the time.

For the next three months, whenever Mateo joined us at the lake or the beach, it was the only time he didn't work and I had his, at least partial, attention. He would teach my sisters and me how to handle his boats, how to water ski, how to do whatever we were doing in a manner that wouldn't embarrass him. I loved being included in his instructions. But he never wasted his time talking with us about boys, dating, life, marriage, or any subject that would be important to young girls.

In a way, I was glad to be left alone with my thoughts as we learned how to comply with his demands. In other ways, not talking about what happened was profoundly unbearable. I missed my mother. At least she knew my truth. It was hard to keep it all in. At times, early in the summer, I found myself crying. Surprised by my tears, I would wipe them away. These were not the colors the adults needed to see. In private, I wrote about Zoryia's powers and the freedom Andor represented and hid it all away.

> They would ride to her most favorite place, a beautiful oasis of lush green acreage she called "Freedom Land."
> Zoryia brushed the back of her hand gently between Andor's eyes. He replied with a nod and a happy snort. She kept her hand on him, ran it along his neck and walked to his left side to mount the saddle. As a sign of willingness, Andor bent his back-left leg to lower himself just enough to make her mount easier. As she lifted her right leg over the saddle and placed her foot in the stirrup, she patted his neck and asked, "Are you ready for a good ride?"

Spending as much time as I could with my friends was acceptable to the adults. My friends saw me as different, but interesting. I had lived in Europe and America. I told them funny stories about the people in these other worlds they had only heard about. I was someone who had fun, hid, smoked, and drank with them, and didn't care about what the adults thought of me. Most teenagers were strictly constrained by adults, politics, safety rules, and expected behaviors. I wondered what they would think if they knew how desperate I was for any kind of attention. How would they have treated me had they known the only time I felt good was when I made an impression on anyone who cared to notice?

At the end of summer, when I demonstrated how well I could command his ski boats, I asked Mateo if I could stay there for the remainder of high school. He replied, "Yes, we talked about it and you would be better supervised and trained as a young lady living with me and Helga."

By that time I had learned that gaining his respect and becoming a society lady had nothing to do with what I wanted. But I was encouraged that I had learned to wear his colors well enough to stay. A part of me continued to hope that he would learn to love me. Another part knew better. I was learning to play a game I didn't understand.

CHAPTER 17

Light in the Dark

That fall, I returned to the American School in El Salvador. I reconnected with a few friends. To stay away from home as much as I could in an acceptable way, I played sports. I was strong and healthy from summer activities and physical challenges were my outlet, especially volleyball. I met Erik through volleyball. He was a year ahead and, on the varsity team. One afternoon during practice, I spiked the ball and scored a point. I heard a guy's voice yell out, "Way to go, Maria!"

I turned around to see who he was rooting for, but there was no one on our team named Maria. During our practice break, I went to the concession stand to buy my favorite drink, Kolashampan. Before I could place my order, someone tapped my shoulder. It was the guy who had shouted out to "Maria."

He handed me the Kolashampan and said, "I know this is your favorite. It's a wonderful product of El Salvador, don't you think, Maria?"

"Why do you call me Maria? You surely know my name since you know what I like to drink." I smiled at him and secretly loved the special attention. And he was cute. I liked his light brown hair and the way he tossed it to the side. He never answered my question, but I let him keep the mystery. The weeks that followed he courted me by getting into my locker, where I found notes, roses, and expensive little gifts. We started dating and regardless of what I was going through at home, he found ways to make me feel special and wanted.

During that year, we were always together. I told him everything about my past: Peter, Mom, and all about Mateo and his family. I even told him that I had been raped at the beach. I had never told anyone about that, but Erik wanted to know everything about me. He was my best friend, confidant, and at that time, the love of my life.

Erik made living in a cold and abrasive house tolerable because I could think about being with him when I was in Mateo's world. Even Zoryia was happy with her boyfriend, Alesso.

She wanted to go all the way with Alesso but knew that would not be possible, for her glowing skin would surely give them away. He delighted her. They would lie together, talk and giggle. He listened to everything Zoryia told him and he never left her side. She had found a love that was deep and honest. They were magical together.

Erik's father knew about the shady side of Mateo's business dealings. In effect, he was Mateo's opponent in the corrupt world of business. I stood no chance of going out with Erik openly. So I learned how to get past the guards and dogs when I wanted to. On the night of our anniversary, in high heels and smoky black panty hose, I climbed up the mango tree in the courtyard to the top. With one high-heeled foot pressed against the security wall, I pulled myself up to a bit of clear ledge and straddled over the two-foot wide, coil of barbwire and cemented glass shards. I pivoted on the opposite bit of clear ledge and threw my heels to the ground where Erik's car waited for me directly below.

Waiting with the engine running, Erik looked up at me through his open window and laughed. "Girl," he shouted enough for me to hear him, "Thank God you are a gymnast. That was a performance the guards appreciated. But next time wear a longer skirt."

I looked down at him and said, "Shut up, get out of the car and spot me."

"What, now you need help? You can't do this by yourself?"

I replied, still balancing on a bit of ledge in a painful situation. "Do you want a massive dent on the top of your car or are you going to help me?"

He slid over and got out of the passenger seat. "Okay, I'll grab your heels. Don't worry about them. They are safe with me!"

I rolled my eyes and jumped backward to the top of his car and slid down the windshield to the hood of his car. Then gracefully hopped down to the ground.

The guards cheered and clapped and whistled at me. Erik said, "That's it? No triple-back layout landing?"

"That's not even a thing," I replied, bowing to the guards and giving them my best gymnastic salute.

I turned to Erik, gave him a salute, and said, "At least, I stuck the landing without a single run in my hose."

He laughed and got back into the car. Before I joined him, I signaled to the guards and they shouted "Okay, Señorita," as they turned the electrical razor wire's current back on, quickly moving through the coils above me. We heard the electrical hiss it always made when engaged. He looked at me with a question mark in his eyes.

"I paid them with my lunch money, honey. How do you think I stay so skinny?"

We drove away to a lovely French dinner that Erik had arranged, at a most exclusive restaurant.

Mateo was waiting outside the gate when we returned. His arms were crossed. I was caught. Fun was over, I was grounded to my room for the rest of the school year. But I found ways to see Erik between classes and when Mateo was on business trips. Helga never noticed when I was gone. My sisters were busy with their friends.

At the end of the year, Erik moved to the U.S. to go to college. I missed him. Writing about Zoryia that summer filled my time but could not fill my heart. I wanted to go home. But I knew I had to finish my senior year in El Salvador. I couldn't move again before I graduated. Mateo and his family were not mine and never would be. I would always be a guest they tolerated out of obligation. Later in life I realized it was a good thing he had stayed out of my life. Accused of money laundering, drugs, and organized crime, he now lives in asylum with his family. He sits in his gilded prison in Switzerland, blaming his situation on others. From what I have heard from his family, the "others" are jealous of him and are out "to get him." I am free and he is not.

In 1993, I graduated from the Escuela Americana High School in San Salvador, and immediately flew back to Atlanta to live with the Witos. Mom was living in Mexico City with her third husband, Hugo, an executive with Coca-Cola. I was accepted to a local college and completed the first semester. Wita, sensing my depression, suggested we take a vacation to Costa Rica, just the two of us. I had no reason to say no. I was nineteen when we flew to Grecia after the Christmas holidays.

CHAPTER 18

Fully Engaged

Just as three years before, the suction of the plane's door released, and sulfuric air filled the cabin. In that moment I didn't know how to feel about being here again. Every time I had left Costa Rica and that smell behind, I was dead inside. This time, things felt different.

Was I past it all? Was I healed from my secrets? Was I denying my feelings? Or maybe deep down inside, I knew this felt different because it would be. Maybe this time, I would leave Costa Rica with life.

"Ay no! Wherrrrd are our luggages? Sydney, go and git di man to help us. Ay no! I see it. Hurrrrry. Go. Git it." Wita demanded with an unusually thick accent. We were in her home turf and it already showed. I laughed and responded, "Wita, just speak to me in Spanish. I can barely understand your English today." I trotted over and got our luggage cart and we headed to Customs.

At the now — familiar curb, I was surprised to see Tomas. Wita had kept it a secret and I figured out why. He was waving with excitement and we hugged and kissed like nothing had ever happened to us or between us. It was strange to be in his arms again and not feel hurt, betrayed, or even awkward.

"Bienvenidos," said Tomas. "Welcome back to Costa Rica! How was your flight?"

Wita answered before I had a chance to say anything. "Oh, estabamos en primera clase!"

"Wow! How nice to have flown in first class," Tomas replied, smiling at me. "Wita …." I quickly interjected, "We had a good flight. Thank you for asking. By the way, where are you taking us?"

Tomas answered, "We are going to Grecia, of course. Everyone is waiting for you."

"Are we having the Grecia specialty?" I asked with a small expectant smile.

"But, of course. Papi remembered how much you enjoyed it and insisted we prepare cow tongue again!"

"Ay, no…wat?" Wita asked. I replied laughing, "It is so good, just wait!"

As we approached the gate to the main house, the wall surrounding the compound was smaller than I remembered.

Tomas honked the horn for the guard to let us in. The winding road up to the house looked much the same, but the trees were much taller and fuller. As in previous visits, the family and their house servants were all waiting for us in their courtyard with smiles on their faces.

I was happy to see them, happy that we were there and actually happy that I came. Yet, I didn't quite understand why we were here instead of staying with Wita's family, and why I was calm, given the last time I had been with all of them. I shrugged it off and decided to leave the memories behind. This was a different time. After dinner, Wita left to visit her family members in Alejuela, where she grew up, about forty minutes away from Grecia. Tomas insisted that I stay with his family to learn more about the area and his family businesses.

I was genuinely interested in what they could teach me. I was older, had some college experience, and thought I had good business sense. At night, we went to parties with his friends. I was happy to see them again. The occasional outings to hotels to gamble were a part of Tomas' life, and at that point they were entertaining. I liked watching the people, feeling their energy and as a young adult, it seemed quite the thing to do, if you had the means.

We spent our days at Grecia swimming, playing tennis, and having fun getting to know each other better. Tomas seemed different — interested in me but seemed less eager than before to have sex. Wita had told me he knew I wasn't involved with anyone. He was twenty-seven and not yet married. His family's and society's expectations could no longer be ignored.

A couple of days before I was to return to Atlanta with Wita, Tomas and I headed to a hotel with a famous nightclub to dance and see friends. It was early January and turning toward the rainy season in Costa Rica. He had asked me to dress up because he was going to take me to a nice restaurant in the hotel. Walking into the restaurant in my black patent-leather heels, smoky black panty hose, tight short black skirt, and a white silk blouse, I felt beautiful and appropriately dressed for the elegant five-course dinner we were going to enjoy. When we sat at our table by a terrace garden window, I imagined that I was in a romance movie, complete with a standing bucket of ice and champagne at the edge of the table. I was delighted when the fancy waiter popped the cork and poured a sip for Tomas. This was special — not one of our casual hotel dinners. This was a classy, upscale restaurant — the kind my father would select to entertain his powerful guests.

Tomas took the sip and nodded his approval. The waiter poured our glasses and I heard the small clink and swish of ice the bottle made as he set the bottle back in the bucket. This all felt right to me and I smiled my approval at Tomas. I had the serious attention of a young successful man from a powerful family. My father's smile crossed the back of my mind. At last, I had his approval, or so I hoped.

Tomas reached across the table and took my hand. His hand was warm and firm. He looked at me for a moment, then tilted his head as if to study my reaction to what he was about to say.

"I have never stopped loving you, Sydney. Since the moment I saw you in Rio Quarto when you offered to pull me so that I could ski. I knew then that you were different and that you would be mine."

He paused. I just looked at him, thinking he wanted to begin a real romance. My heart raced. I wasn't sure I wanted to hear what he was going to say. Tomas spoke quietly and I tried to breathe.

"Do you want to continue your studies? Do you want to go back to Atlanta? What is there for you anyway? What are your plans for the future?" He asked these questions without giving me any time to think or answer.

I sat back and let go of his hand. "I know this is a lot, but I need to know your answers," he insisted.

I closed my eyes to think. He took my hand again and held it tightly. "Sydney, look at me," he commanded softly.

I looked at him and spoke as honestly as I could. "Tomas, I really don't want to study, I don't know if I want to go back to Atlanta, and to be honest, I don't know what I want for my future."

His eyes lit up, and he excitedly stated, without hesitation, "Then let's get married!"

I inhaled, shocked, surprised. and completely certain all at once. Consciously, I had no suspicion, no fantasy, no imagining that Tomas was going to propose to me. In fact, I was not able at that point in my life to actually create an image of a life I wanted. I was not self-aware enough to know that such a thing was possible. But I knew I wanted to be loved, appreciated, spoiled, adored, and cared for. Zoryia had taught me that we deserved these things and, together, we had been holding our breath for nineteen years.

Tomas' proposal was unexpected, but a deeply longing, bold, and adventurous part of me wanted it. This was mine. I exhaled. "Yes!" and closed my eyes. I watched Zoryia rush past the dark fog of constant fear that shaped the landscape of everything we knew and jump.

The word vibrated in my brain as we landed on our feet, then rolled to the ground. We tumbled gently in a soft green field, looked up and giggled at a very blue sky. We were loved by a wealthy young man and his powerful family. The fog was behind us and we never needed to look back.

Tomas squeezed my hand. I looked at him at first through a haze of blue. It cleared quickly and I looked around the elegant restaurant. I had sat down in this chair as a cautious, wounded, teenager across from a man I liked and trusted only enough to show me a good time. When I said yes, I became a young woman looking at a man I trusted enough to show me a good life. I knew he wasn't perfect. I wasn't in love with him. But I had made my own decision and trusted where my life was going, without question. It wasn't a leap of faith. It felt right. It was a certainty.

"Did your parents know you were going to propose tonight?" I asked him calmly, as if asking what he wanted for dinner.

Tomas kissed my hand. "Yes, they encouraged me to go ahead and not wait another minute."

I mused how he had not asked me to marry him in the traditional, romantic sense. We had never shared a preamble or "what if" conversation couples may have when they are deeply in love. He had told me he loved me before tonight. Granted, each time he had been trying to pull down my panties.

None of that mattered. This rich romantic setting, the wine and candles, the fine china and white linens, was where I belonged. Everything seemed romantic should anyone ask, but throughout our time together, he never asked me how I felt about him. And more importantly, I had never told him my truth. Our truth; mine and Zoryia's.

Wita would be pleased. As one of the most important contributors to my safety and well-being in life, I wanted to make sure her greatest dream — having a family member continue her Costa Rican legacy, would come true. I knew that I had been a burden on her and Wito and hoped that by marrying Tomas, I could pay back at least some of what I owed my grandparents. My father would have to approve. At that time, the Fulcos were his equals in business and influence in their country's government.

CHAPTER 19

Our News

At nineteen, I was young enough to believe I knew where my decision would lead — an easier path to a white picket fence, babies, friends, and a supportive family that would take care of me forever. It felt wonderful to be approved of by the Fulcos. I was also old enough to suspect their true motives — our marriage could help their son get ahead in business and society. That was fine with me. If I would never be a real part of Mateo's family, I would be an integral part of Tomas' family.

I woke up in the guest bedroom in Grecia with sun streaming through the windows. Speckles of dust floated in the air. I stretched. Excited for my new life ahead, and relieved that I didn't have to wear Mateo's colors anymore. I didn't need to live with Juliana or the Witos anymore. I would be a married woman and part of a wealthy, powerful family. The Fulcos were more honest and real, to me, than any family I had lived with before.

I got ready for breakfast. As I dried my hair, I smiled in the mirror and imagined Wita's face when we told her our news. Dressed and ready, I heard her car pull up outside my window. I quickly checked myself one last time and ran out of the room without making my bed. The maids would take care of it. I greeted her at the front door.

"Wita, I have such wonderful news!" I hugged her tight.

"Que pasó,"? she asked.

"Let's go to the terrace," I smiled.

"Okay, pero, I should say hello to the family."

"Don't worry about them right now. Come with me." I said and grabbed her hand.

We sat down in the covered terrace. It smelled of morning mist from the midnight rain. The kitchen maid approached and asked, "Buenos Dias, doña Adriana. Quieres algo de tomar?"

"Un cafécito, porfavor," Wita responded. The maid took note and looked at me expectantly.

"Yo tambien gracias," I replied.

"So, what is dis exciting news jou have for me?" Wita asked.

I leaned toward her across the table and said quietly, "This is just between us."

She opened her eyes wide, nodded quickly and leaned toward me. "I am all earrs...."

"Tomas took me out last night and we had very elegant dinner." I paused to scan the terrace. "We talked about my future," I leaned forward a little deeper and spread my hands on the table between us. Wita took a deep breath.

I continued. My voice was a high-pitched whisper, "He asked me to marry him."

Wita's clasped her hands together. "Ay, oh, oh, what did jou say?"

"Well, it looks like you might lose your money for my return ticket," I paused dramatically and sat back in my chair.

She sat still and said nothing. I realized in that moment that she had wanted this for me from the day we arrived in Costa Rica for our family vacation, four years earlier.

"Of course she did," I thought. "Wita," I said quietly, I will be staying here. I said yes."

"Si, I am so happy for jou," she said warmly, stood up and clapped. "This family is so wonderful. Jou are going to have de most incredible life. This makes my dreams for jou come true. I knew it. I knew it would be so. Does jour mother know? Where is the rring?"

I replied laughing, no longer concerned about being heard. "I'm sure he will give me a ring soon. You are the only one who knows. He wasn't sure I would say yes. But, he did ask about my plans for college before he proposed."

"I'm sure he will get de very best ring for jou, as jou are *my* granddaughter. I promise not to say anything until his parents know and agree to this union."

We hugged and Wita pulled out her kerchief from her bra and dabbed her eyes.

The sliding glass door from the main house to the terrace slid open. Tomas came out, greeted Wita, and looked at me expectantly. I nodded yes. They hugged and Wita whispered in his ear but loud enough for me to hear, "I am very happy for jou both. Jou have my and Wito's blessing. A happy life to jou both. Many childrren and moments of joy togetherr."

Tomas replied in a quiet voice, "Thank you, Wita. I will always cherish your granddaughter and what she means to this family."

His parents came out to the terrace for breakfast. Their mood was light, and the conversation revolved around Wita's visit with her family. I noticed that Tomas was attentive but kept clearing his throat. Wita asked for a glass of orange juice, smiled and said politely, "I need to call Wito, if jou will excuse me." With glass in hand, she walked back into the house.

Everyone grew quiet as they focused on breakfast eggs, sausages, tortillas and coffee. I tried to imagine Wito's response, then relaxed and listened to the birds in the background chirping. A slight cool early morning breeze lifted a stray wisp of my hair.

The smell of sulfur had not yet touched the air. It was my favorite time of day. At that point in life, it was my happiest moment ever.

I took a sip of coffee and wondered if Tomas was going to wait for Wita to return to announce our engagement. Just as I put down my mug, Tomas stood up and said, "I have some news."

Melia reached for Otto's hand mid-flight to a plate of cheese. Otto looked up intensely. Their eyes met in agreement. "Go ahead son, we are here."

Tomas touched my arm. I stood up and took his hand. Melia's free hand brought her napkin up to wipe her eyes, already filling with tears.

"We have decided to get married. Sydney has agreed to become my wife."

Otto sat back in his chair and crossed his arms. He looked intently at me with his bird-sharp eyes. Tomas and I sat down, still holding hands.

"Are you sure you are ready for marriage?" he asked me. "This is a big commitment and you are still very young. I don't know your father, only about him and who he is. Will he approve of this union? Will he give you his blessing?"

Otto's question made me more than uncomfortable. I grew very warm, thinking about my answer. I didn't know what to say because I didn't want Otto to know Mateo's opinion of me or my dismissal from his home. I looked at Otto and shook my head no. "It doesn't matter," I replied slowly. "What I do or don't do is of no concern to him."

I honestly believed that I didn't matter to my father in any way, whether I married, died, or had children, it simply did not concern his world or what he cared about. Sweat seeped down my chest and underarms. I wanted to take a shower.

Otto narrowed his eyes and didn't say a word. His expression was very subtle. He seemed to shrug his shoulders with his face. Other than what I had shared with Tomas about my father, I'm sure Otto had his own sources. Yet it was proper and customary to ask the question. Just as that non-expressive feeling passed, he pushed back his chair and stood up. With a bolstering, deep broad voice, he said then, "So shall it be. Another union of the Santo and Fulco families will be blessed."

Tomas stood up and hugged his parents. Melia hugged me. Wita, listening just beyond the terrace, walked in, hugged Melia and said, "Que felicidad! This is good news."

Otto looked at Melia and said, "Let's start planning the engagement party." He turned back to Tomas and asked, "When do you want to have the ceremony?"

Melia answered his question. Later I realized that she had already planned everything because directing major family events was her purpose in life and, no one could get in her way once she had permission to proceed from Otto. "We should have it in March. The orchids will be in full bloom in Grecia and there are no big church events. I will ask Archbishop Villalobos to perform the ceremony at Iglesia de la Nuesta Señora de las Mercedes and I'll invite President Rafael Angel Calderon Fournier, for he should be there as well."

"Oh, how nice," said Wita. "I will tell our familia. We will have to send out invitations as soon as possible so that everryone can come!"

I was already feeling overwhelmed and excited. Our wedding was going to be a grand affair. That night in my journal, I imagined the flowers and colors I wanted for my wedding, and for Zoryia's wedding. She smiled at me under a crystal blue sky. Her arms held an array of white wildflowers tied with a lavender ribbon.

CHAPTER 20

Their Glory

As if from a side balcony, I watched Melia command the stage. She orchestrated all the details of the plans for our wedding and reception. I was not the star — she was. Tomas had little to say about anything. But I don't think he cared very much. His mother had it all under control, as it should be.

Matriarch of this influential and wealthy family, Melia's youngest son was to marry the great-grandniece of a former Costa Rica president. A full Saturday afternoon Mass would demonstrate the family's importance to the political journalists strategically invited to cover the wedding. Hosting a reception for more than 400 prominent families and government dignitaries on the grounds of their home in Grecia, the Fulcos would be envied by Costa Rican society and talked about for many months.

Nothing was too expensive. Melia's guest list grew as we got closer to the day. Every time she confirmed the attendance of a diplomat or associate he wanted to impress, Otto's pride was as obvious as a peacock's plume.

Melia brushed aside my ideas and questions with a dismissing flick of her hand. "You are going to be the perfect, beautiful bride," she said repeatedly in an unconcerned tone. She did allow a respected local seamstress to work with me to design my dress and her event coordinator asked what I wanted for my wedding colors. Melia approved my choices and I hoped that her concessions meant that what I wanted mattered, at least to some degree.

My lack of Spanish fluency with the seamstress resulted in a dress that had wings as sleeves instead of fitted sleeves that cupped my shoulders. I thought she understood my request during the fitting. When my wedding dress was brought to the house, I told Melia the sleeves were wrong, and I wanted them altered. She replied curtly as she walked out of my room, "There is no time to make such trivial changes. The sleeves are lovely, and you will be lovely." A dark fog flooded my stomach as I looked at the dress suspended on my closet door. It was suddenly clear to me. All the warmth and kindness she had shown me up to our engagement was her attempt to encourage me to want what Tomas wanted. He got his wish. Melia saw me as a necessary part of fulfilling his wish, but not the center of it.

"I don't care," I told myself. "It's just a fucking dress." I sat down on my bed. My stomach hurt. I knew I was in trouble. "What the hell am I doing? Am I running away, or getting what I really want? Or both?"

In my heart, I knew I wasn't in love with Tomas. Every time I asked for something, but was politely corrected by those in charge, I felt a familiar stab of disappointment. Every day, my initial certainty of a grand life that I wanted slipped away in pieces.

I didn't know how to say to anyone — or have anyone to say it to — that from the moment I said "Yes," to what I thought had been promised, a life of love and security, had little to do with the world happening around me.

In my journal one night, I told Zoryia everything. She listened carefully, then told me she also was engaged, to a Prince she didn't know well enough to love. He seemed to be a good but older man who shared her intolerance of evil Mandragons and the influences of the powers that threatened his land. But she knew her only hope for happiness required giving birth to a son. Once a male heir was in place, she might be able to use her influence of truth to help her husband govern well.

The evening before our wedding, Mom and Hugo, Wita's family and my cousins, were received at the Fulco's apartment compound in San Jose. Tomas and I greeted our guests and, as far as anyone could tell, I was the fortunate and beautiful nineteen-year-old, bride-to-be of Otto and Melia Fulco's youngest son. After all, any young woman of good standing would be honored with such a prestigious and prosperous union. No one questioned anything. The evening was filled with food and mariachi music. Everything was clearly perfect, including my dress and eyeliner. Dancing continued after midnight.

The next morning — my wedding day — I placed a call to Erik's home in El Salvador. For some deep reason I could not explain, I needed to know that I was doing the right thing. In fact,

I needed to know there was no going back to the love, heart, and passion for a man that I had experienced with Erik. Something within me longed to connect with what we had shared and I in no way experienced with Tomas. I only knew that Erik was not ready to commit to my life, what my life needed to proceed with enough certainty to commit to what I needed. A family with the means to offer me a life where I could be an asset, where I could be of value to the family members and what they wanted to achieve in society. At least being tied to a family in Costa Rica separated my opportunities to be independent from my father's ties in El Salvador.

"Hola, Doña Gilda, this is Sydney." I said to Erik's mother's voice which I was so relieved to hear. I trusted our relationship and knew that she would give me an honest answer to my questions.

"How are you and your family? I am so glad to hear your voice!"

"Why, Sydney, hello, I am well. I trust that you are as well. I understand from Erik that you are getting married. So, forgive me if I ask, why are you calling today?"

"Doña Gilda, I am getting married actually today. That is true. But also, to be true to myself and your son, I need to know something. I hope that you, someone I deeply respect, can give me an honest answer because it affects your son's future as well as my own."

Doña Gilda responded, "I don't think it is proper to respond or to discuss anything at this point. There is no need. Live your life as you choose and let Erik do the same. There is no need to talk to him. Please, never call here again."

"But is he there? Can I talk to him?" I asked.

"No, he isn't." she answered.

"I understand," I said quietly. "I respect your wishes. But please, should Erik ask, please, let him know that I called and that I wish him every happiness."

141

Doña Gilda paused, then replied, "Sydney, I will do nothing of the sort." And hung up.

I got back in bed and pulled the covers up. I was confused and scared, determined and completely without any idea of what to do next, except to move forward with the decision I had already made. I should have called Erik days ago, but I did not. I simply had to call to know that this young man I had loved from the moment we had first connected was no longer available to me.

Juliana came over shortly after my call to Erik's mother. She came into my room to check on me. I rolled over in bed. She saw my eyes, red and swollen, and asked, concerned, "What's wrong Muñeca? Did you get some sleep?"

I answered in a low voice so no one else could hear, "Not really. Mom, I'm scared. I don't know if I should do this."

She crossed the room and stood beside my bed.

"I feel like it's not my wedding," I said as I sat up and pushed the quilted cover aside.

"Melia just expects me to go along with what she wants. We didn't have a rehearsal. I don't know what to expect during the ceremony, I don't know what to do," I implored, hoping she would give me some guidance.

Juliana replied, trying to sound lighthearted, "Well, large wedding ceremonies are kind of set in stone here. Do you have a coordinator? Someone to help you?"

"Yeah," I replied. "But in America couples rehearse things — like where to stand, what to say and when to say it." I sighed. "Everyone laughs when I ask about anything. Like I'm supposed to know. Seriously Mom, I'm scared."

Juliana shrugged. "I'm not sure how to help you, Muñeca. Can you follow their lead? Do what they tell you to?"

"I guess I'll have to. If Melia thought I needed to know something, she would have told me by now."

"I wouldn't be so sure of that," Juliana replied with a nervous flip of her hair. "But I'll help if I can," she shrugged again.

"It's not just what I'm supposed to do," I said as I got out of bed and slipped on my house shoes again, focused on what Tomas needed.

"Mom, I need you to know that if you and Hugo weren't here, I don't know if I could do it," I smiled at her, then looked at my feet. "My father isn't here, and I don't understand why."

She replied with a subtle but quick edge to her voice, "Your father has reasons I don't understand, either. Really, I've never understood his reasons for anything." She shook her head as if saying "no," then paused to look at me and took my hands. "He should be here for you, Muñeca. In my heart, I'm pretty sure it's not because of me."

She took a deep breath and said slowly, as if she was committing to something, she didn't want to but had to. "One thing I do know, is that you do not have to marry Tomas if," she paused, "you don't want to."

"Mom," I asked, "can I back out now?" I wanted her to tell me that it wasn't too late. That I could walk away and go back to Atlanta. That it would all be okay.

She said nothing and bowed her head. I told her my deepest fear. "The Archbishop, the President, Wita's family, and four-hundred people I don't even know are here for this wedding. I don't want to be a laughingstock. I don't want to hurt Wita and embarrass the Fulcos." I sighed aloud, crossing my arms, holding myself tightly, hoping for a way out she couldn't provide.

Juliana stepped to me and folded me in her arms. I laid my head on her shoulder and tried to feel the comfort she offered. A few quiet moments passed as she stroked my hair. She whispered and I listened closely, "Marriage isn't easy, even when you are in love. It's much harder when you aren't. You haven't had enough time to get to know Tomas or what kind of husband he will be.

And he doesn't know the special things about you that make you so lovable."

My throat ached with her words. "Tomas wants what he sees and imagines," she laughed gently and hugged me tighter, "and he thinks that he deserves what he believes."

She stepped back and took my hands. "One thing I've learned in my life, is that certain men love what they believe about a woman." I pulled back and looked at her puzzled, not sure what she was trying to say. She continued, "Some men believe they deserve what they want, regardless of what you want." She paused and gave me a little smile. "But Hugo and I will support whatever decision you make."

I realize now that this was the most sincere thing my mother ever said to me. Her wisdom and vulnerability hit me hard in that moment. I looked at her puzzled — and loved her more for her sincerity. In the next moment, Melia's makeup artist, hairdresser and wedding coordinator knocked politely and entered my room. Anything Juliana or I needed or wanted became an instant swirl of gratification. When I asked for a mimosa while my hair was being pinned into a French Twist, they brought it to me right away, freshly made from oranges grown in the Fulco's backyard.

With the drink in my hand, I turned to my hairdresser. "Please give me a moment, I need to get something."

"Of course, your hair will be fine, just don't touch it," she replied.

Juliana asked, "Sydney, where are you going?"

"Oh, I forgot. I have to take a little pill every day. I guess I should start now. Is it okay to take it with a mimosa?"

With a small gasp, Juliana asked, "What little pill are you taking?"

"Melia took me to her doctor so I could get on birth control. I thought I should start today."

Mom's jaw dropped, in shock, and asked, "How long ago was your appointment?"

"Well, it was when we got engaged, so about two months ago."

"Uh … ok, I guess this is as good a time as any. And sure, why not, take it with a mimosa!" She looked away.

I popped the little pill from its pack and swallowed. The doctor had told me that as long as I took one every day at the same time, I would not get pregnant. I put the pack back in my honeymoon bag to make sure I stayed on schedule. Mom kissed me and left to get ready for her role as mother of the bride.

At breakfast on the terrace, which I simply could not eat, I watched the servants put linens on the tables, with fresh-cut flower center pieces and white china. Melia moved around the house making sure the food was covered in mosquito nets until ready to be served. Her orchids were in full bloom and surrounded the entire gazebo. Little floating candles were placed in the pool. The DJ was setting up and I could hear him testing the microphones and speakers. Our reception in the backyard would offer a roasted pig, meticulously laid out in the center of the gazebo. Tents had been put up the day before and staged with tables and chairs.

Traditional Cumbias played softly throughout the house. It seemed to energize all the staff and they moved with a bounce in their step. I was in a kind of trance when I returned to my room to get dressed.

I was almost ready to go when Juliana came back to my room wearing her white, traditional dress of the mother of the bride. She looked happy and radiant. Wita and her family were already at the church. Wito was waiting on the church steps to give me away.

Two maids helped me dress, lowering it so I could step into the folds. As Juliana buttoned each satin covered button on my back, another servant lifted the bottom of my dress and guided my feet into high heels covered with the same satin as my dress.

Juliana stood back, looked at me and tried not to cry. I wondered if it was because I was getting married, or because she knew the truth about how I felt.

I remember very little about the wedding itself. I stepped into and out of Otto's mother's old blue Mercedes. Melia had selected that car for its nostalgic class and elegance. The long Catholic Mass, much of it in Latin which no one understood but the Archbishop, happened without my attention. I do remember Aunt Isa by my side as my Godmother, and her husband Pedro, the man who called me a dirty girl when I was fourteen, stood beside Tomas as his Witness. I remember we exchanged traditional vows and our wrists were tied by a ribbon. I smiled at an endless flash of lights while we posed for photos.

I remember standing in line for hours as we greeted hundreds of guests at the entrance to our reception. I remember mourning my favorite pig, Alfonzo, cooked and displayed belly down with full body intact, on a banquet table surrounded by grilled vegetables and decorations. Otto had given me Alfonzo as a Christmas gift and as a token of his affection. I loved that pig. Otto laughed when he saw me bend over and gently kiss its sweaty, dead head. I remember dancing with Tomas, his friends and Otto's guests. Finally, I remember saying goodbye and riding in the back of a long black limousine. I knew I was married — and that I had made a mistake. The biggest mistake of my life. I knew that I had to create new colors, colors I could not see.

CHAPTER 21

Honeymoon Ends

Exhausted, Tomas wrapped his arm around me, and we relaxed together on our way to San Jose. The pressure of the wedding and reception began to fade. We could just be ourselves. I wanted to feel happy. Happiness will come, I told myself. *This is our lives now*! I thought and began to pay attention.

We checked into a local hotel and Tomas said he was going to sleep. That sounded good to me. It was a bit awkward because I took off my wedding dress and hung it on the hook on the back of the bathroom door. I pulled on the special gown Wita had given me and slipped in beside him and reached for my husband's hand. He held it for a moment, squeezed it gently, and turned away from me. That felt good.

The next morning, we flew to Jamaica for our honeymoon. Getting through the Kingston airport was challenging. Tomas guided us through with his hand on my lower back. I felt better as we pushed past the beer and marijuana sellers wearing the traditional colorful Rasta caps. We laughed a lot. Married but not yet lovers, we found our way through the paths that lay before us to our honeymoon. I wondered if he felt as uncertain as I did about our first time together.

We enjoyed the scenery and private transfers from the airport to the Sandals Ocho Rios resort. The roads were rustic and bumpy, and it took more than an hour to get there. When we arrived, the staff treated us like long — awaited royalty. Our suite was large, just one floor below the penthouse. It faced the ocean with a wide patio.

I was excited to be there with Tomas. We had always enjoyed the beach as friends. We swam in the ocean, relaxed in our luxury beach chairs and had drinks by the pool. Watching the early rays of the Jamaican sunset, I wanted to stay and eat by the pool. Tomas said we had to get cleaned up for dinner. He had made reservations at a resort restaurant and suggested I would like to go dancing afterward. I was pleased that he had made these plans for us. *This is a good sign*, I thought. *We will always be friends.*

In the shower, I knew Tomas wanted to have sex that night. I thought he was being very respectful to wait. I relaxed, hoping that given our history, he wanted to take things naturally.

I stepped out of the shower and wrapped the towel around me. He knocked. I opened the door. He walked in and stared directly at me. Tomas reached behind my neck and drew my body into his. He kissed me hard and tasted like Scotch. I could feel his bulge under his bathing suit, and I could feel my heart race as I kissed him back. I knew I had to commit and give in, and I knew he wasn't going to wait any longer. *He is my husband*, I reminded myself.

Before the wedding, Erik had been my only lover. When we were intimate, he made love to me, and I made love to him. He helped me know what lovemaking with someone you care about should feel like. Erik and I were intense, passionate, careful, and connected to each other. I was eager to learn how making love with my husband would feel.

Tomas led me out of the bathroom and over to the bed. He pulled my towel off. He took a step back and stared at all of me. He breathed quiet, shallow pants. My stomach dropped. I'd seen this kind of behavior before. I was about to be pushed off a high diving board by my husband.

"You are driving me crazy," he said. Tomas pulled down and kicked off his bathing suit. He lifted me up by my waist and laid me back on the bed. His moves were so fast I kept my eyes on his face for clues about what he wanted me to do. He flipped me over and did what he wanted to do. Then it was done. He left me lying there. He had not taken any time or made any effort to show me love, or even that he cared for me. He was done. He got up and said he was going to take a shower. We were going to be late for dinner.

Without explanation or expectation, I understood that our marriage would have nothing to do with me or what I wanted. My body was now his vessel for ejaculation. His family had secured my services by allowing me to be his wife. I felt only the need to crawl into a closet and just leave when it was time to fly back to San Jose.

Tomas was happy and needed to make an appearance. I kept my shame and disappointment to myself, got ready in silence, and walked out of the hotel room. My head was up and eyes were dry. I now wore the colors of Tomas.

In the resort restaurant overlooking the ocean, we were seated at a nice table. We ordered some drinks and appetizers. I looked up to see a young man slapping Tomas on the shoulder saying, "Dei Mae!" Tomas jumped around and realized it was a high-school friend.

"Dei, what are you doing here," Tomas asked, surprised.

"I'm here on my anniversary trip with my wife, and you are here on your honeymoon. Congrats Mae, I read in the papers that you got hitched!"

Tomas stood up, hugged the man, and introduced me to his friend. "This is my wife, Sydney. Sydney, this is my good friend, Santiago, and his wife, Gloria." I smiled at Santiago and greeted him and Gloria European style with kisses on cheeks. Tomas said, "Why don't you join us. Grab some chairs and let's have dinner together."

Santiago, said, "No, you two enjoy your dinner. We can catch up tomorrow at the beach."

With that settled, Tomas smiled at me and told me all about his high-school friend, a story about Gloria and how they all met.

The following week was not what I expected for my honeymoon. Tomas spent most of his days playing tennis with Santiago, and I spent time with Gloria. She even joked that it seemed as if she and I were on a honeymoon. On the one day Tomas spent with me, we explored Dunn's River Falls and snorkeled on a reef. We laughed a lot and remembered how it felt to be good friends again. Each evening he would have me, his way.

It got a little stranger every time. No preamble, no foreplay, no getting close or communicating before he would take me from the position he wanted. I wondered if I would feel this empty for the rest of my life. I knew that it was somewhat my fault. I kept hoping that he would eventually want to take us to a place where we could make love, not just have sex, his way. I never told him how I felt. Maybe I kept silent because of my past, or maybe because I had learned to comply to get what I wanted.

In this marriage though, I wanted a family who would care about me. I wanted to be free from dependency on Juliana, Mateo, and even the Witos. But now I realized I was completely dependent on Tomas. And it was painfully clear that he had needs I could not understand.

What have I done? echoed in my head every quiet moment I spent listening to my heart. If Tomas rejected me, where could I go? I said nothing and smiled when expected to do so.

Zoryia would never marry for security. If she married to perhaps resolve a debt, she would have spoken her truth to the man out of respect for him and for herself. She wore her own colors. I was ready to go back "home." But what was home for me? I was about to find out.

CHAPTER 22

Abandoned

Otto and Melia had given us their San Jose apartment as a wedding gift. It was part of a compound they owned with two other apartments. The compound was surrounded by a high brick wall and two guarded, gated entrances.

Tomas' older brother, Rene, his wife and two daughters lived in one apartment, and Di-Ana and Tino lived in the other with their two daughters. Each apartment had three upstairs bedrooms, a guest bedroom and a master on the main level. Beyond the kitchen were servants' quarters. We didn't have any servants at the time, so my father, making a show of support for the Fulco's benefit, sent me one of his best maids, Marina, to live with us as a wedding gift. She was sweet, kind, and from what I could tell, very loyal. I loved her company.

When we moved into the apartment, it was overflowing with gifts from friends and Otto's business associates. It was a well-designed and decorated living space, suited for entertainment. I felt privileged to live there, but the kitchen smelled of a thousand meals shared by so many people I had never met. At night when we turned on the lights, the cockroaches would scatter. This was supposed to be our servant's domain, not mine.

Juliana returned to Costa Rica to visit me, friends and family. Tomas usually stayed at Rio Quartro on business. For fun, I went river rafting with Juliana and her friends on the Reventazon, a category-three river. That day, it became unexpectantly rough half way through our adventure. I fell out of the raft for a moment; then the guide pulled me back in. It was quite a ride. As the river slowed down to a smoother ride, I turned to Juliana and said, "I think I might be pregnant."

She stopped mid-stroke and gasped. "We have to see a doctor when we got back to make sure everything is okay."

On the ride back, she asked me if I was sure, and I said, "I'm pretty sure, I feel funny, and I'm late."

She looked at me questioningly, "I thought you were taking your birth-control pills."

I said, "Yes, I started the day I got married."

She put her head in her hands and shook her head back and forth. "Didn't the doctor tell you to start taking the pills at least a month before you had sex?"

I said, "No, I started taking them the day I got married, with my mimosa. No one told me to start taking them a month before, how would I know?"

"Well, if it's meant to be, then I'm happy for you. I will support you and the family will be so thrilled."

I replied, "I'm not so sure about his family. They will think we got married so quickly because I was already pregnant." I shrugged and looked down.

"Honestly Mom, we haven't even had sex since the honeymoon. I don't like the way he wants to do it." Mom asked, "Have you told him what you do like? How else would he know?"

"Not really Mom, I'm too embarrassed to mention it. He doesn't know about Peter, and he doesn't ask me anything. It's always all about him."

"Well, what was it like with Erik? Did you enjoy it with him?" Juliana asked quietly.

"I did. But it was very different. I dated Erik for years before we made love. He knew my past and waited until I was ready. When we were together, he always asked me how I felt and if what we were doing was okay with me."

"Well, you need to tell Tomas the same things so he can understand what you are comfortable with."

I knew I couldn't do that. Erik loved me and wanted me to love him. Tomas wanted something else.

She continued, "As far as other people are concerned about the pregnancy, they will do the math and know that you didn't marry because of a baby."

A couple of days later, the doctor confirmed I was pregnant.

CHAPTER 23

We're Pregnant!

Tomas had been away at Rio Quarto during the week and returned on a Friday night. We had talked on the phone about the apartment, his work, and his family. I had wanted to tell him about the baby, but decided it would be better in person. I waited until he was home. Juliana was there to support me and to show her excitement.

He was surprised to see Juliana but greeted her warmly and kissed her cheek. I handed him a card. "Open it," I said and led him to the couch. I sat down in the middle between him and Juliana. She held my hands as he read the card. We smiled waiting for him to finish reading.

When he was done, he put it down and stared at me. I reached for him, thinking he would want to hug me.

His cold stare scared me.

"What are you thinking?" I asked hesitantly. "Are you in shock?"

"How could this have happened?" he asked very coldly.

"What do you mean? I am having your baby. We must have gotten pregnant during our honeymoon." I grabbed his hand.

He didn't take it and stood up now visibly angry. "I thought you were on the pill to avoid this!" he stated sternly.

"I was," I said in a low soft tone. I was surprised that he reacted this way. "I started the pill the morning of our wedding. Isn't that what I was supposed to do?"

Tomas turned and starred at Juliana in disbelief. "Did you not teach your daughter about these things before we got married?"

Juliana didn't know how to respond to his accusation. "Tomas, this is a wonderful thing. You two are going to have a baby. That's the only important thing right now. You should be excited. I know you must be shocked at the news that you will be having a baby so soon after your wedding, but this is what it is." She tried to explain and soften the news.

"This wasn't the plan and now what are people going to think?" he glared at me and threw the card to the floor.

Tomas was pissed, angry, filled with upset. Juliana was scared by his reaction.

"Well, you are getting an abortion," he pointed at me as if he was telling me to clean up a mess.

I felt my world spin out of my control. I ran to the bathroom to throw up but couldn't. I sat back on the bathroom floor and rocked with my hands on my stomach and all I could see was Zoryia's face, the smooth whiteness of her skin and her black eyes crying.

"No" she rasped. "You are going to be a wonderful father. Your family can never make us destroy this one thing we love more than anything. This baby is a part of us, and they can't take it from us!" Zoryia watched her husband's face. He reached for her and pulled her to the bed. They held one another tightly. "As you say," he whispered.

Tomas left and returned the next morning. He grabbed some of his things and left without saying a word. Juliana and I talked about how he had behaved and tried to understand his reaction.

She asked me where he had gone. I said that he would either run to his parents or to Rio Quarto.

"When do you think he will be back?" she asked.

"I don't know," I replied. "He wants to be at Rio Quarto more than with me here."

"Well that is his main source of income. Maybe you should think about staying with him and getting used to being his wife in his business life."

I thought about it for a while. *Could I do that and have a baby he didn't want?* Juliana made tea for us.

Finally I responded, "I don't like living there. Vacationing at Rio Quarto is one thing, but I don't know. I hate bugs and it's hot. And what if something happened to the baby? We are so far from civilization."

She laughed a little, "Well, Muñeca, think about it and in the meantime, at least you will have maids to help you there and you can relax. I have to leave in a few days, but you can always call if you need me."

After she left, I called Tomas and asked if he wanted me to move to Rio Quarto. He didn't dismiss the idea. I knew it was because living with him there during the week would be acceptable to his family. He may not want to be a father. But he knew how to play his part. If I refused to get rid of the baby, he had no choice.

I moved to Rio Quarto and for the next couple of months, I did absolutely nothing. I was so bored I believed I would lose my mind. I played a lot of solitaire. I entertained myself by taking a lighter and my hairspray and flaming the humongous bugs that were determined to share my space. When burning bugs stopped being fun, I swam in the cold pool, which actually soothed my nausea. When Tomas came home to eat lunch and tell me all about his pineapples, I listened. We ate chicken with grilled pineapples for lunch, steak with pineapples for dinner, pineapple cake, pineapple pie, and waffles with pineapples for breakfast.

I think there was even a time that I took the family BB-gun and shot pineapples on the farm, just for fun. From the day I left Rio Cuarto, to this day, I have never eaten a single bite of pineapple.

I stayed at Rio Quarto until my fourth month of pregnancy. We got along like roommates until I told him I wanted to make our apartment in San Jose my home. Tomas said he was fine with the idea and actually came home from Rio Quarto on weekends. I think Melia and Otto must have told him to make the best of it. I was putting up an appearance and so should he.

We went out with his friends on Saturday nights and he acted proud to have my belly in tow. His friends seemed happy for us and, he bragged about being a father right out of the gate. I knew better.

During the week, I kept myself busy decorating the master bedroom to make it more my own. I didn't care what he wanted. Tomas wasn't around enough to care about. I decided to convert the downstairs guest room, which we used as a TV room, into the nursery.

Physically I was more comfortable, but emotionally more alone than ever. Other members of his family lived in our compound, but they became strangers who, after looking in my direction, didn't bother to wave or smile when they passed by. When Melia stopped by to check on me, she was polite but distant. Marina, my maid, spent most of her time in Grecia, offering meager excuses about why she needed to stay there. I kept quiet to keep the peace and focused on my health and the baby.

When I knew we might be able to find out the sex of the baby at my next OB-GYN appointment, Tomas said he had appointments that day. I asked Melia if she would like to go with me. She agreed and when the ultrasound was complete, my doctor asked if we wanted to know the sex.

Melia said, "Oh of course, we were hoping to find out."

I was so excited and giddy, I practically forgot about everything else I had been feeling.

"Please, doctor, yes, tell us," I agreed.

"You are having a boy," he said excitedly, knowing this was the first grandbaby boy for the Fulcos.

Melia hugged me tight, like she used to. With tears in her eyes, she exclaimed, "The Prince of the Fulcos! We will celebrate. He is our first namesake!" I wondered what she would have said had it been a girl.

Immediately, I became important to the Fulco family. But not necessarily Tomas. His mother called and gave him the news. She had this covered and he didn't need to worry about anything. He told her, not me, that he was pleased to be having a son, and would continue to live at Rio Quarto during the week.

I responded to his lack of attention by spending his money. I had carpet installed in the nursery. I had a muralist paint really cute bears on the walls. And I added privacy curtains and bought baby furniture.

I was having his son, the first namesake of the Fulcos. Melia had said so. Apparently I had deluded myself into thinking this would make a difference to Tomas.

During my second trimester, when I could finally feel the baby moving, I wanted to celebrate and prepared a special meal for Tomas' Friday-night meal with us. That evening we ate mostly in silence. I don't know if he was bothered by something or just tired. I wanted him to be as excited as I was. After dinner, I felt a flutter that I was sure that he could feel too, so I grabbed his hand. Tomas said he couldn't feel anything and to leave him alone. "You'll be able to feel him when he gets a little bit bigger," I said happily, forgetting that I was the only adult in the room who was actually happy. "It's wonderful, Tomas, almost like magic. There's a baby growing inside of me and I want you to know what it feels like."

"I'm sure when that time comes you will let me know. Could you bring me a drink? It's been a long week."

I handed Tomas an after-dinner drink and told him I had a big surprise. At this point I was absolutely desperate for some kind of positive response from the father of my baby.

"Close your eyes, I want to show you something," I said. "All right, I'll play along." He closed his eyes and I led him to the nursery. "Okay,, you can open your eyes now."

His mouth and eyes opened to a growing rage. "What the hell?" he exclaimed. "Where is my TV? How could you have done this without asking me first?"

"I didn't think it would be a problem," I replied quietly. "Your mother helped me. We moved your TV upstairs so you could have your space if the baby was crying. I thought it would be good to have him downstairs with us. Don't you like it?" I asked, trying to stop the tears burning my eyes. I didn't want him to see how scared I really was or how hard I was trying to make this apartment our family home.

Tomas rocked back on his heels and with his hands on his hips he looked up at the ceiling. "It doesn't matter if I like it or not." He gestured widely, encompassing the room. He turned to look at me and placed his hand on his hips with his chest out and shoulders back. "Your family hasn't given you any money. So, I want to know how much of *my money* you spent on this." His voice grew louder and higher with each word. He emphasized "*my money*" with his mouth and leaned forward, as if speaking to a child who couldn't hear.

I had no idea what to say and shook my head. He walked back and forth, pushed hard on the crib railing and, not realizing I was crossing the room behind him, turned into me and knocked me to the floor. I shouted accusingly, "You are out of control. You could have hurt your son."

"You're damned right I'm out of control," he shouted. "I go away and work my ass off just for you to sit here and spend my money on a baby I wasn't ready for. I have to get out of here."

He left in a huff, then came home late that night drunk and insisted on having sex — the first time since our honeymoon. I pushed him away and said, "No, I am not doing it with you. I don't love you, and I know you don't love me, either!"

He tried to say something. Even though his speech was heavy and slurred, I knew what he meant. Tomas stumbled upstairs and dropped asleep on the guest bed, fully clothed.

Since the honeymoon, the air between us had been soured by sexual tension. Over the months, we had somehow come to an unspoken understanding that we both wanted a good marriage, something that would serve both of us. But the individual expectations of what "a good marriage" meant had become an impossible nightmare of near despair for both of us. In those days, I had no idea how swiftly "the powers that be," in Tomas' world, could move to support his position.

The next morning, I wasn't sure what he remembered, and I was afraid of what he might do. Tomas said nothing and did what was easiest for him. He packed some clothes, got in his truck, and left me to figure out my own position. I pulled out my journal.

"How can you say that?" Zoryia asked her husband. "This is your son. I am your wife. I have sworn to defend your crown. Your child is innocent. He is not a weakness or threat to your power. Grow up and recognize the truth — he will be your greatest strength!"

The next morning, I realized how weak Tomas really was. He was completely dependent on his father's influence. I didn't know how to carry a baby inside me with a man I didn't respect.

Tomas was not my hero. He wanted nothing to do with either of us. He was bound to us by family expectations to publicly play the part, and the expectations of the society of which he wanted to remain a part. The illusion fully dissolved, I wanted a divorce. I needed Juliana to stay with me.

That afternoon, my stomach hurt, and I called Melia. She told me to see the doctor right away. I didn't mention that Tomas and I had argued or that he had accidently knocked me down. My doctor determined that I was in pre-term labor at only 21 weeks and admitted me to the hospital. He insisted on complete bedrest to help the baby's lungs develop in case I went into labor. For a few weeks, I was on an IV and could only drink broth to keep from throwing up my medications. During this time, Tomas visited me twice.

I could not attend the baby shower Melia had meticulously planned. She was disappointed but happy to know the baby was safe. At least she was concerned about us. I had no idea what Tomas said to her or if she defended me in any way. I did know that she understood my desire to prepare a home for her family's little prince.

At 28 weeks pregnant, I was allowed bedrest at home. A few days later, Juliana called to say that Hugo was being transferred to San Jose. It was the most incredible and unexpected news! I felt safe again, and Juliana told me that Hugo wanted to help me and the baby and that, no matter what happened, I would always have a home with them.

CHAPTER 24

Baby Bliss

Almost a year after I had arrived in Costa Rica with Wita, Marco was born. I told Tomas that morning our son would be born very soon, but on that day, he chose to play tennis in Grecia with friends.

Marco had fair skin, light eyes, and no hair. Tomas' German and English ancestry had made its mark on my son. From my side of the family, he was part Swiss, Norwegian, Italian, Greek, and Mayan. He was a unique, international blend of both our families. He had high-brow, pronounced cheek bones, and well-honed features. He had no hair, but most importantly, he had all his fingers and toes and I loved every ounce of him.

I was disappointed that Tomas missed the birth. And with the irritation and command allowed a new grandmother, Juliana called him and said impatiently, "Tomas, you have a son. Come see him today." He visited his son in the hospital that evening, and stopped by to kiss me on the cheek. "He is a handsome boy, and seems quite healthy," Tomas grinned, offering this one remark before leaving my room.

Two days after Marco was born, we were ready to go home. Juliana drove us to the apartment and stayed for the rest of the week. The following weekend, Tomas and I took Marco to Grecia

164

to meet his grandparents and their family. They were excited to see and hold him.

Melia went into full planning mode, asking me questions about the arrangements for his baptism in the local church. I had no expectations for a baptism with his family and resented her questions. Growing hotter by the minute, I realized that I needed to wear Tomas' colors for a while longer. I blamed my resentment on hormones, since Melia was so enthusiastic about the upcoming celebration.

A few days later I was in full baby mode and totally exhausted from breast feeding and lack of sleep, but excited when Melia called me to let me know, without asking me, that she had extended the invitation to my father and his family. I was surprised he had accepted the invitation and they would come to meet their grandson. It was a short few weeks later that I was driving Marco and myself back to Grecia, back to the little guest room where I stayed when I prepared to marry Tomas.

Mateo and his family came to the pre-ceremony reception at the church and I approached them with Marco in my arms. Mateo, Helga, and their daughters looked up and seemed very happy to meet Marco. I introduced Tomas to them, and we exchanged pleasantries. I looked into my father's eyes for a greeting of warmth, if not love. Nothing. I glanced at Helga, she smiled and looked back at Marco. My father's colors were worthless here. With a polite excuse, Tomas and I left to prepare for the ceremony.

At the reception in Grecia, everything was perfect, especially the food, music, flowers, and decorations. We took family pictures. I was glad that Mateo and his family were here for Marco's baptism, but confused about what their presence meant. I was restless, as if something was about to happen. Despite my deeply held disappointments, I told myself to enjoy the people and the moments for Marco's sake. This was, after all, his day.

Today, as I finished writing about this, I shook my hands to bring the circulation back. I leaned back on my chair and searched the box of memorabilia on my desk for photos of the baptism. I looked at them carefully and asked my memory to return to that backyard gazebo where our wedding reception had been held almost a year to the day. I smelled the orchids in the photos and remembered how deeply I had wanted the smiles on their faces and the appearance of everything being perfect to be real. Now, I understand why I was so unsettled that day. Something was definitely wrong. Just as a volcano spews little bits of smoke before it erupts, I should have seen it coming when Otto stood up to give his toast.

Clink, Clink, Clink!

Otto's toast was in Spanish, but my memory of what he said, and my feelings were all in English. "If all my guests could gather, please. Raise your glasses and let us toast to our first-born grandson, "Tomas Marco Fulco Achilles!" Everyone followed his command and raised their glasses to enjoy his speech.

Brushing my heart aside, I smoothed Marco's baptism gown and propped him up high so people could see his beautiful little face. I stood next to Otto holding my son in my arms.

"I am honored to finally have our namesake to carry on our family legacy and businesses. He will be no doubt, strong, smart, and dedicated to our family lineage. May God bless him and keep him with us always. Let there be no man or woman, (he turned and looked at me) interfere with his commitment to us." He grabbed Marco's little hand and bent down to kiss it lightly. "You, my grandson, are a blessing to us." Melia, at his side, smiled and stood up a little taller, showing pride and her full sense of belonging.

I missed the Witos. They had been unable to attend.

I remember feeling bad for Juliana and Mateo, because they were not given the opportunity to toast or add to Otto's remarks. In that place and moment, for some reason, I felt that Marco wasn't mine. I grabbed him tightly and refused to let Otto carry him. I held him as if I would somehow lose him if I let go. I was young but could not deny these intense feelings.

Tomas stood next to me and said nothing. He beamed on cue at his father's words. He had given his father what he always wanted, a family namesake. Later I realized that my parents had given no money to the Fulcos on my behalf, ever, and were present only by their permission to keep up appearances.

As the light fell and people began to take their leave, Mateo walked over to me with a proud smile as if something had been settled in his mind. He bent down to kiss Marco. Mateo grabbed his grandson's two little hands and whispered in French, "Maintenant, sois un bon garcon pour ta maman." I smiled at the request he was making of my son, "Now, be a good boy for your Mommy." Holding back tears in my eyes, I grinned at my father and, for the first time in a long time, felt a small connection. I leaned over and kissed Mateo's cheek. He patted me on the back and said that he would keep in touch. As he walked away with his family, my entire being hoped that his words were true and that his presence was not only for appearance sake, but for mine and his new grandson.

Just then, Juliana came up behind me and said, "This has been a wonderful day, I am so proud of you. Hugo will be staying at his ranch, for a few days. When he leaves, why don't you stay with me for a while because Wita will be there, too. It will be fun, and I can help you get some rest at night."

I replied, "Oh, that will be great. I think Tomas will be staying at Rio Quarto for work. He has told me that there is a huge shipment to prepare for and I don't feel like taking the baby there just yet. He is still too young."

"Perfect, then it's settled. Why don't you come Monday morning?"

We kissed goodbye and I gathered my things to go back to our apartment in San Jose. I thanked Otto and Melia for the wonderful party. Melia beamed at me and said, "I am happy to have the opportunity to celebrate Marco. You are not staying here, this weekend?"

"Oh," I replied. "I didn't bring things for us to stay the weekend."

Melia asked, "Didn't Tomas tell you we are all staying here for the weekend? I know Di-ana was looking forward to helping you with the baby."

"Where is Tomas? I haven't seen him for a while."

Melia smiled, "Why, he must be saying goodbye to the last of our guests. I'll go get him."

"No need." I shrugged. "Tomas didn't tell me to plan and stay the night. I'm tired and really need to get Marco home. He's going to wake up hungry and fussy from all of this."

"Okay, dear, I understand. We'll see you soon," Melia replied, some disappointment in her voice.

As I was putting Marco in his car seat, Tomas walked up to me and grabbed my shoulder firmly. Startled, I turned around. "You scared me!"

His stern face made it clear that he was unhappy with my preparations to leave. "Why aren't you staying the weekend?"

"You didn't tell me to plan on staying. I can't read your mind, Tomas."

"I did tell you; you just don't listen."

I shrugged my shoulders, pushed his hand away. I wasn't going to get into an argument, since there was no way I could stay without our things.

"I'm sorry, but we can't stay now anyway. There is no point in arguing in front of everyone. Are you coming with me?"

Tomas replied with quiet intensity, "I'm staying here with my family."

"Fine, we'll talk in the morning."

"No, call me when you get there."

I drove away feeling once again that we weren't his family.

CHAPTER 25

Wita Won

Monday morning, I woke up exhausted from being up all night with Marco. He sure did have his nights and days mixed up. I stumbled out of bed, taking advantage of his morning nap. I packed our bags to spend a week at Hugo's small ranch home about thirty minutes from the apartment compound in an area of Alajuela northwest of San Jose.

I told Tomas that we would be there for a week or maybe longer, because Wita was visiting and Juliana wanted to spend some time together with Marco. I said that if I was going to stay there longer, I would let him know and would be back to pick up more things for the baby. I also encouraged him to come visit if he had a chance because Wita wanted to see him. Tomas reminded me that this was the busiest season for the pineapple farm and the supply was in huge demand. He was extremely excited to have a new partnership with a North American company.

During my drive I felt really happy for Tomas and his work, but more excited to be seeing Juliana and Wita. I was finally going to get a full night's sleep.

As soon as I pulled up to the dirt road leading to the ranch house in El Cacoa, I rolled down my window to smell the sulfuric air and the delicious fruit trees that lined the driver's side of the road. I could see the clearing where I would turn into the gravel driveway to park the car. It was in front of a basketball court and the pool. To the left side of the house and pool was a covered rustic patio lined with hammocks and picnic tables and an open barbeque grill.

The sound of the tires crushing the gravel beneath the car was loud enough to be heard from inside the house. The moment I put my car in park, Wita ran out of the house with her arms in the air saying, "Ay, Yay, Ay ... mis bebes! I am so happy!"

I got out of the car and hugged my grandmother. It felt like home and I was instantly safe. I felt like I belonged. Juliana came out behind her with a big smile and went directly to get the baby out of his car seat.

I was a new person that week. I slept well and talked with Juliana and Wita about the differences between the Fulcos and our family. Wita was concerned about Tomas' behavior. From sunup to sundown every day, it was the best week I had experienced in a long time.

The week came to an end. Juliana asked if I could stay longer. I said there was no reason to go back home to be alone. Wita invited herself to join me back in San Jose to get more diapers, clean clothes, and formula. Juliana would stay at the ranch and take care of Marco to make things easier for us.

On the way to the apartment, Wita and I laughed and had a good time "shooting the shit," as we called our special way of communicating about things that are important; but needed to be humorous. We pulled into the entrance of the gate to the apartment. I did my usual light tap of the horn for the guard to open the gate and let us in. That day, he opened the little window of the guard stand, looked at us and closed it again. I looked over at Wita and said, "That's strange. He's never done that before and why didn't he open the gate?"

Wita, an impatient woman, reached across and honked the horn loudly, several times. The guard opened the window and closed it again. I looked at Wita and said, "That's the strangest thing. Should I get out of the car?"

Wita narrowed her brows and said, "Wat di hell is wrrong wit this man? Is he jour rregular guard?"

"Yeah, he is," I replied and rolled down my window and yelled out to him. "Is there something wrong with the gate, are you Okay?"

The guard station door slowly opened and Juan Demeo, our usual guard, looked around suspiciously as if he didn't want to be seen. He walked very quickly to my window and put his hand on my arm. I knew something was very wrong. His face said everything. Wita leaned over and demanded that he open the gate at once. He leaned into the window and said with his head down and in a low voice, "I'm sorry. I have strict orders to not let you in."

I did not understand what was going on. This was the gate to my home. I had done nothing wrong, nothing to warrant being kept outside of my own home. My heart began to pound hard in my chest. My face grew pale and my hands shook. I didn't know what to do or say. I was totally confused.

Wita, with her hand on my shoulder, pushed me back against the seat, leaned over and shouted, "Wat du jou mean? Jou can't let us in? Is there something wrrong wit jou? Arrre jou estupid? Open di door rright now."

He replied under his breath, "Trust me, if I could I would, but they will take my job away and I have eight children to feed."

Wita asked with as much indignant attitude and height as her small frame allowed, with slow deliberate speech, "Who gave jou dis orrder?"

"I cannot say, Doña Devold, I am sorry."

She spoke sharply, "I demand dat jou tell me rright now, or jou will lose jour job rright now."

"Doña Devold," he paused. "I have my orders, but I respect you very much and love your granddaughter. She has been so kind to me. Okay, but please don't say anything. I will let you in for ten minutes. Be quick, grab as much as you can, because they are trying to make it look like Sydney has abandoned her home."

"Pero," Wita replied, "Who orrdered dis estupidity?"

He looked down and whispered, "Don Otto Fulco."

Wita said, "Open di gate, quick. Sydney, jou go in and get everrything jou can. Dis is bullshit. Hijo de putas. Sydney, git jour passports, marriage certificate, and all jour documentos for Marco. Git only dis dings."

She turned to the guard, her face now red, "I want jou to write down dat it was el estupido, Otto Fulco, dat gave jou dis orrder and Sydney did not abandon her home." She pointed at the palm of her hand, "Dey will not get away wit dis!"

The guard looked at Wita and swallowed hard. He said with a sigh, "I will do this because I love Sydney and the new baby. They don't deserve this." He shrugged his shoulders, "If I lose my job, I'll find another one. I don't want to work for people like this. I have children and they are more important than what Don Fulco thinks is important."

Juan opened the gate and let us in. I pulled in to our apartment driveway. I got out of the car. My hands trembled and my legs felt like noodles. My mouth was too dry to swallow. I tried to think. "Why did Otto want to cut me off from my home without any reason or notice?"

Wita's voice pushed me forward, "Hurrry, git di documentos. We don't have time. Oye, now, Sydney, andale!" I trusted her instincts, but my body wasn't cooperating. I was swallowed in quicksand. Everything was spinning. Her voice was the only thing that gave me direction. Her voice was the only thing that mattered. I had no choice but to do as she commanded.

I grabbed a duffle bag and stuffed Marco's baby book and documents, which were in the same drawer and some supplies into the bag. I got my passport and legal documents and put them in a backpack. I grabbed some clothes and shoes, but the guard yelled into the door and said, "You need to get out now! Rene always comes home for lunch. He will be here any minute now. Go!"

I moved faster. My hands shook but somehow, I got back in the car. I had to put the key in the ignition. I took a deep breath and wiped my eyes so I could see what I was doing. We pulled away and headed towards El Cacao. The first fifteen minutes, Wita and I said nothing. Then she put her hand over my hand, gripping the stick shift. She said, "I don't know wat's going on, but together we will git through dis and those Hijo de putas will pay. I am sorry I didn't hearr wat jou were telling me before about living wit di Fulco familia."

I shrugged, "I didn't do anything to deserve this. I just don't understand why they hate me so much."

Wita pointed to her chest with her free hand and said, "Wita won! They won't git away wit dis. We have prroof. In life, Sydney, jou have to fight and dink ahead, and always be estrong enough to ask forr wat jou need. Asking is not weakness, but estrrength. Because only those who arre estrong enough to ask, have the capacity to receive wat they arre asking forr."

I realize now that she was right. I had, understandably, reacted as a victim. Not only because I was a young mother attacked by my baby's father and his family, I had been hurt and disappointed by almost every man I had ever known. My self-doubts, immaturity, and insecurity made me desperate to find someone who would take care of me. But I didn't know what I was doing.

When I said yes to Tomas, I had forgotten myself. But on the other hand, had I said no, I would not have my beautiful son or, as I was soon to learn, how strong I really was.

Driving back to Hugo's house gave me time to calm down and realize that I would have to rely on my gut more than ever. I didn't know how it would happen, but there would be a reckoning. Marco and I would find our way together, alongside Zoryia, who would show me how to act with strength and courage. Her power was truth. My truth was all I had. In both our worlds, a volcano was rumbling and about to erupt.

CHAPTER 26

Hugo, Just in Time

The following weeks were a blur. Juliana and I were in shock and kept trying to make sense about what happened. We went over everything, again and again. What had I done or said to make the Fulcos kick me out of the apartment? I never thought staying with Juliana at Hugo's ranch house in Cacao threatened Otto's claim on his family heir. One thing Tomas said he liked about me was that I was different from other women he knew. Apparently, Otto knew that as an American, I didn't share their values. I had no intention of living under Otto's rule and he knew it.

I called Tomas many times, but he never answered. Weeks later, he called me and insisted that we find a way to co-parent with a legal agreement. I asked him to explain why Otto had barred me from the apartment. Tomas said only that due to our separation, co-parenting Marco was the only thing we had to discuss. I was confused but wanted to cooperate, thinking a legal agreement would protect my status as Marco's mother. For Tomas and Otto, co-parenting was a legal grey area they intended to play to their family's advantage.

Hugo's good friend, Umberto, a family lawyer, told us that in Costa Rica, the law stated that we couldn't get a divorce until we were married for a minimum of three years. Separation was a grey zone. Legally, there were no parameters or guidelines for co-parenting. He confirmed my fears.

Tomas and his family suggested that they pick up Marco every other Friday afternoon and return him to me on Sundays before dinner. Juliana and I decided that this would be fair and verbally agreed to it.

Wita returned to the United States. Living in the little ranch house in Cacao reminded me of when I was pregnant and living in Rio Quarto. I was bored and frustrated, but happy to be safe with my baby. When Marco slept, I would sit outside in the almost complete silence and wonder what was next.

A few weeks later, Juliana called me from Mexico City where Hugo worked. She was so excited she could barely get the words out. She said, "You are not going to believe this."

"What?" I asked anxiously. "I need some good news. I'm going absolutely crazy. Please tell me some good news."

"I don't even know how this happened, but Hugo has been transferred back to Costa Rica!"

"What does that mean?" I didn't understand, but it sounded promising.

"Don't you see, we can buy a house in the city large enough for you to live with us. You can find a job. I can take care of the baby. You can start to figure out something for you. And we will be together."

"Oh, that's incredible!" I laughed nervously. "Did he ask to move to Costa Rica? And is he okay with us living with you?"

"He just got promoted and transferred. He wants to support you and the baby, at least long enough for you to get on your own feet and find a place of your own. But you won't be alone. Out of all the places in the world that Coca-Cola could transfer him to, they chose the place you needed us to be."

I will forever be grateful to Coca-Cola and to Hugo, who had the capacity and the strength to support me and my baby during this time. This was a huge blessing!

Things moved fast at that point. Tomas and I were polite with each another and he stuck to his commitment. He picked up Marco on Fridays and returned him on Sunday afternoons like clockwork. Mom and Hugo bought a house in Santa Ana, just outside San Jose near Escazú, an affluent area. It was surrounded by a large brick wall and had acres of land. It was in decent shape, and Juliana worked to renovate the interior. She hired a local couple to live in the guest quarters. The husband, Carlito, was our guard, gardener, and sometimes chauffeur. His wife, Leo, was our housekeeper and cook. Leo absolutely loved Marco. When I needed a break, she gladly jumped in. They became part of the family.

Marco woke up every hour on the hour. He was energetic and curious about everything. He ate breakfast, took a nap, played for a few hours, took another nap, had lunch, took an afternoon nap, had dinner and fought to stay awake at night. It was hard for me, but I wouldn't have changed that time for anything. On weekends, when Marco was with Tomas, I went grocery shopping or visited Sofia, my only friend. She was from El Salvador and now lived in Escazú. When I had Marco on weekends, Sofia and her two-year old daughter often visited us. She was a light and a refuge for me, as I tried to be for her.

One afternoon while I was visiting Sofia, she asked what I was going to do when Marco started school. Her question hit me hard. Recent conversations with Tomas and Melia flooded my head. Until that moment, I had naively assumed my future was assured by my marriage to Tomas. Trying to answer her question, my stomach began to hurt.

I sat quietly on her couch. I shook my head and looked at Sofia with tears. She explained that unless I was a citizen or legal resident of Costa Rica, I had no rights as a mother. If Tomas had never registered me as a resident of his country, I would not be able to get a job, buy a home or rent an apartment. I couldn't even register my son for school. As far as Costa Rican agencies were concerned, Tomas was in control of Marco's identity. I sat there, spiraling down a corkscrew again, but this time, my son was riding down with me.

I knew that I had no legal standing in Costa Rica. But it never occurred to me, until Sofia asked her question, that we were in trouble.

If Hugo got transferred again, what did that mean for us? If Mom divorced Hugo, what would that mean for us? Very clearly, I saw us standing very close to a ledge that we could be pushed over at any time. I had to grow up, right now, and find our way out. I had to change. Sofia grabbed my shoulders, looked me straight in my eyes, and said, "You are fucked!" I nodded in agreement and said, "I am, unless I do something about it."

Sofia knew my father through her husband's business. She insisted that I call Mateo and ask for help. "Don't wait another day, Sydney. He needs to know what you are going through."

She was right. Zoryia agreed. Somewhere, a volcano was waking up.

CHAPTER 27

Awe and Shock

I pulled up to the gate but didn't remember driving home from Sophia's house. I had been imagining scenes where I asked the Fulcos for what I rightly deserved, as Wita taught me. Carlitos opened the gate. I parked and sat in the car trying to figure out what to say.

I was sick with a gut-wrenching truth — the family I had trusted and joined in marriage, was intent on taking my life. How long I got to be Marco's mother would be determined by people who had no idea how much I loved him. I had to wake up. Now.

I decided.

I yelled for Juliana to come to the kitchen. She thought something was wrong and came quickly. Hugo followed and sat down at the island. I told them about the conversation I had with Sofia. They were stunned.

"Muñeca," Juliana said steadily, "your friend is absolutely right. What do you need to do?"

I looked at Hugo, hoping for guidance. He picked up on my cue. "First of all," he said, "you need to ask Tomas what he plans to do. He needs to step up to the plate and make sure you have a place here in Costa Rica with some legal standing. You are the mother of his child. It is his obligation to see to your well-being. And, I will call my lawyer friend Monday morning."

"Thank you, Hugo," I replied and tried to smile. "I'll talk to Tomas tomorrow afternoon when he returns Marco."

We talked more about these concerns and I took notes. We sat outside enjoying classical guitar recordings. I felt more at ease, as if we had accomplished a good plan. In that moment, I believed we could have a decent future in Costa Rica. I slept well that night and woke up the next morning energized and confident about what I had to say to Tomas.

I took a long shower and brought my laundry down to Leo to wash. I gave her a hug. She looked at me curiously when I said, "Thank you for everything you've done for me," feeling gratitude for having someone close to me that didn't judge me. I was confident things would begin to move toward what I needed. I didn't know why I felt so close and connected to everyone that day. It was real and strong and palpable. Leo felt it too, when she smiled at me with affection. I almost felt like a young girl again with the whole world ahead of me. I walked into the kitchen. Mom was in a similar mood. She made my favorite breakfast, Huevos Rancheros.

Hugo came down to join us and the conversation was light and fun. After breakfast, I asked Mom what she needed from the grocery store and left to shop. I got what was on her list and a little something special for Marco, his favorite teething crackers. They were American-made and beyond my budget, but I wanted him to enjoy something that gave him pleasure.

To this day, I still can smell his baby breath and those crackers. They would get so soggy and run down his chin and get stuck in the crease of his neck until I fished the mush out with a damp cloth. I enjoyed these moments.

The sunsets in Costa Rica are unexplainable. They are beyond description. Rays of hues of blues and pinks become indelible memories that can't be communicated with normal language. It's a visceral feeling that must be experienced to even begin to understand. The most you can hope for is to bring up the subject with someone who has also experienced this magnificence. Then you can share without words an emotional and physical event that others can only imagine to the best of their abilities.

On this particular afternoon, Leo entered the kitchen, grabbed my and Juliana's arms, and rushed us out to see the sunset. We all gazed at the shooting rays behind one of our largest palm trees, splendid with bursts of colors. All of us stood there in amazement. Mom held my hand and said, "This is the beginning of a good future for you. I just feel it."

Hugo walked out the door with Carlitos following and started preparing a barbeque on the patio grill. Juliana, Leo and I sat watching the sunset. We giggled and reminisced about happy times we remembered while we waited for Marco and Tomas to arrive.

The sun finally set. The barbeque was ready. I turned to Mom and said, "What time is it?"

She looked at her watch and said, "It's time to eat and it's about six thirty. Shouldn't Tomas be here by now?"

"Yes," I replied sitting up straight. "Maybe they had company at Grecia, but he could have called to say he would be late. I'll go check the machine."

I went inside and found no messages. Juliana came in and I told her there were none. "That's odd," she said, "he's never late. Call Grecia now."

I called. The maids said that Tomas was not home. I thought they were probably delayed for some reason. I'll wait another half hour. The time came and went. Still no message, no call, no information. I called Grecia again and asked if they had left later than usual. The maids had nothing to say. I asked to speak to Melia. They told me she was busy.

I started to panic. I turned to Juliana and said, "What if they were in an accident? What if they are lying in a ditch? What should I do?" I couldn't breathe. "This has never happened before, surely something is wrong."

Finally, Juliana called Grecia and asked to speak to Melia. They gave another excuse, but Juliana insisted that if they didn't put Melia or Otto on the phone, she would call the police.

After a long pause, Melia came to the phone, "Alo," she said in an even voice.

Juliana said, "Alo, we are worried because Tomas and Marco are not here, and we don't know where they are. Do you know anything?"

"No, Tomas should be on his way back here by now. They haven't arrived yet?"

"No, we are worried that something happened to them. We are going to call the local police and hospitals. Something is definitely wrong."

Juliana covered the mouthpiece, "Sydney, call the hospitals," she yelled. "Hugo, call...."

"Wait," Melia abruptly interrupted, "don't call anyone."

Juliana turned to tell us to wait, confused. "What are you trying to say?"

"Don't call anyone," Melia said. "I'll put Tomas on the phone."

Juliana asked, "Tomas is there? Muñeca! Tomas is at Grecia. Come here. I'll put the phone on speaker."

Hugo interjected, "What? He's in Grecia? Are they okay?"

Juliana shrugged and pushed the speaker button.

Tomas spoke with a cool, almost sarcastic voice, "We are okay. No need to get dramatic."

I yelled into the speaker phone, "Dramatic? I thought something happened to you. Why aren't you here? Where is Marco?"

"He is here, of course, with me," Tomas replied for all to hear.

"I don't understand what's going on," I shrieked. Again, I was helpless. I couldn't get into the apartment. The gate was closed and a guard, Melia, was blocking my way to my son.

The room spun, my hands shook, and nothing came out of my mouth at that moment.

Mom took over and started asking questions, "What the hell is going on? Why isn't Marco here, what are you up to?"

Tomas spoke, but it was his father's words I recognized — adamant, definite and defiant.

"Marco is a Fulco. Without your father's money, you will never be able to raise him properly. For us, you are dead.

"He will be taught that you died in childbirth. Forget about Marco and leave this country. You are a poor American girl who knows nothing. You have nothing, and are nothing to us, or to him."

Tomas hung up the phone. Mom cursed loudly in Spanish; Leo yelped in disbelief. Hugo put his hand over his face.

I was caught wearing white shorts again and had just been told to take them off.

CHAPTER 28

A Legal Battle

Click, dial tone . . . We stood looking at the phone. Hugo reached over and hung up the handset. The noise stopped. In my head it kept going. No one moved. I cried out. My cheeks were hot. Juliana hugged me and rubbed my back. She insisted that everything would be okay. Leo put her arms around us both. Hugo rubbed his temples, got up and crossed the kitchen.

"I'm getting a drink. Does anyone want one?"

I could have used a drink but took a deep breath. I wiped my tears and said, "This is bullshit. They can't do this. Marco is mine. He's my entire life! They are going to tell him I died?" I went from shock and disbelief to overwhelming sadness. Then boiling anger. Nobody was going to kill me off!

I pushed Juliana and Leo away. Blood pushed through my veins. I found Juliana's keys. Hugo grabbed them first.

He said softly but with sharp eyes, "This isn't the answer. You can't go over there right now. That is the worst idea. We have to be smart about this. You will come out of this and you will win. I will do everything I can to make sure of that."

"How?" I cried. "You don't understand these people. Look at what they've done. I've done everything they've asked. I haven't complained. I haven't made a fuss. I've been more than fair with them."

We sat in silence for a minute. The fear pressing against our hearts made it hard to think clearly. Then I said, with a thick lump in my throat, "I am nothing here, I have nothing in Costa Rica. The one thing I do know is that I am Marco's mother and will always be his mother. I can't let them keep him. I don't care who they are in this country. He is my baby." I looked at Hugo, took a breath, then asked him slowly. "How can you help us? Can you fight the Fulcos?"

Hugo wrapped his arm around my shoulder. "I may not have as much influence as Otto does, but I do know some people who can help us. Tomorrow morning, I will call my friend Umberto. He used to be a superior judge but now practices family law. I'll tell him what happened. He will take your case. Don't worry about the cost. In the meantime, write everything down."

He turned around to Leo and Carlitos leaning against the kitchen counter and said, "Things are going to change around here. I will give you a list of things to do to secure the property. You should both get a good sleep tonight." He turned to Juliana and said, "You need to be smart with what you tell your family. Remember your cousin is married to these people. Make sure you both stay calm and don't do anything drastic." He looked down at me again and asked, "Do you understand?" I nodded and wiped under my eyes with both hands. "You can't act afraid or vulnerable. You have to be strong, resolved. Show no emotions. Most important of all, be calm. Don't yell or argue with Tomas if he calls or shows up. If they think they can't shake you, they will make a mistake trying to shake you. Trust me. I've seen this kind of thing before."

I was so glad that Hugo was in our lives.

"It will be hard," he hugged me then dropped his hands to his hips. "But I know you can do it for Marco."

Looking back, I never understood why my mother married Hugo, but in a way the synchronicity of it all is quite uncanny. Had it not been for their marriage and his transfer to Costa Rica, I would have either been at the mercy of the Fulco family, or alone with my fear and anger. Wita's family might have taken me in for a while, but they would never have helped me get Marco back. I was amazed at how much Hugo cared about us. Now in reflection, I see how important he was in securing the course of our lives.

Tomas was Otto's son and would always be under his control. He had proven to me many times that he had no integrity and no courage to stand up to his father for any reason. I touched my right-hand ring finger. I lost my grandmother Titita's ring on that mountain and almost lost my life. I shuddered. I knew that I had the strength to never allow that man to ever take anything away from me again. Marco was mine. Tomas had no real desire to claim him as his own. Otto made him act like a father to maintain their position in society. If not for that, Tomas would have walked away from us. It was Otto who needed a male heir to continue his family line.

I watched the sunrise cast its rays on the empty crib at the end of my bed. For all the sleepless nights with Marco, I would give anything to have been awake all night with him again. He loved to get into my bed and play rather than close his eyes and fall asleep in my arms.

My eyes were swollen from crying all night and I was completely drained. But I remembered Hugo's advice, I had to be strong.

Zoryia's heart grieved and her body trembled. She reached inward and moaned outward. "This hurts too much!" She leaned back against the wide trunk of an old Hassion tree and shook her fist at its brittle limbs cracking and flying away from her, one by one, with each gust of wind. "I am the granddaughter of Laertes and Isadora!"

*she shouted. Her only concern was moving the pain out
of her heart and belly. "It is my right to raise my own son.
No one else can have him!"*

I whispered her words out loud, stopped crying, and put my
journal away. Today I would meet Hugo's friend and find out what
was possible.

Juliana and Leo were eating breakfast. I sat at the kitchen
island and listened quietly to their conversation. Leo got up and
brought me some orange juice, freshly squeezed as always. I
sipped it but could barely taste it. Hugo laughed in the other room
and I looked at Juliana. She nodded and explained that he was
on the phone with Umberto. "Oh," I sighed with relief. "I thought
he had forgotten."

Just when I hoped things are getting better, they got worse.
"Mom, I want to get my baby and never come back here. It hurts
too much. I can't do it. Tomas hates me because Otto hates me,
and I don't know why."

"Muñeca," she said as she leaned across the kitchen island
and took my hands. "I don't know what the hell their fucking
problem is. I've seen you bend over backwards for them, even
after everything they did to you. Let's just focus on what we have
to do today. In fact, I sent your father a fax. He knows you need
his help. This kind of thing could make him look bad if he lets it
happen."

Just at that moment, Hugo strode into the kitchen, threw
an imaginary cape behind his shoulders and stood in a wide
superhero stance with his hands on his hips. "Ah ha! Umberto has
agreed to take your case, and he's made time to see you today."

I blinked and look at him, not ready to smile, but the fast
pounding in my heart made me catch my breath. "Thank you so
much," I managed to say.

"Well, don't thank me yet," he replied. "Umberto did say this is going to be a long process and it won't be easy. Remember, in Costa Rica you must stay married for a minimum of three years before you can get a divorce. There is no legal separation and or guidelines as to who keeps the baby. As far as the law is concerned, you both have equal right to have Marco. You will have to prove that Tomas is not taking care of him. If he cannot, then the baby should be with the parent that can.

"Well, I'm sure Tomas is at Rio Quarto during the week, but his mother and their maids are tending to Marco," I said tentatively.

"Exactly!" Hugo replied. "Now we just need to prove it."

"But how?" I asked. "You think it matters that Melia is taking care of Marco?"

Assuming the smirk of superhero who knows something others don't, Hugo cocked his head to the side and said, "It might. Yesterday, Juliana hired a detective to spy on Tomas' every move. He will document everything. Trust me. You will have proof one way or another. Now eat some breakfast and take your mother's car to meet Umberto. I'll write down the address."

As he reached for his coffee, Hugo whipped his head around sharply and said, "Those assholes don't know who they are messing with. But," he said, raising his finger in the air defiantly, "a good strategy is to keep them thinking that we know we've lost and accepted our fate."

I giggled a small concession to his plan and saw a small but distinct light at the end of the tunnel.

At the meeting later that morning, I felt better as soon as I shook Umberto's hand. He was tall, slim, with light brown skin. He spoke fluent English and I could barely detect a Spanish accent. He seemed very confident and reassuring.

"Call me Umberto, please. And may I call you Sydney?" he asked respectfully.

"Yes," I smiled and for some reason started to breathe a little easier. His voice was warm, and I instantly liked his dark green eyes and distinguished short grey hair.

"I know you are worried but it's actually a straightforward case. Your private detective, Chulo Estevez, a man I've worked with before, will follow Tomas until he has proof that either he is, or is not, Marco's primary caregiver. If he is not, I will file your claim and stay on the case until Marco is in your arms again."

I started to cry but didn't care.

"You've been through too much, Sydney, to lose your son," he said gently. "The Fulcos have a lot of friends in high places, as they say, but I am going to do everything I can to win this case for you."

We stood up and I hugged him, trying not to wet his suit jacket with my tears. He hugged me back politely and walked me to the door of his reception area.

"You don't need to do anything but keep busy and wait to hear from me. Don't call the Fulcos or anyone working for them. You can visit your friends and go shopping, that kind of thing. But stay close to home with Hugo and Juliana. Do not leave the city. For all we know, the Fulcos could be watching you."

I laughed a nervous laugh when he said that, but I had nothing to fear as long as they were looking for the truth. I went home and gave myself permission to keep hoping things would work in my favor. I thought it would only take a week or so. The legal system had other ideas. It doesn't move as fast as a mother's heart. By the time Umberto and Chulo were able to show that Tomas was not an active father, then get the judge to rule in my favor, then finalize the court order, I had missed a month of my baby's life. I may have missed his first words, his first steps, without a picture, or touch, or whiff of my baby's head to remember. My soul was as empty as my arms. My heart barely kept my blood moving while my mind tried to move things along faster. It was excruciating.

I wanted to get my baby back before his first birthday but could only wait for the news I had to hear. At 9:00 a.m., Wednesday, December 6, one week before Marco's birthday, the phone rang. Umberto proudly told me he was coming to pick me up — *now*. I shrieked and jumped and yelled "Mom!" She ran into the kitchen, "What, Mi hija?"

"Everything went through. Umberto's coming to pick me up, right now. I have to get dressed and get a diaper bag ready. Are you coming with me?"

She replied, "No, I think I should stay here. You should do this on your own."

I looked at her briefly and wondered what the hell her problem was. She had helped me so much — why wouldn't she go with me? I didn't have time to think about it. I had to go get my son.

The gate buzzed. Leo yelled out to me. I grabbed my purse, the car seat and diaper bag, and ran out to the carport. Umberto was standing beside a long, black sedan. His driver nodded at me and waited. Behind him, two more black sedans waited with men inside. They looked at me and nodded. I was surprised but greeted him excitedly. He said, "I see you've noticed the caravan," his voice was a little tense.

"Why are they here?" I asked.

Umberto shifted his feet and looked down for a moment. "I felt we should have some backup."

"What do you mean, backup?" I asked. A sharp pain ran up my stomach and lodged in the back of my throat.

"Well, things can happen quickly when the media takes an interest in these things."

"The media?" I raised my eyebrows in surprise and asked, not understanding why anyone would care what happened to me. Then I realized it wasn't about me or my baby. I realized I was glad to be a "nobody" in Costa Rica.

Umberto continued in a low voice. "The Fulcos know we are coming now. If they refuse to give Marco to you, I will have to have Tomas arrested. Also, the judge's decision in this case is very unusual for our country. You are an American young lady who is fighting a very powerful and political family. The media is out to get the news."

I replied quietly, "Okay, let's get this over with." Again, I asked Juliana to come with me. She shook her head no and said that I would be fine.

During the 45-minute ride to Grecia, I felt everything from extreme happiness to extreme fear. My hands shook and I had no idea what to expect. I never imagined that I would have to take back my son with a getaway driver, the police behind us, and the media watching.

But I had faced *Mandragons* before and escaped with my life. It was all in my journal.

Umberto talked very calmly and wanted me to understand that in this situation, the law was actually on my side. I had nothing to be afraid of but he emphasized several times, "Let me do the talking. Don't say anything. As soon as you have the baby, get in the car, lock the door and keep your head down." I knew how to do that.

Even though Umberto seemed calm, I could tell he was worried. He looked out the back window every few minutes and ran his hand over his hair every time he turned around. I did everything I could to focus on the fact that we had won the legal battle and it would soon be over.

We approached the town of Grecia. I could see its familiar shape as we drove down a hill just outside the "Welcome to Grecia" sign. My heart raced faster. Umberto leaned forward and touched the driver's shoulder. "Take a side road to the Fulco home." The driver nodded and turned the wheel sharply down a narrow dirt road.

"Why? What's wrong?" I asked.

Umberto said, "Look over there," pointing over my right shoulder.

I turned and saw several vans with media logos and satellite dishes on their roofs waiting for us to drive down the main road. I tried to swallow but stopped midway. Umberto placed his hand on my shoulder to reassure me. "Maybe they didn't see us, and we can get in and out before they notice."

In a few minutes, we pulled up to the gates of the Fulco compound. The guard came out and spoke to Umberto through an open window. Umberto showed him the legal order for us to enter and get the child. The guard waved to the guardhouse to open the gate. We pulled up through the winding driveway, through the same trees I had seen the first and many times I had visited as a welcomed guest. Right on cue, as we neared the house, Melia, Otto, Di-ana, the maids, and workers met us just outside the carport. No smiles or gestures of invitation greeted me as they always had before.

Otto stood out like a flame. He was on fire. He stood with his feet spread apart, his arms crossed over his puffed-out chest, a deep-furrowed frown on his face. I wasn't just worried about what was going to happen, I was numb to my core, about to throw up, ready to jump out of the car, too scared to move. The horrible men Tomas and I barely escaped from on that mountain four years ago were nothing compared to the horrible man in front of our car. I met his eyes for a moment, then looked away to keep from being burned by the intensity of his stare. In truth, he was less of a dragon than some I had met before. And, this one took my son.

He has no power over you, said Zoryia.

I looked for Tomas and Marco, but they were not there. Umberto told me to stay in the car. He got out and handed the order to Otto, who shoved the paper back at Umberto and shouted angry words of refusal and belligerence.

I turned to look back at the surrounding property wall. Telescopic lenses and microphones were pointed at us, but I was too far away to make out any hands or faces. What I did know was that we were being recorded by the media. My personal life was being invaded by strangers. The guards were working to get them off the wall and away from the wrought-iron gate through which they could see the house.

Two officers got out of one of the cars behind me and walked forward. It was their job to enforce the court order. They approached Otto steadily. He reached for his back pocket. The guards stopped — he could be reaching for a weapon. Otto put his hand up and took out his handkerchief to wipe the sweat off his face. The guards relaxed and Otto turned and called for Tomas. I waited to jump from the car and grab my baby. Tomas came out with empty hands.

The legal jargon in Spanish was hard for me to understand through my rolled-up window. My heart pounded faster. Confusion, anger, and a look of panic crossed Tomas' face. He yelled and waved his hands in denial. His behavior was strange to me. A show of machismo for his father and the media. Otto gestured as if trying to settle Tomas down. A show of concern for his son and the police.

An officer grabbed Tomas' arm, swung him around and handcuffed him behind his back. Melia put her hands over her face, cried out, and ran into the house. The officers walked Tomas back to their car and put him in the back seat. I watched this take place in complete shock.

Umberto got back into our car and said, "They refused to give up your baby. We have arrested Tomas and are taking him to the judge in Grecia. He knows the consequence of defying the order. But he says he is friends with the judge and will never have to give Marco to us."

I interjected, "This is what I was afraid of. They have everyone in their pockets." I sobbed and tried to catch my breath and speak at the same time. "What are we going to do now?"

"Ahhhh," Umberto said, letting the sound trail slowly to emphasize the importance of the word. "You don't know who I am and neither do they. Tomas will not win because I appointed that judge when I retired from the courthouse. Rest assured, he may be friends with Tomas, but he will not go against the order of a judge from the capital. And, he owes me one."

I smiled a real smile for the first time since Marco did not come home that Sunday afternoon. Umberto patted my hand and relaxed. The worst was over. I relaxed a little and realized my hands were sore from holding them in tight fists.

Two hours later, in front of the Fulco carport, with media in attendance from the outer wall, Tomas handed Marco to Umberto. Except for Otto, the entire family, servants, and workers were crying like babies, overly dramatic for the cameras. I laughed nervously. Umberto's driver opened my car door. I got out and held my arms out. Umberto gently placed my baby boy in my arms. I shook and cried and held him so close. I kissed his face and got back in the car and locked it without hesitation. We looked at each other and laughed as we I put him in his car seat and we made cooing noises at each other. He had missed his mother's face, and I had missed his entire being.

We circled around the courtyard and carefully pulled through the gate onto the main road. The police cars came along side to escort us through the crowd. I covered Marco's face to keep him away from the media and kept my face down. Once past the town square, the two sedans followed behind. I pulled Marco's blanket back and examined my baby. He was a little heavier and a bit longer. He was perfect, pink, and healthy. On the highway, a car came beside us and paced our speed for a minute. I turned to see Di-ana in the back seat growling and shaking her fist at me through her window. I had never seen such hatred in my life.

I turned away and caressed my son's face. We were on our way home.

"I told you," Zoryia laughed.

I laughed too, from relief and joyful reunion with the deepest, most meaningful part of my life.

A few days after we settled in, Umberto advised me to set up a legal, documented arrangement for Tomas to have visitation rights. This would help the courts protect both parents and the child, and avoid any question of who takes Marco on occasions such as holidays and birthdays. This made sense to me and gave me some confidence that if something were to happen, getting him back would be an easier extraction. I could never trust the Fulco family again, but I knew I had to comply with the most reasonable terms the law could allow in my situation.

Marco's first birthday was a small gathering with some of Hugo's and Juliana's friends, Sophia and her daughter, and of course, *The Lion King.* It was my favorite Disney movie when I was pregnant and seemed to be Marco's favorite cartoon. Lion King decorations, Juliana's homemade cake, and a Simba piñata were the hits of the party. That evening Tomas picked up our son and brought him back the next afternoon. We worked out the terms of our visitation arrangement through our attorneys and, from that day forward, the Fulcos complied.

A week later I overheard Hugo and Juliana talking in the kitchen about some unusual things she had noticed recently. I stepped into the kitchen and interrupted them when I heard my name.

"What are you talking about?" I asked.

She looked at Hugo cautiously and he nodded in agreement.

"What?" I asked again. "What's going on?"

Juliana slowly replied, "Well, um ... we weren't sure about telling you because we aren't really certain about our suspicions."

I rolled my eyes, "Suspicions? Again, there is something else? What now?" I threw my arms up in resignation and sat down at the table.

"We decided to have Chulo look into why, every time I'm on the phone, I hear a clicking noise. Hugo has heard it, too. It's faint but there. And there has been a car out by the main road with someone sitting in it for the past few days. It's the same car every time I see it. The windows are tinted, and I can't see who it is, but there is definitely someone in there. And then ... there's this."

She walked to the other end of the kitchen and opened a drawer and grabbed a crumpled piece of paper, smoothed it out and handed it to me.

"What's this?" I asked.

She replied, "Just read it."

I read the note. My hands started trembling, and I looked up at them. "Where did you find this?"

She answered, "It was taped to our front gate. Leo found it and gave it to me. I was about to throw it away but stopped, thinking it might be useful."

"Why didn't you tell me about this?" I asked. "This is really scary. Who on Earth would want to harm us?"

Hugo replied, "I think the Fulcos are behind this. You know they were very embarrassed by what happened in front of the media. They were certainly shocked that they lost custody. That family is used to getting what they want, regardless of the cost. Otto didn't think you had any power or ability in this matter. But you proved them wrong and now they are pissed."

My voice cracked, "We have to show this to the police. I need to make a copy for my lawyer. Is this the only one?"

Hugo said, "Yes, it's the only one, but . . . " he turned to look at Juliana. She nodded okay.

"People we don't know have called and made threats."

Oh, I realized, that's why she's been jumping to answer the phone for the past few days, before I can get the call. It all started to make sense to me why Juliana would send Leo to the grocery store even though I wanted to go, and why Carlitos would quickly close the gate behind any of us coming or going.

Juliana grabbed my hand and said, "I think this is just temporary. Nobody cares about this type of gossip for long and they will forget about it. Plus, we have a legal arrangement with Tomas, and you are being much more forgiving than I would ever be."

In the following weeks, things were tense in the house. We jumped at noises. Carlitos carried his gun and patrolled the grounds when he heard the dogs barking. The house was surrounded by a security wall, but nothing was un-scalable.

I shared everything with Umberto at our next appointment. He said having Chulo look into these things was a good idea for our records. He also explained to me that this was just an intimidation tactic and should blow over in a few weeks.

"Remember," he said, "you are giving Tomas legal visitation with Marco. You are not doing anything to spark more drama. Just continue being a good mother and we'll figure out your legal status in this country when everything settles down. Let's not move forward with that yet."

Just as Juliana predicted, we returned to a kind of normalcy. The only bothersome concern was the faint clicking on the phone. We were always very careful about who we talked to and what we said. Juliana bought a fax machine to communicate with the family in the United States when we couldn't connect to the internet. At that time, it was a dial-up connection that was by no means consistent or reliable.

A week later the car down the street showed up periodically, but not every day. We thought they were paying less attention because they realized the ammunition they needed — catching me with other men, staying out late, buying drugs, abandoning Marco — was not going to happen.

When Otto couldn't get his hands on any ammunition against me, he reached for the most lethal weapon the law would allow. Without hesitation, he took aim and fired.

CHAPTER 29

Measure for Measure

One day after I fed and bathed Marco and played with him on the family room rug until he grew sleepy, I decided to put him down for a nap and take one myself. Just as I lay down, I heard the gate bell ring. It startled me and I got up to see if the baby was still sleeping. He was, thankfully, and I tiptoed out of the room and closed the door. I started walking down the stairs when I heard Juliana yelling loudly for me. *Geez, what the hell?* I thought. *She's going to wake him up.* Rushing down the stairs I shushed her. "Don't wake him up, please!" I whispered loudly. "What do you need?"

She replied grabbing my elbows. "There's a police officer at the gate. He said you have to sign some documents." She rushed me outside, and I asked her, "What? Do I need to call my lawyer? I can't sign any documents without his approval."

"I'll call him," she said quickly. "You find out what's going on."

"Okay," I agreed and trotted down the driveway. I could see Leo standing next to the officer with a worried look on her face, waving for me to hurry. When I got to the gate, the officer showed me his badge. "Are you Sydney Devold de Fulco?"

I responded, "Yes. What is this about?"

He responded coolly, "The contents of this document are of no matter to me. I am here to ensure that you receive them. Please sign here that I have properly served you."

I signed and took the thick, legal-sized envelope and looked at Leo. She closed the gate and the officer drove away. I stood there uneasy for a moment, but hoped this was just copies of our agreement documents. I walked into the kitchen and threw the envelope onto the counter. Juliana looked at me quizzically. "Aren't you going to open it?"

"I will but what did the lawyer say? Did he send us a copy of our agreement?"

Juliana asked, "Why would he serve you a copy? This is from the Fulcos," she pointed to the label. "You need to open it."

My heart pounded and my mouth went dry. I slumped down on a kitchen chair and opened the envelope. Unraveling the string from its two buttons seemed to take forever. I pulled out the papers and held my breath. The cover page made no sense. It announced the deposition of a Doctor Mirez, Department of the Psychiatric Ward of San Jose.

I read it again silently. Juliana snatched it from me and read it out loud. I heard the words but did not comprehend what they meant.

"Mom, I don't understand. Do you think they made a mistake? Why is this psychiatrist being deposed and what does it have to do with me?"

"Hold on, Muñeca, let me read this."

She scanned the first page, swayed, and grabbed the table to steady herself. Leo ran up beside her in case she might faint. Juliana sat down hard and kept reading with her head in her one hand and turned the pages slowly with the other, trembling. I stood up and looked over her shoulder to see what was so upsetting.

The document was a completely falsified psychiatric evaluation of me. One of the most prestigious psychiatrists in Costa Rica had recommended that I be committed to an institution based on his observations and tests conducted on me over the past year. He stated that I was incompetent to take care of Marco or myself. His credibility and the evidence presented in the document would convince any court that I was indeed a mental patient of his and he was seriously concerned about our well-being. The final page had the date of when the Fulcos were going to receive the child and my apprehension. It did not state the duration of my stay in the mental hospital but implied it would not be a short one.

Chulo, watching our house, saw the officer serve the papers to me. Carlitos let him through the gate and he came inside to find out what it was all about. Juliana handed him the documents. He skimmed through them and asked me if this deposition was true. I assured him it was not. I had never been to a therapist, much less a psychiatrist, for evaluation.

He drove Juliana and me to Umberto's office. I was so grateful that he was able to see us right away. After reading the deposition, he slumped back in his chair, took his reading glasses off and wiped the sweat off his forehead. He looked at me intensely and said, "I am so sorry. I know this is all fabricated. I never thought this family would go down this path. Unfortunately, this is a credible and prominent doctor, and no one would believe that he was paid any amount of money to fabricate these documents."

I stood up and walked to look out the window behind his desk. "What can I do? Can I fight this?"

Umberto replied, "Sydney, I'm so sorry but there really isn't anything you can do."

His words, carefully and slowly spoken, hit me hard. I grew numb and cold. Juliana led me back to my chair. We sat there. Shock was setting in.

"So," I said, more in defeat than asking a question. "Because some man I've never even met said I'm crazy, I lose Marco to the Fulcos? These people will never stop until they get what they want." I looked up at Umberto and shrugged. "There has to be something we can do. I'm not going to end up in some mental institution." I turned to Juliana, "Mom, do something. You and Hugo have to do something. He has connections. He knows people in power. Call him now, call him at work!" I jumped up and held my head between my hands trying to think while I paced in front of Umberto's desk.

"Wait, Mateo can fly us out of the country or come and get us. I have to get away from these people for good. They are the ones who are bat-shit crazy. How can they be so fucking mean to me?"

Juliana laughed in a strange, sad way and shrugged her shoulders. "Your father is not going to help in this situation. You know it, and I know it. We have to find another way."

"Umberto," she implored, her voice cracked. "Can she leave the country and take the baby?"

He replied, "Sydney can leave. But any child born in this country needs the father's permission. There is no way Tomas is going to allow it."

He paused and drummed his fingers on his desk. "Give me a moment." Umberto pushed the intercom button on his phone, "Estela, call the immigration office and check on the status of Sydney's and Marco's passports."

He looked at me and said, "There might be something we can do, but I need to make sure your passport has not been flagged."

"Flagged?" Juliana asked. "What do you mean flagged?"

"The Fulcos have been one step ahead of us this whole time. They have surely been advised in many ways. Otto would want to make sure Sydney could not leave with Marco."

I said quickly, "I also have a Swiss passport, and I registered Marco as a Swiss born abroad. My grandfather suggested we also register Marco as an American born abroad. So he asked his friend, the American ambassador to Costa Rica to expedite Marco's American passport."

Umberto looked amazed, sat up straight, and pulled his chair closer to his desk. "So you are telling me that he has three passports, right?"

I replied, "Yes, except Tomas has his Costa Rican passport, and I believe he knows about the American passport, but I never told him I registered Marco under my Swiss passport."

Juliana crossed her arms and with a satisfied smile said, "Muñeca, you never told him? Brilliant. Does this mean she can leave with him with her Swiss passport?"

He replied, "Unfortunately, he will still need the father's permission because the child was born here."

Estala buzzed his phone and he put her on speaker. "Senor, it seems that Sydney's and Marco's passports are flagged. Is there anything else?"

He replied, "Can you check the status of Sydney's Swiss passport? And find out if any updates were made to it in the past twelve months."

"Swiss?" she asked to clarify. "You mean from Switzerland?"

"That's right." He smiled at me and asked, "When did you register Marco as a Swiss born abroad?"

"He must have been three or four months old. It may not be registered with the Swiss Consult here yet because the papers are sent to Switzerland and processed there, before they are sent back to the Swiss Consult in Costa Rica. However, we can use the passport they gave me when I registered him because they added Marco's photo and information."

Umberto told us that Chulo may be able to help get us out of the country together, but it would difficult and dangerous. I told him I didn't care, that I would take any risk necessary to get us safely out of this country. Estala buzzed again. "Her Swiss passport has not been flagged and no updates have been made. Anything else?"

"No, that will be all, thank you." He turned to us and said, "This could be very good news. You might be able to leave the country with your Swiss passport. If it is flagged in the meantime, it could only be flagged for exiting Costa Rica, but not for entering another country."

Juliana slapped her knee and laughed, "The shit-head must have forgotten that you have dual-citizenship."

I didn't laugh, but I was relieved and the words, *"I do spy a kind of hope,"* echoed in my head. I decided that as soon as I put the baby to bed tonight, I'll write about Zoyria's plan to escape.

Umberto told us he was worried about the tapped phones. He needed a little time to pull together a plan and research my options for using the Swiss passport. Getting around the need for Tomas' permission would not be easy. Their strategy would be to call our house and let it ring twice, hang up, and repeat. When we heard this pattern of rings, we were to go to the nearest pay phone and call Chulo for instructions.

Later that evening, I heard two rings and my heart began to pound. Then two more rings. "Mom!!"

She was already getting her purse and keys. "Let's go!" I quickly responded, "No, I'll go on my own. You stay here with Marco."

"Okay, please be careful and make sure you aren't followed," she urged.

I got in the car and raced to the local grocery store just down the street. It had a row of pay phones in the entrance area where the carts were lined along the opposite wall. I chose the middle phone and called Chulo. He immediately answered.

"Were you followed?" he asked.

"No, I don't think so, there is no one around," I replied. "What did you find out?"

"Well, the good news is we can potentially use your Swiss passport to get you partially back to the United States."

I frowned, "What do you mean, 'partially?'"

He replied, "The only way for you to leave the country is if we use a Coyote. Do you know what I mean?"

"No," I replied.

"A Coyote is a person who helps people get across national borders illegally," he said slowly.

I gasped and said nothing. A stab of fear ran through my stomach.

He continued, "This is the only way for you and Marco to escape this mess. You will give the Coyote money to pay the border patrol to un-flag your American passport for five minutes. It will be a short window and you must act quickly to cross the most difficult border into Panama. He will explain it all to you step by step. It is going to be very dangerous, but I know this Coyote is the best and you will be in good hands. Do you really want to do this?"

"No, but I don't have a choice. I will do what it takes to keep my son with me and away from those horrible people. They've done enough to us," my voice shook.

"Do you want to sleep on it and get back to me tomorrow?" he asked.

"No. Let's do this," I stated, trying to sound as confident as I could with my knees shaking. "What is the Coyote's name?" I asked.

"No one knows," Chulo replied in a flat, serious tone. I understood what he meant.

He said, "Okay, write this address down. It's difficult to find but you are very resourceful, I can tell. You will find it. Go meet with this Coyote tomorrow at 10:00 a.m. I'll let him know to watch for you. Make sure you are not followed. Take roads you've never taken before and circle a few times to be sure no one is behind you. And please, don't wear any jewelry or clothes that show your social status. You must go alone and tell no one, not even your mother."

CHAPTER 30

My Coyote

The next morning, I borrowed Hugo's old pickup truck and headed to an area of San Jose I had never been before. Society referred to this part of town as the "barrio" neighborhood, or what we would call a slum. I tried not to be frightened as I followed Chulo's instructions. I drove past rows of dirty shacks that seemed to be standing only by leaning on each other. Some had no roofs. Most of the children on the street had no shoes. Skin-and-bone dogs rooted around mounds of trash. Dirt and grease stains crawled up the buildings as if reaching for daylight. Power lines drooped dangerously low across several intersections.

The situation that sprawled around me was painful to look at. It made me appreciate Mom and Hugo more than ever. Even though I was going through what might break me, I knew at least I had family and opportunity. I had support. The people in this part of town had almost nothing.

I had to focus on this meeting, not think about tomorrow, and keep focused on the end goal — all at the same time. It was a lot for me manage. At twenty-one years, my life had been dominated by powerful and respected men who had given me little reason to trust them or their intentions. Very few had ever looked out for my well-being. Hugo and Umberto were two of them. Searching for the Coyote's shack, hoping that he would actually help us get out of Costa Rica, was the hardest thing I had ever done.

I circled the area three times, going in both directions until I was certain I wasn't being followed. Driving slowly down the dirt road that led to his location, I saw a tall, dark figure step out into the road and dart quickly back inside. I knew that was the Coyote. There was a gate to the side of a dark wooden shack. He rolled it back and motioned me inside. I pulled in and he closed the gate. I was in a covered garage. It was dark and took me a minute to adjust my eyes. I watched him move toward a door. He opened it and said, "Please come inside." His voice wasn't threatening. It sounded muffled in a way, like a speech impediment. His black sweatshirt hood covered his head and almost covered his face.

The smell of rancid grease and decayed food hit me before I stepped into what looked like a makeshift kitchen. It made me nauseous. The thick dust covering everything realized this was not where he lived. It seemed abandoned and not a place where anyone would live, at least not voluntarily.

He sat down on an old plastic chair next to me but not too close to me. "Sydney, I hope you are not scared by these surroundings. This is not a place where the police would think to look for someone who does what I do." I nodded and said that I understood, it was fine and Chulo assured me that he could help.

"Sydney," he said so quietly I had to lean in to hear him clearly, "this is where we will meet when Chulo calls to tell you we are ready. He will also explain what to bring with you. Will you be ready to do as he says?"

He looked carefully at me from my feet to my head waiting for my response. I took a deep breath and said, "I have to do this, I have to be ready, I have no choice. In a way, it's a matter of life-and-death for me and my son."

He sat there for a long moment. "I accept your answer and the danger to myself. I will see you soon. Please go now, be careful and make sure you are not followed. Tell no one of this meeting."

My hands had finally stopped trembling by the time I pulled into our driveway. I knew Juliana was going to communicate today with our family in Atlanta. I was anxious to hear what they had to say. She called me into her study and said, "Tell me about your visit with Sofia later. Right now, I want you to read these emails so you are in the loop and we can make a good decision."

"Okay," I said. "Where is Marco?"

"Leo has him in the back yard," she replied.

I looked out the window and saw them together playing with the dog.

While writing this book, I researched papers Juliana had kept from me at the time. These are the email exchanges between family members who were helping us navigate the logistics of what we were planning. Below are some of the actual email strings that were meant to be confusing to anyone outside of the few who knew what they were up to. They illustrate our desperation and the extraordinary effort we all were willing to make.

Marco was about to slip from my arms. I was an innocent about to be sacrificed to the guilty.

To: Henry
From: Juliana
Date: 12/03/95 13:25
Subject: Sydney

Hi Henry!

Here's the deal ... the ambassador never called! But we have been on the move. This morning we went to the small airport of Pavas and Hugo saw an old friend of his there who just so happens to be the manager of the airport. We told him of our problem, sort of, about Sydney. We asked if she could leave in a small airplane from this airport even though their U.S. passports have been flagged. We told him that they could leave using their Swiss Passports. We are to call Hugo's friend at 4 pm today. If he agrees they could be leaving on a private plane tonight.

Here's the favor I need either from Witos or you but should be done right now since the time is running out. Please check from your end with American Airlines if they have a flight leaving tonight from CR to Miami and if it's available. Don't make a reservation because if Sydney isn't allowed to leave the country and somehow the reservation gets seen at this end there could be lots of trouble. Just find out if there is a spot.

We shouldn't call from the house because we feel big trouble is coming our way. Hugo is the one that thinks we should leave ASAP. If that's not possible we will just have to stay and fight but in the meantime, it'll be horrible for Sydney and everyone involved. I don't know what the consequences for Sydney and the baby will be in the future, but at this time we feel frightened and feel that this is the best way out for the time being.

We must be very quiet about this and not a soul. The less people know the better. It's serious. I have this horrible feeling. Anyway, I do want to say that if in case SOMETHING WERE TO HAPPEN TO ME OR SYDNEY, YOU KNOW THAT THE FULCO FAMILY IS INVOLVED. Please print this page so that you have it with you. They are out for revenge and they are planning something. But I sure as hell don't want to sit around as we have in the past to "wait and see what happens".

Give me your input please.

Love you, Juliana

To: Henry
From: Juliana
Date: 12/03/95 14:10
Subject: Sydney

Dawn

>I JUST CALLED LACSA & THEY HAVE A FLIGHT LEAVING
AT 4 TO MIAMI

We'd never make it on time. I must wait until 4 to get a
reply before we know if Sydney can get on a private plane.
It would be very serious trouble if Sydney attempts to leave.
Then she would be under accusation of kidnapping and would
be horrible for us. We HAVE TO BE VERY careful.

>WITA SAID FOR YOU TO CALL NANCY (ambassador's wife)

I can't at the moment since I'm using the line to correspond
with you. Anyway, I don't seem to get anywhere with them.
They know already because I had a long conversation just
the other day about everything. Maybe they are afraid of
getting involved and I don't want to push the issue with them
especially since I'm not getting any feedback at all.

>HENRY & I AGREE SYNDEY & BABY HAVE GOT TO
LEAVE ASAP. AGREE MORE THAN EVER.

>NEED TO COOL DOWN & THEN THEY COULD GO BACK
BUT RIGHT NOW IT IS SCARY.

Don't agree. Once Sydney/baby leave, they'll never be
able to put feet back into the country because she'll be put
in jail.

>STILL ON HOLD WITH AERO C.R.

They are probably masturbating or practicing getting BUCK TEETH!!! HA HA HA

Love , Juliana

To: Henry
From: Juliana
Date: 12/03/95 14:15
Subject: Sydney

>HEY HEFFER,

>1. AERO C.R. HAS A FLIGHT LEAVING TONIGHT AT 7:30 ARRIVING IN MIAMI AT 11:15.

> FLIGHT #216 AND THEY HAVE SPACE.

Great! I won't make a reservation. I'll just show up at the airport.

>2. WITO CALLED THE AMBASSADOR HERE & THEY SAID IT TOOK 10 DAYS FOR SOMEONE TO PUT A STOP ON ANOTHER PERSON LEAVING THE COUNTRY. SO NOW IS THE TIME FOR HER TO LEAVE.

OK I think we're going to try to get them off tonight then. Good work and thanks so much for your help. Just pray that they don't stop her at the airport. I'll inform you via e-mail any time after 4 pm whether or not there is a stop on her leaving with the baby today is the 10th day!!!!

>O.K. KEEP US INFORMED. THANK GOD FOR E MAIL.
OK.
>LOVE YOU, DAWN

ME TOO. Juliana

To: Henry
From: Juliana
Date: 12/03/95 14:43
Subject: Sydney

>HEY HEFFER
>
>I JUST GOT OFF THE PHONE WITH MARIA. THEY WILL
BE THERE BUT THEY WILL BE GOING TO SOME BEACH
LATER. BUT SHE TOLD ME TO CALL HER OR E MAIL HERE
WITH THE FLIGHT INFO SO THEY COULD PICK SYDNEY
UP. SO, THE AERO C.R. FLIGHT WOULD BE OUR BEST
BET. SINCE THEY HAVEN'T PUT A STOP ON HER LEAVING
OR I SHOULD SAY IT WON'T SHOW UP, UNLESS OTTO
THE PRICK PULLED SOME STRINGS. WILL WRITE BACK.

FROM, YOU KNOW

   OK Dawn. We still don't know if that's the case. But we
have to be patient. Maybe we'll find out in ½ to 1 hour whether
or not she'll be able to leave tonight.

See ya.

To: Henry
From: Juliana
Date: 12/03/95 14:58
Subject: Sydney

>HEFFER,
>
>IT IS THE 10TH DAY BUT IT IS ALSO A SUNDAY. I BET IT IS 10 WORKING DAYS. THAT'S THE WAY IT IS HERE. THEY WOULD NOT COUNT SAT. OR SUN. AS A DAY BECAUSE THEY DON'T WORK ON THOSE DAYS. WELL GOOD LUCK & PLEASE KEEP US INFORMED SO WE CAN CALL MARIA. I TRIED TO CALL THE WITOS & THEY WERE NOT HOME, I BET THEY ARE ON THERE WAY OVER HERE TO E MAIL YOU. I PRAY EVERYTHING WORKS OUT. LOVE & KISSES, DAWNO
>
>P.S. TELL SYDNEY NOT TO WORRY ABOUT BABY STUFF THAT WE CAN GET HER SOME STUFF HERE FROM FRIENDS ETC. THE BABY WILL HAVE CLOTHES ALSO. YEP. She won't worry about clothes don't worry.

Love Juliana

To: Henry
From: Juliana
Date: 12/03/95 15:42
Subject: Re: Sydney

>HEY HEFFER,
>

    Listen guys, we're off to look for Hugo's pilot friend, Briant to see how his lawyer friend can help us out. We're almost 100% sure the airport has been blocked for Sydney to leave. But Pavas small airport is still open. We just have to find someone to fly her out. So I won't be in touch till later. Bye for now.

Love, Juliana

To: Dawn
From: Juliana
Date: 12/03/95 17:45
Subject: Re: Sydney

>HEFFER,

>MARIA CALLED & I GAVE HER THE INFO ON AERO COSTA RICA. I TOLD HER I WOULD CALL THEM WHEN WE KNEW SOMETHING FOR SURE. GOOD LUCK FINDING BRIANT. DID YOUR FRIEND SAY THAT IMMIGRATIONS HAD A BLOCK ON SYDNEY?

>LOVE & KISSES...

Cont.

OK Dawn, after talking to Briant to fly her out, his lawyer friend highly advised Sydney not to escape. If Sydney gets caught, she'd go to jail. If she escapes and I stay behind I could be taken in for conspiracy in helping a crime be committed. It's a crime to take a child out without consent. I'm the one living here and I would have to suffer consequences that could affect many people. The airport is blocked for Sydney anyway and she can't leave from the small airport without getting authorization from the main airport (they must report all people aboard). She'll get caught and it would be terrible. We're going to have to stay and fight it out with the law. Sydney isn't doing anything wrong. They are!!! We shouldn't have to run away. I think we're doing the right thing. We got both your letters in hand now and we'll use those letters also. Tomorrow morning we have an appointment with the lawyer and will begin process to try to leave the country legally.

Comment please!!!

Love, Juliana>

I read through the emails on the CRT monitor while Juliana watched me closely. I looked at her, confused. She leaned on the edge of the desk and said, "It's okay, we aren't going to try this. Briant refused to fly you and we have no choice but to stay here and fight this through the courts."

I stood up, walked to the window, but Leo and Marco must have come inside. "Mom, there is another way. I didn't tell you last night because I wasn't sure if I could go through with it and he made me swear not to tell anyone. Do you know what a Coyote is?"

She blinked a few times as if to conjure up what I could mean other than the animal. "Do you mean the men who help people got out of a country illegally?" Her face grew pale. I helped her sit down on the coach under the window.

She said, "You can't do that. You could get killed. You could get the baby killed. It's too dangerous!"

"I know it's very dangerous, Mom." I replied. "But Umberto and Chulo are convinced that it is the only way we can get away from the Fulcos. Remember, you said he was afraid they might want to kidnap us. If nothing else, I will wind up in a mental institution and you will never see Marco again." She shook her head "No," got up and walked into the kitchen. I gave her a minute to think about what I had told her.

A few minutes later she returned with two glasses of wine. She handed one to me, turned to shut the door and sat next to me on the couch.

"Let's talk about this for a few minutes before Hugo gets home from work."

"Mom, you know that I don't want to have to do this. I'm scared and don't know what will happen. But you should know that I met with a Coyote today. I did not go to see Sofia. Chulo told me he was the best in the business, and has never failed to help anyone to escape. He has been doing this for a long time and I trust him. He is a strange man, but he was respectful and confident. He agreed to put himself in danger to help me and I made up my mind to let him help me."

She looked at me for a long time as we sipped our wine in silence. We heard Hugo come into the house, call for her, then go upstairs.

"Well," she sighed, "I guess it's done then. When does all this happen?"

I answered, "I don't know. I will be waiting for the signal call. At that point, he and Chulo will tell me what I need to know when I need to know it."

Juliana grabbed my hand and said intensely, "I know this was a very hard decision to make. I don't want you to do it, but I will help you any way I can. We can't tell Hugo, or anyone." She got up and left me sitting in the room. I heard noises in the kitchen as Leo prepared dinner. A little while later, I heard Hugo's voice in the kitchen and dishes being set on the table. Marco banged his sippy cup on his highchair tray. I wondered if this would be our last family meal in Santa Ana. I decided to enjoy it as much as I could.

CHAPTER 31

Dry Run

February 22, 1996. Like every other Thursday, I woke up, got dressed, sipped my coffee with Juliana and waited until Marco announced he was ready to get out of his crib. I fed and bathed him, then took him outside for fresh air, safely behind the eight-foot security wall that surrounded Hugo's home. He toddled over to the Weimaraner's lounging in the corner of the courtyard, sat down abruptly and reached for a long, soft, silver ear.

After some time, outside, he grew sleepy and I put him down for a nap. I had lunch and did some chores until he woke again for lunch. In the early afternoon, we played in his play area with all of his favorite toys. I tried to engage with him and be excited when he showed me something, but I had a sense of restlessness and anxiety that grew stronger throughout the day.

After Marco's afternoon nap, Leo took him for a stroll in the driveway. Juliana returned from the store with steaks and some wine for dinner. She leaned over and told me she had given Chulo the money for the Coyote, and handed me a thick envelope and mouthed the words, "For your escape. He understood why I had to help, but insisted that what you are doing is far too dangerous to tell anyone else. Not even Leo or Carlitos can know."

"Don't worry, Mom," I assured her and shook my head. "I haven't said anything to them or anyone else."

"How are you feeling?" she asked.

"I am getting really nervous," I replied. She said, "I am, too. I keep thinking the Fulcos are going to try something any minute."

"I don't even want to think about those people," I said, rolling my eyes.

Leo brought Marco into the kitchen and Juliana scooped him up and held him tightly. She kissed his face and walked with him to the piano. He sat on her lap and patted the keys. I talked with Leo and set the table while she cooked. Hugo came home and we enjoyed a quiet dinner.

I didn't have much of an appetite and neither did Juliana. Hugo asked, "Ladies, why aren't you eating anything? You are just poking at your plates. The steaks are really good."

"Um, they are good," I agreed. "We're just worried about what the Fulcos will do next."

"Yeah, I'm worried too. It could get out of hand pretty fast." He raised his glass and said loudly not caring who could hear, "Fuck the Fulcos!" he took a sip of wine and laughed. We laughed, too.

"Good one, Hugo. Fulco does sound a little like fuckos," Juliana laughed. We all snickered. I appreciated how easily Hugo could lighten our mood. Mom and I ate dinner with an occasional giggle between us.

Just as Hugo was getting up from the table to go watch a soccer game, the phone rang twice, stopped and rang twice again.

Hugo was out of the room but stopped and looked back at me. Juliana said, "Sydney, it's your lawyer. Go to the store and call him back. I'll get Marco ready for bed."

Hugo continued down the hall to watch his game.

Juliana and I looked at each other, knowing that this could be it. My heart was pounding. Juliana said, "Go!"

I heard her words, but as much as I wanted to get up and run to the car, I felt like everything was moving in slow motion and my legs were stuck in mud. It was as if the room were warped and I couldn't really focus. I took a deep breath and told myself I had to do this, that we would make it out of Costa Rica safe, and together. It's what I had to believe. Anything else was unbearable.

Carlitos opened the gate and I looked around to make sure no one was watching. It was dark and I couldn't see much, as there were no lights on our street. Oddly, time sped up. My five-minute drive to the store felt like half a minute. When you are about to do something that will change your life forever, nothing is normal.

At the store, I called Chulo from the payphone in the middle of the entrance. I know people were walking in and out of the store, I heard a young man laughing and the crash of carts being shoved into place. I heard Chulo's voice. I was glad to hear it.

"Were you followed?"

"No. I made sure."

"Go home, get a small travel bag that you can carry on your shoulder. Put some clothes, food and water in it. You want to look like a Swiss tourist. Wear comfortable shoes. Bring your American and Swiss Passports." He paused and continued, "Do you understand so far?"

"Yes, I got that. But...."

He said a bit sharply, "You are going to leave the baby with your mom. This is a trial run so you know what to do, and for us to know if anyone is following you. If they are, we can switch to our second plan. Either way, Sydney, you are getting out."

"But, I need to leave Marco here?"

"That is correct. You'll be entering Panama without him, this time. I'll explain on the way. Get these things now and drive Hugo's truck to the Coyote's meeting place. Be careful you aren't followed. Do you remember how to get there?"

"Yes."

"Good. I expect you at the meeting point in one hour."

I put the receiver back on its hook and walked as fast as I could, without drawing attention, to Juliana's car.

I wanted to race back home but drove slowly, cautiously, and looked around for anyone following me. There was no one. When I got home, I pulled in quietly and left the gate unlocked. The house was quiet. Leo and Carlitos were in their quarters. I tiptoed up to my room and grabbed my backpack. I looked down at my sleeping baby and wanted to kiss him but didn't dare. I couldn't risk waking him up.

I went across the hall to Juliana's bedroom and saw that her light was on. "Mom," I whispered. She opened the door slightly. "It's time. I'm taking Hugo's truck and will be back tomorrow night." Juliana nodded, kissed two fingers, turned them to me and shut the door quietly.

I put Hugo's pickup truck in neutral and pushed it back. We didn't call his truck "the crapper" for nothing. Thankfully, it moved slowly enough to stop at the edge of the driveway. I got in but didn't close the door, cranked the engine hoping no one would hear, backed up and turned toward the gate.

To say I was nervous would not describe the panic that rose in my throat. If someone had tried to stop me, I probably would have run them over without thinking. I couldn't hear anything and except for the old dim headlights, it was completely dark outside. No moon guided my way. I had memorized the route in my head and knew exactly how to drive to the Coyote's meeting shack.

I circled the Barrio three times to make sure no one was following me. I saw the black hooded Coyote step out and open the gate. Once inside, he closed it behind me, and I got out. "Chulo will be here soon," he said. I was so glad he was going to drive us to wherever we were going. My hooded Coyote motioned for me to sit in the same dirty kitchen as before. One candle flickered in the shack. The shadows it cast gave me goosebumps and I wondered if there was electricity in this place. The Coyote sat in the corner where the candle couldn't reveal his face. It was awkward and uncomfortable, and I could see large cucarachas crawling on the table drawn to the candle.

I asked him, "How much longer do we have to wait?" He shrugged and put his finger on his lips to quiet me.

I wanted to ask his name, but remembered Chulo's words, "No one knows."

I understood why he couldn't reveal his identity. We sat in silence for a long time. I was getting tired of sitting in that plastic chair, hoping the cucarachas weren't crawling on me.

Finally, Chulo came through the door and put his hand on my shoulder. "Let's go," he said quickly. "Where are the keys? We're taking your truck."

I handed him the keys and he got in the driver's side. I sat between Chulo and the Coyote. The last thing I had ever imagined for myself was to be sitting between two large men I barely knew, in an old pickup truck going somewhere in the dark, all night long.

It was an eternity before we got beyond the city and onto back roads through the mountainous region of Costa Rica. I could tell we were climbing because my ears were popping and Chulo drove slowly around curves knowing there were cliffs on our right side. The Coyote was asleep for most of the drive.

Several hours later, Chulo stopped for gas at a wooden shack with what looked like an old propane tank on the side of it. He siphoned what had to be gas from that tank into our truck and I worried that he was stealing it. The Coyote got out of the truck and went around to the back of the shack, I supposed to relieve himself. When he returned, I did the same. Chulo finished filling the tank and disappeared as well. I was glad to see him put Colones in a can nailed to the shack to pay for the gas. I drank from my water bottle and offered it to the men. They declined and we proceeded up the mountain for another hour.

Finally, we leveled out and drove on through fields, past huge plantations and small villages. I was falling asleep but felt uneasy between these two men. To stay awake, and find out what I needed to do, I asked Chulo to tell me everything. I couldn't wait any longer.

"I will tell you now," he replied.

The Coyote said that we needed to go faster to make it in time.

"Make it where?" I asked, a little frantic.

"Our friend here, has arranged to have the stop on your American passport dropped for five minutes as soon as the Costa Rican border station opens. You need to be the first person in line. Smile and give them your passport. If they ask why you are crossing to Panama, say you are a tourist and you have a cab arranged to pick you up inside their border."

I looked at him not sure how I felt about doing this. "What if it doesn't work? What if they stop me anyway?"

He replied with an air of confidence, trying to reassure me. "Yes, anything can happen so you must be prepared. But our friend has done this many times and has never lost a traveler."

I turned to look at our friend. He looked at his watch then straight ahead, "You must go faster. We cannot be late."

"What do I do if they let me pass?" I asked.

"When they let you pass," Chulo replied.

"When they let me pass," my voice cracked, "What do I do?"

Chulo told me to walk along the bridge between the two border stations. At the Panama station, I was to present my Swiss passport and tell them that we were meeting my husband in Panama.

"But Marco isn't with me," I protested.

Chulo replied. "It doesn't matter. The Panamanian station is very small and won't look too closely. But you have to get the book stamped for you and Marco. This "dry run" will show that you entered Panama sooner than you really will. It will confuse things if they try to look for you. The Panamanian border is the most difficult border to pass. They will look at the Nicaraguan border first, since that's where most fugitives escape the country."

To calm myself sometimes I tell a joke or make light of a situation. "Are you calling me a fugitive?" I laughed.

"Well, actually you will be when you cross that border. You shouldn't laugh at this. We're putting our lives on the line for you."

I hung my head down. "I'm sorry, it's just how I cope with fear sometimes. It's gotten me in trouble before. Please don't think that I'm not completely serious about this. I am."

Chulo grunted. Our friend said, "Go faster, if we are late, we have to turn back."

I stayed silent. More hours passed and I was still unsure what to do when I crossed into Panama.

I could see the sky beginning to brighten and asked Chulo how much longer until we arrive. He said that we were almost there. In a quiet voice I asked, "What do I do when I get to Panama?"

Chulo said, "I'll tell you when we get there, I need to concentrate on driving faster." He glanced at the Coyote who looked at his watch and nodded.

Still on winding roads, I could feel the truck straining to stay at high speeds. I glanced behind us. A dust trail filled the air reminding me that we were in the middle of the dry season. It was a higher and thicker dust trail then I had ever seen. I wanted to glance at the speedometer but didn't dare. There was no speed limit, but I knew that a big pothole could send us rolling down a hill, and there could be a cow or donkey in the road. It was a wild country for most of the way.

Just when I thought the truck couldn't go faster, it did. My heart raced with the truck. I closed my eyes tight, pretending I was on the Mindbender, a fast-moving roller coaster in Atlanta's Six Flags amusement park. It turned upside down as it ran along looping tracks. It was the only thing that kept my mind from where I was, how fast we were going, and the danger I was in.

We finally stopped in front of a small border-patrol station and a suspended rusty metal bridge about fifty yards long that hung several yards over a dry riverbed.

"Sydney," Chulo said dryly. "Do you have your disguise?"

I nodded yes and opened my backpack. I pulled out an auburn wig to match my hair color in the photo in my Swiss passport. I put the wig on and smoothed it around my face. I tied a soft, lightweight scarf around my neck in a European style fashionable at that time. I put a wide brimmed sun hat over my wig and finally, put on a pair of large round plastic sunglasses. It calmed my nerves to have something to do.

"When you get your Swiss passport stamped, walk into Panama until you see a green painted shack with yellow letters on your right. It's a general grocery store. Go in and give this to the man behind the counter. He will know what to do with it."

He handed me an envelope with a name on it.

My head hurt worse than before and I thought I was going to faint. I didn't want to get anyone else in trouble. I put the envelope in my backpack and looked up at Chulo. I looked at the border station and the bridge, and reminded myself that I could do this, that I had to do this. "Then what?"

"Then, he will show you to a small bathroom in the back of the store. There, you will look out the window. Leave your disguise in the bathroom. Crawl through the window and stand with your back against the wall of the shack. I will be directly across on the other side of the riverbed. When you see me raise my cap, run back to me straight across the riverbed as fast as you can. It's rocky and not very level. It is dry so you shouldn't have a problem if you watch your step. You need to understand that it doesn't matter what happens, if you fall, get up and just keep going. You cannot stop for any reason."

"Won't the guards see me run across the riverbed?" I asked, imagining I could be shot.

Chulo said, "The Panamanian side has too many trees blocking their view of the river. And our friend is going to disturb the guards in Costa Rica and keep them busy trying to get rid of him." The Coyote actually chuckled briefly and turned away.

Chulo continued, "The time is now. Go, Sydney. You have to do this now."

I nodded and took a gulp of water. My mouth was so dry I couldn't speak. Tears tried to come but didn't. I froze.

He grabbed my arms and leaned into my face. "You have to do this. You have to succeed. Your son, your life with him, depends on what you do in the next minute."

I wanted to hug him. I felt completely vulnerable. My life was in his hands. The edge of the cliff was just beyond my toes. There was a safety net below me that I couldn't see. I had to jump. Now.

The Coyote said, "Four minutes left."

So, I jumped. I threw my backpack over my shoulders and walked straight up to the border station window. I was the only person in line. I smiled and laid my American passport on the window ledge. The guard, a heavy bearded dark faced young man was sweating and I hoped that I was not. I put my hands in my pockets so he wouldn't see them shaking.

He opened my passport and typed on his computer. He looked at his monitor, then at me without turning his head, as if comparing me to a photo on his screen. I smiled again. He smiled back, turned my passport to an empty page and stamped it so hard I jumped. He laughed and I saw he had a gold front tooth. "You like it?" he asked with a wide grin.

I laughed my nervous laugh, something I have little control over in times of stress. I said, "Sure" with another laugh. He winked at me and asked why was leaving Costa Rica. I stopped laughing and said without thinking, "I'm a tourist and I used to live in Panama City. My husband is meeting me there tonight."

He looked me up and down and said, "Well then, enjoy yourself." He handed back my passport and I put it in my backpack behind my Swiss passport so I wouldn't pull the wrong one out when I got to the other side of the bridge. He signaled to the guard by the bridge to let me pass.

I walked over the bridge, trying not to fidget with my wig or scarf and kept repeating to myself, "I'm almost there. Just one more station to get through."

The Panama border station was at the end of the bridge. I could see the little green sign with white letters that simply spelled PANAMA. By now my hands had stopped shaking, but I was concentrating on my next move. There were a lot of people around the station and there were no lines for me to stand in. I had crossed the bridge toward Panama alone, so these people must have been trying to get into Costa Rica. It was noisy and chaotic. It was hot and no air moved to cool the crowd. The guard station was on the end of the bridge but sat higher, almost as a second story. I pushed my way forward toward a guard who motioned for me to approach through a wide-open window. I had to reach over several small sized adults to give him my Swiss passport.

He looked at it then at me. "Is your son with you?" This time I had prepared my answer. I replied "Yes," as if I was very tired, which I truly was. "But he has diarrhea." I crinkled my nose and shrugged. "Do you want me to go get him?"

The guard curled his lip and shook his head no. "That isn't necessary." He stamped my passport, once for me and used another stamp for Marco's entry as a minor.

"Thank you," I said. "I have a taxi waiting. Can we go through?"

"Yes, of course, Señora." As he handed back my passport he added, "Get your son and be on your way."

I turned as if to walk over to the side for my baby. The guard had moved on to the next person who pushed past me.

I walked down the dirt road alongside all the shacks holding tightly to the envelope. Within a few minutes I saw the green store front with yellow letters. I went inside. It was dark so I gave myself a minute to let my eyes adjust.

The store was more like a large pantry with rows of canned goods and some produce. I looked around and a man's voice asked me, "Can I help you find something?"

"No thank you, I just need to give you this." I held out the envelope toward a thin man with a thin mustache who stood behind a narrow counter. He took the envelope, opened it, read the paper inside quickly, folded it, put it in his pocket and said, "Señora, the bathroom is back there." He pointed to the back of the store.

I said, "Thank you." I locked the door and turned around. The bathroom was quite small, the window I had to crawl through was an open hole in the clay wall. I pulled off my disguise and dropped it in a corner. I stood on my tip toes and could just see out the window. It was small, but I thought that I could shimmy through it. I looked for Chulo. He was standing directly across from me but seemed so very far away. I looked down at the steep bank below me that led down to the riverbed. I dropped my backpack out the window, pulled myself up and balanced on the window ledge on my stomach and slowly worked my right leg through to the outside. Pressing against the sides of the window, I pulled my other leg through and dropped to the ground. I congratulated myself for not breaking my neck and thanked my high school gymnastics training.

I pulled my backpack over my shoulders and stood, pressing myself against the outer wall, faced the riverbed and watched Chulo for his signal. My eyes were wide from fear and anticipation of the dash I was going to have to make to get across that riverbed.

I was poised, ready to spring into the fastest run of my life over unfamiliar ground. I was terrified.

Twice I thought Chulo waved his hat as my eyes caught every glint of a change in the reflection of the sky. I wanted to see him wave his hat. Waiting was killing me. I could hardly breathe. It was too hot, and I was very thirsty and uncomfortable standing exposed like a victim about to be shot.

I could not even try to pull out my water. I had to be ready to move.

It happened. Chulo waved his cap in the air. I jumped and slid as fast as I could down the bank but didn't fall. I hit the riverbed running and kept running and running. I passed several big rocks but saw them ahead of me in time to go around. I stumbled a few times but did not fall. My legs burned from running and from the heat coming up from the riverbed. It was hell, but I didn't have time to think about it. I skipped over puddles of water that must have seeped up from earlier rains. There weren't many, but enough to make me aware of the possibility of water standing in my way the next time I had to cross this path. I wasn't even sure that I would have to run this path again — or if crossing over here would be something I would do again.

I thought about Zoryia's crossing in her world.

"It's dry now, but clouds can change. We must be aware that sometimes, what is dry, must become wet. Pay attention."

I understood her warning as a feeling that hit me somewhere, but right now, in that moment, getting across the riverbed that lay before me was the only thing I could do.

Chulo got inside the truck ready to drive away as soon as I could reach the passenger's side. I scrambled up the bank and ran to the truck. The door was open. I climbed inside and slammed it shut. He said, "Put your head down. I'm going to get … our friend. Stay down." He drove a short distance and stopped abruptly. I heard a thump in the back of the truck, and we pulled away. Gravel moved against the wheels. I heard only the sound of hope.

CHAPTER 32

Escape

But now what? I was back in Costa Rica, in pursuit of freedom. For me, for Marco, for us. For Zoryia. "What am I doing?" was my only question, my only thought, my only concern the entire way home.

Chulo woke me up as we pulled into the Coyote's shack. He told me, "Don't go anywhere, stay home, don't be seen. If we call you with the signal, make sure Juliana goes to get the message, and you stay home." I looked at him and nodded agreement. I was incapable of any further response.

I drove home and tried to stay awake. It was dark and almost midnight. No one followed me, all had been accomplished for this trial run. I didn't understand why we had to do it this way, but Chulo and the Coyote certainly had their reasons. I felt good that I had been able to do what I was asked by these men I didn't know well, but had to trust because I had to. I had no choice.

At home, I checked on Marco. He was sleeping peacefully in his crib by my bed. I was so glad that I could just go to bed and sleep. What would happen next was tomorrow. Right now, I could sleep next to my beautiful son, and really sleep. Sleep was everything. Tomorrow could be so different.

The next morning, I went down before Marco woke up and was happy to enjoy my coffee. Leo had prepared a breakfast that smelled good, but I was not interested. I drank on the patio alone. Leo asked," Where have you been?"

I knew she meant well, and not wanting to lie, wondered why she even asked, it was none of her business. But she was like family to me and asking out of love, not curiosity. I took a deep breath and lied, "I was with my friend Sophia. With everything going on with Tomas, I needed a break."

"Oh yes, of course, but why did you take the truck?" Leo asked.

"Well, if Juliana had visitors, I wanted her to have her car. Hugo said I could use it whenever I wanted? Did you need it while I was gone?" I asked.

"No, I was just curious. You have never just left without asking me to keep an eye on Marco, before. Is everything okay?"

"I'm just stressed out right now. It was a last-minute invitation from my friend. And Juliana knew, she said it was okay." To change the subject I said, "Can you get me some more sugar please, for my coffee?"

Leo smiled and brought me the sugar bowl. "Here you go. Would you like for me to put the sugar in your coffee?"

"Leo, I can do it, you don't have to do it for me," I said, looking up at her, understanding her approach.

She said, "I know you are keeping something from me, but that's okay. You don't want to talk about it."

Her feelings a bit hurt, she started to turn away. I grabbed her hand and tenderly stroked the top if it with my other hand. "I love you, Leo. Always remember that. I appreciate all that you do for us."

She turned around with a little shine in her eye and kissed me on the cheek. She smiled and said, "I know. I love you too. And one day, you will trust me enough to tell me what is going on."

Leo walked into the house and I felt a pang of guilt, but I had to say nothing for her own safety. I knew that she would understand one day soon.

I fell into the usual schedule with Marco. Late that afternoon when he was down for his nap, I had a moment to tell Juliana everything I had experienced on my "dry run" crossing the border. Hugo wasn't there. It was just the two of us.

Juliana looked at me with wide eyes and concern. "I can't believe that you had to go through that!" I was somewhat surprised at her reaction. Was something else going on?

"I had to, Mom. You know the detective and the Coyote were sure there was no other way at this point, given the death threats that you told us about. And the Fulcos had a psychiatrist say all those things about me. To get free of that family and the law, and return to America, I have to get out of Costa Rica now." It hurt, I was scared, but something inside me said this was what I had to do. It wasn't about Tomas or Otto or Melia, it was about Marco and me.

She looked at me with both fear and amazement. I didn't understand her fear as much as I understood my position as Marcos' mother was no longer a certainty under Costa Rican law. That was a certainty and the only thing I had to go on. My decision to flee was based on what I knew, and what Juliana had had told me.

"No, Muñeca, of course, you have to go. I'm just sorry that it's come to this. I never expected the Fulcos to do this kind of thing. It's crazy. They're crazy."

She shook her head and hugged me. I knew for sure that this was indeed what I had to do. It didn't matter anyway, according to my Swiss passport, Marco and I were already in Panama. The course was set. There was no other way to go.

Before I said, "Goodnight," to Juliana, she asked, "What's going to happen now?"

Exhausted, too tired to care, I answered, "I don't know much. All they said was to stay in the house. When the phone rings the signal, you are supposed to call them back and get the instructions for me."

"Okay, I can do that. I wish we knew more, but I know they are protecting us, and making sure that everything goes well. I hope nothing happens to you and Marco. I will light a candle and pray."

The next morning, I woke up wondering when the phone would ring.

It rang that evening.

Juliana went to get the information. She came back ten minutes later. I was waiting for her. She said, "Get the truck. Get your stuff and get your baby. It's time." Her eyes were wide, and I could tell she was scared. To protect her and Hugo, I had not told them any specific details. I knew by looking at her face that keeping my secret was the best decision. I almost fainted but did what I knew I had to do. She hugged me hard and said, "We are all going out now, and you will be alone. I love you, Muñeca. Take care of Marco. Be safe."

I watched my mother turn away and walk out the door.

I grabbed the note Chulo had me write and put it on my nightstand. It explained why I had left with Marco to make it seem that Juliana had no idea what I had done. My handwritten note was to be found by the "OIJ," the FBI of Costa Rica, not Juliana. It worked because the unsealed letter had been opened by the OIJ only after we escaped the country.

"February 25, 1996

My dearest Mommy,

I hope that you are fine and that you are not worried about the baby and I. I know that by the time you get this or find this letter, I will be long gone. I want you to know that I hid this letter so that you wouldn't find it right away. I had to have ample time to go away without much trouble and without them going to look for me.

Don't worry about me!!! I am fine. I met some very nice people while you were in the United States and became friends with them. They knew my story about my life, past and present. They didn't want me to continue suffering, so they are helping me.

Please, don't try to find me. I don't want you to get involved!!! It's better if you don't know anything!!!

I will however, tell you some of my reasons for my departure….

Well, I guess to start off, my number one reason for leaving is NOT because I am afraid of Tomas or his family, I have done NOTHING wrong, and my conscience is very clean! But, I don't have to prove anything, plus you as well as I know everything that I have been through.

I hired a detective to get some information on Tomas. I found out some INCREDIBLE facts. Anyway, I'm just afraid that Tomas is planning to kick me out in to the street and take my precious baby away from me. I DON'T TRUST HIM! Besides, of what the detective found out and told me, Tomas has been delaying and backing out of most of his promises. The deal between him and I was that he could see and take the baby whenever he wanted to and the lawsuits would be thrown out. He said that he would buy me an apartment and a car. Now he says that the lawsuits will be gone after the legal separation, he's only renting an apartment and NO car. I will not settle for this type of lifestyle!!!

I am going out there into the world and make it ON MY OWN. I don't want to depend on anyone anymore. This might sound selfish, but I will be happy and therefore my son will grow to be a happy gentleman. I don't want him growing up with such bad influences and example from Tomas. Plus, I want to teach him to be independent and having the same honest morals as I was so well brought up with. The one thing that I really do want for my son is STABILITY!

It hurts me to think that Marco will not grow up with his natural father and I will never speak badly of Tomas EVER to Marco. He is his father. But knowing now what Tomas is, I'd rather him not be around a father who is going to teach my son that it is fine to lie about innocent people, especially his own mother at the drop of a hat. Plus, every other thing that I have found out about Tomas. I would rather die than know that my son would walk in his father's dirty footsteps!!

This is not about revenge! It is about saving my son from a life filled with lies and manipulation, not to mention the bad examples that would grow up with him. It is about getting my own life back.

Mom, always remember that I love you and that we are both safe! Thank you for all your help, love, and understanding! I will truly miss you with all my heart! Please take care! Hugs and many kisses….

Your daughter and grandson,
*   Sydney and Marco*

P.S. Please let Hugo know that I am very grateful for all his support, hospitality, and for all the help that he has given me! I will always be grateful for everything he did for Marco and me! Give him my love as well!

Thanks again! Sydney

CHAPTER 33

Coyote's Angel

The route and risks I would take over the next thirty-six hours — the excuses and stories I needed to cover any gaps — were planned by Chulo and the Coyote. It was up to me to actually escape. Any wrong step could rip Marco from me. Every unexpected challenge could land me in a mental prison.

To this day, every time I remember what happened, I am grateful for the unaccountable "incidental" actions of strangers, the "accidental" occurrence of distractions, and the unexpected help of strangers. It's been said the Universe supports acts of boldness. I am a believer. It was as if my decision to leave, to trust, to dare, to take the first step away from what I did not want and could not allow, intensified the relationship between Marco and me.

Everyone we encountered along our journey to freedom was a relationship. These relationships weren't apparent at the time. I was too focused on getting past my fear of being caught and drained by the effort. Today I see more clearly.

Marco fussed and cried during the last few hours of the drive to the border. He wanted to stand up and climb around the truck. I kept him busy with his favorite stuffed bear, the only toy I packed for our crossing, and a bottle. Five minutes before we arrived on the far side of the riverbed, he sat quietly and chewed on his teething ring. His eyes closed.

"Sydney, we are almost there," said Zoryia. "I see a horizon and it's similar to the one that you see. The sun is setting here." I blinked. My sun was about to rise. "This is where we cross over from fear to power. We don't often realize just how magical we really are. But we always have the power to hope. There is nothing extraordinary about what we are doing, except that in this moment, we choose hope. We choose to take an extraordinary journey." I took a deep breath. We were at the end our ride. "Do you understand?" she asked, or I asked.

The moment we parked, I slipped my journal into my backpack. What I wrote from this point forward would be what I lived. This was it. This was the moment in my life, in our lives, where we claimed our freedom, or we survived under the control of others. This was it. There was no alternative. There was no turning back. There was no forgiveness. There was only the hope we brought with us. This was the moment where everything changed. Or everything died. I was good with either outcome for myself. But not for my son.

I got out of the truck and pulled on the front baby sling I had carried Marco around in for fourteen months. He had outgrown it a bit, but I figured it was the best way to manage him, my backpack, and the two cloth bags I carried filled with the supplies I could only imagine we'd need as refugees sneaking out of Costa Rica. His bare feet dangled below my waist. I was barely 90 pounds myself and carrying almost as much as I weighed.

Chulo had placed us in the hands of our Coyote. Two feet from where I had climbed the riverbed in my return from the "dry run," I stood with the Coyote, my only support.

Sangre de Cristo, contemplo y medito con todo mi corazón la llaga de tu costado por la abundante sangre que de ella derramaste, te pido salud del alma y cuerpo, que las enfermedades que tanto afligen; no se apoderen de mí, ni de los que amo, devuélve la salud a aquellos que han perdido especialmente.
(Aquí se pide por alguno que tengamos enfermo y deseamos devolver su salud del alma y cuerpo)
Padre Nuestro, Ave María y Gloria

Sangre de Cristo, ya he meditado en tus santísimas llagas y con fe la que otras mis súplicas, te ofrezco propagar esta tu eficaz devoción y ser tu fiel devoto.
Padre Nuestro, Ave María y Gloria

Nota: Esta devoción se reza durante siete lunes, háganlo con fe y obtendrán lo que pidan si es para Gloria de Dios y bien de su alma, ni en vano es la Sangre de Cristo.

EN ACCION DE GRACIAS
A LA
SANGRE DE CRISTO

SANGRE DE CRISTO

Heme aquí postrado ante tu Divina presencia, meditando tus santísimas llagas y por ellas imploro tu piedad y misericordia en mis tribulaciones y sufrimientos para que bendigas mi hogar, mis hijos y demás familiares hacernos dignos de tu perdón y misericordia, y que tu martirio en el Gólgota y la sangre que derramaste por redimirnos nos lave y purifique de toda mancha.

Sangre de Cristo, Contemplo tu llaga de la mano izquierda, y con todas las venas de mi corazón te pido Señor me ayudes en todas las penas que hoy me afligen y te pido consuelo y misericordia.
Padre Nuestro, Ave María y Gloria

Sangre de Cristo, contemplo la llaga de tu mano derecha y por ella Señor te pido bendigas mis negocios y mi trabajo para que no nos falte el pan de cada día, especialmente te pido.

(Aquí se pide por algún negocio especial que se tenga en manos)
Padre Nuestro, Ave María y Gloria

Sangre de Cristo, Contemplo la llaga de tu pie izquierdo y por ella te pido que mis pasos y los de quienes amo, sigan tus huellas para alcanzar la salvación de nuestras almas y saques del Purgatorio las de nuestros seres queridos con tu santo amor.
(Aquí se pide)
Padre Nuestro, Ave María y Gloria

Sangre de Cristo, Contemplo la llaga de tu pie derecho y por ella te pido la paz de mi hogar, y la buena armonía de mi familia para mis hijos, y todos los que amo se encaucen por el camino de la virtud, para que sean tus buenos hijos y gocen de la felicidad que das Tú con tu santo amor.
(Aquí se pide)
Padre Nuestro, Ave María y Gloria

· 1 ·

· 2 ·

"Wait," he whispered with a slow breath. His head, always bowed and turned away under his dark hood, was directed at me. In the twilight of the dawning light, I still couldn't quite see his face. He offered his hand to me in a broad, gentle manner. His movement was unexpected, but it didn't startle me. Rather it seemed as if, I thought, he was inviting me to dance. I took his hand. It was rough and callused.

"Don't be afraid. You are where you need to be," he said quietly. We stood on the riverbank I had crossed in dryness days before. Our entire future depended on crossing the same riverbed that now, I could hear, was flowing with water. It was, in fact, the dry season in Costa Rica. But it had, in fact, rained for two days. Again, a reminder that no matter what was in front of me, or threatened to pull me down, I was going to have to face and overcome the danger, the fear, being uncomfortable and carrying more weight than I could have dreamed possible. It was the weight of our worlds.

I looked but could not see how deep the water flowed below me. Perhaps what my Coyote sensed was overwhelming fear and he felt the need to offer what comfort he could.

This mysterious man, whose expertise I was completely dependent on, pulled back his hood. In the early dawn, this man revealed himself to me.

His face was almost missing. His ears were gone. There was no hair on him anywhere. His skin was a mottled mess of scars. Red and grey and dark. His deep brown eyes showed me no threat, no cause for concern. No need to run for safety. They reflected pure kindness. Whatever this man was had nothing to do with how he looked. To me, he was my angel.

This man, whose breath I had felt in our earlier meetings, whom I had ridden beside through many hours and never thought to violate his need for privacy, chose to trust me, a twenty-one-year-old American woman with his most precious self. He showed to me what he rarely showed to anyone, ever.

"I look like this because I protected my wife and children against a fire. There were people in our town who wanted to kill us and stop us from leaving the country. Our cause was innocent, but it didn't matter. I tried to save them. They didn't make it. I was left for dead but woke up in the hospital. I was in and out for days. One day, I was able to open my eyes, or so I thought. I saw a nurse dressed in white. She came to me and I felt her touch. She placed something in my bandaged hand. I heard music and thought maybe it was her voice. I heard her say, 'Keep this prayer. It will protect you. One day you will know to give it to someone who needs it more than you. You will know who that person is.'

"I don't remember how many days I was in the hospital or when she came to visit or if she was even real. I do know that when I got out of the hospital and fully recovered, reading the prayer became a new habit and I realized that my life would be always to help innocent people get away from injustice. I live my life in honor of my wife and children to the best of my ability. I have been doing this for many years. I know that this prayer now belongs to you. With what you have to change in this world, I give her prayer to you. To protect you and keep you safe. The Angel is with you."

I looked at the small slip of paper he handed me. It was a palm-sized, white piece of folded paper with blue print. I nodded and put it in my bra, close to heart.

I hugged him and he allowed my touch and with his body, seemed to embrace and support my baby. My Coyote said, "Go now, I will see you one day, and we will laugh. Vaya con Dios. You are in my heart."

He continued, "There is water in the riverbed. Don't be scared, you can do this. It will be easy for you. On the other side is your freedom."

I turned and looked at him and said, "Tu tambien. I will never forget you and will be true to our Angel." I hugged Marco to my chest, tucked his little legs up against me. Lifted our two bags with both hands and sloshed heavily into the water. There was no time to think, only to act.

CHAPTER 34

Freedom Point

It was cold water, running against me, very muddy up to my knees. Cold mud splashed against my thighs with every step. I did everything I could to stay upright and just take another step. My next thought was to put my next foot forward. Marco as usual sleeping against me, had no fear or reaction against our reality. Every moment and every step I caught my own breath. "What if they see us?" "What if they catch us?" "What if we die in this river?" As scared as I was, the only thing that I could do was to keep putting one foot in front of the other before the dawn grew light. Where I put my next step was everything. The next step was everything.

The next step was everything. The next step went down much farther than I expected. My next step was an effort to pull my foot and my shoe out together to the next step. The next step I felt an up rise in the riverbed. The next step was a little bit higher. The next step was a rise away from the current. The next step I knew that we were almost beyond the current. And the next step I knew we were on the other side. Just barely. I needed two or three more steps and took them. No one stopped us. No one flashed a light. No one held us down. No one said anything. I stepped up and out to dry land. Within two steps I was working my way up the embankment. I stepped around and over shrubs and rocks. With two more steps, Marco and I were free of the river. Two more steps and we were almost to the shack wall that I had climbed over before when I faced Chulo in Hugo's truck during our "dry run."

I turned around in place taking up as little space as I could. I made sure we were in darkness and took a half step back directly under the window. Only then did I take a breath, and look out across the river for my Coyote. He was gone. How it was possible to feel an overwhelming sense of gratitude, sadness, and fear for our lives at the same time? But that is how I felt.

Everything was up to me now. The sun was coming up. There were no distractions from what I had to do, so I had to do it now. No thinking, no thoughts were allowed. I turned and dropped my bags through the same bathroom window I had climbed out before. I took my backpack off, dropped it through the window, then considered the best way I could drop Marco through the window. I carefully lifted him up and pulled the straps off my shoulder. I stood on tiptoes to gently guide him through the window without waking him up. As carefully as I could, I lowered him to the care of the grocery store's bathroom floor. In what seemed to be one second, I pulled myself through the window and found Marco on the other side looking up at me quietly. I smiled at him and whispered, "You did well, sweet baby. I love you."

I gathered him up and squatted on the floor panting, crying, scared to death and desperate to wipe the mud off my jeans and sneakers, but it was hard because the bathroom floor was a dirt floor and I was covered in mud from the thighs down. I kicked both legs out and mud went flying. I didn't care. I took some baby wipes out of my backpack and cleaned the mud off Marco's legs. I knew he would be hungry again soon, so I opened the bag with his powdered formula and a bottle of water. I made him a bottle and propped him against my backpack. He happily took the bottle and watched me sleepily while he drank.

Because the store was closed until later that morning, I pulled out my journal to find the note where I had written my next instructions from Chulo. I wanted to be sure I knew where to go, what to say, and what to expect when we left the store. It was my first moment to really think since starting out this morning.

I found the note and read it a few times. Once I felt confident in what I had to do, I knew what Zoryia had to do.

> The shawl that wrapped around Lexin's body and kept him tightly bound against Zoryia had rubbed a sore on her right shoulder. She shifted her son to her right hip and adjusted the shawl over her left shoulder. She lifted a length of its cloth and draped it over her baby's head. She could hold her breath, but his breath would summon the sapient snakes that swim in the river rocks.

My hands shook as I wrote. She needed to know that it was almost done, we were on the other side, almost safe.

> The shimmering sapient snakes drifted behind her. Zoryia could almost see through the black water to the

bottom of the riverbed below her knees. No longer able to hold her breath, almost fainting and falling into the water, she stumbled ahead two more steps. She was going up. She had reached the side of the riverbed and it was far enough. Her inhale was sharp and fast. It was the sweetest air she had ever tasted. Mud squished around her boots. Two more steps, the mud became, simply, dirt.

I heard a sound in the store like keys opening a lock, and a man whistling a local Cumbia.

"What if it's not the store owner?" I panicked. "What should I do? I need to make a little noise, so he knows I'm here and not startle him by just walking out of the bathroom."

I looked around and found nothing to make noise with, so I stood up, turned the water on in the sink, and waited. I still heard whistling in the store, but it didn't sound like it was coming toward us. I turned off the water and flushed the toilet. Just then, I heard the man stop whistling.

"¿Quien esta allí?" The voice asked.

I opened the door slowly and peeked out saying, "Soy yo, the woman with the boy."

"O, si. Pasa adelante," he signaled with his hand.

I pulled everything together, tucked Marco back into the front sling, threw my backpack on and stepped out holding both bags.

As instructed by Chulo, I knew I had to pay the man. He greeted me with a handshake, and I put one of the bags down between my feet and returned his handshake. The envelope with his payment was in my backpack. He stared at me awkwardly. I realized his gesture was less of a handshake, and more of a payment request. Looking back, it was almost funny. At the time I was self-conscious and swung my backpack around and pulled out the envelope. The last thing I wanted was any trouble.

He looked at me and cocked his head to the side and smiled. I smiled back and looked down at Marco's head. He was beginning to squirm and I knew we had to get moving.

"Adonde consigo el bus a Panama City?"

He shook his head and replied, "No, no bus a Panama City. Tienes que tomar un taxi o micro van blanco a la cuidad de David," and pointed outside. "No," he shook his finger at me. "Taxi no Bueno. Es mejor tomar micro van y es menos dolares," he winked.

"David?" I asked.

"Si, gran bus a Panama City."

I thanked him and ran out to get into the first mini-van waiting on the curb.

Fortunately, it was so early there were only two other passengers in the van. I sat right behind the driver on a padded bench with room to put my bags, hoping to discourage other passengers from sitting next to me.

The trip to David took about two hours and, on the way, I looked out of the window at the clouded sky and wondered if it was going to rain again. It was an air-conditioned mini-van. The ride was fairly comfortable. Marco seemed happy and enjoyed the bouncing and tilting of our progress along dirt, paved, pot-holed, and eroded roads. At least it was a flat area and fairly straight.

We finally pulled into a large bus station. People were everywhere. Finding their loved ones, carrying baggage, shouting for attention, running to catch a bus, or a ride away from the station. There were vendors selling trinkets, streams of passengers moving together toward unseen destinations. We pulled up to a ramp that led to the ticket booths. Two big signs said "Panama City." One sign said "Regular — $20" and the other said, "Express — $30."

I didn't know what the difference in price was for but decided to pay the extra $10 for the Express to hopefully get to Panama

City faster. I got my ticket and bus number. It was leaving in ten minutes, just enough time to find the bus and get on it. This bus was very big and very old. Faded stripes of red, blue, green, and yellow paint decorated the sides. The steering wheel was huge and round and wrapped in lengths of multi-colored plastic rope. I imagined these helped the driver grip and control the wheel. The seats were tattered and not so clean. I imagined these were a cesspool of germs and who knows what else. Already full of passengers, I spied two seats near the middle and reluctantly sat down. I didn't want to call attention to us by cleaning the seats with diaper wipes. I took a deep breath and placed Marco and our bags in the seat next to me hoping no one else would want to sit there.

People piled in quickly. I noticed a handful of babies, toddlers, older people and teenagers. And chickens. Upside down chickens, squawking chickens, unconscious if not dead chickens, waiting for their conversion-into-dinner chickens. The windows were open but as people piled on, the smell of fast-fried street food and body odor made my stomach hurt. Some men coughed. Some teenagers sneezed and wiped their hands on their shirts. Some babies cried. Some women shouted. I looked around for a place to throw up. Only the window was a possibility.

Marco laughed at the flapping and squawking chickens. He watched closely and reached out as feathers floated past his face. I watched closely to make sure he didn't manage to eat them. I needed the bus to start moving and air to flow. Fresh, damp, hot airflow would be better than the cesspool sauna bus air filled with who knew what germs and viruses. I had to think quickly.

We were actually sitting on a beach chair somewhere, and a cabana boy standing at attention was ready to fill my cocktail glass with frozen margaritas, or better yet, chilled Cuba Libre with just-squeezed lime. It was a difficult choice to make. I chose the margaritas.

This daydream was far away in any reality, but it was a kind of hope that kept me from crying. If I could dream of a "future" life, this "present" life was temporary.

Finally, the engine groaned and we backed away from the station. I had been told that we were only five hours from Bus Station 46 in Panama City. From there all I had to do was take a taxi to the airport and fly to the United States.

With the windows open, the most important thing I had to do was keep track of those feathers. I picked them out of Marco's neck and kept my mouth shut. It was a constant incessant barrage of almost dead chickens. It was their way of exacting revenge on the humans that dared to put them in such precarious positions.

They had no choice but to hang by their feet from poles that spanned across the aisles anchored to the baggage racks above our heads. To this day, I can see their little beady eyes staring at me, protesting their situation by rapidly flapping their wings. At first, I felt sorry for them. About twenty minutes into the ride, the chorus was so loud I wanted to scream at them. Everyone else ignored the fowl cacophony. Or maybe they had been deafened by too many bus rides.

The aisles were blocked by passenger bags. One caught my eye. It was made out of plastic tubes of different colors woven into a sort of cultural pattern. Something liquid oozed out of the bag through the webbing and onto the floor. I couldn't identify the color of the liquid, but it matched the floor of the bus.

Above us, three heavy thumps made me jump and hard scuffling sounds moved over head. I had seen people ride on the outside of buses in El Salvador, but never imagined that people could do that for long-term rides.

For a couple of hours, we traveled over flat roads. They were paved and straight, but bumpy and not well maintained. It started to rain hard and sideways. It was a rainforest after all. Everyone closed their windows. We had to, the sting of hard rain on our faces and heads made it necessary. I didn't even think about how the rooftop passengers dealt with the onslaught until after it stopped. I just had to hope that they knew how to deal with such things.

The smells, heat, humidity, sounds, and hours of discomfort filled our old aluminum tube of a bus and grew in such intensity, I could not breathe. Marco cried too; his face grew so red I thought he would explode. Well, he did. In his diaper. I had to change it in his seat while he kicked and screamed and tried to roll over, over, and over again. He wanted to get out, I didn't blame him. I rolled up his dirty diaper, folded the tape down to contain the hazard, and put it on the floor under my seat. I wasn't about to throw it out of the window like some other mothers I watched. I knew we were coming to a bus stop soon and I would throw it away. A cow, confused by the rain, had other plans and suddenly crossed the road. The driver slammed the brakes and that dirty diaper rolled somewhere toward the front. At least now, it wasn't underneath my seat.

Finally, we pulled into a bus stop and I wondered, but only briefly, where that diaper had landed. It was out of my hands now. The rain had subsided and many of us had opened the windows again. I worried that his diaper could give us away. Marco might be the only passenger sporting disposable Huggies.

We waited as patiently as we could for those in the front of the bus to depart. I had to get out and breathe air not filled with chicken feathers and farts from sleeping passengers. I brought our bags with us and headed for the public bathrooms. Inside I shuddered; they looked very much like the shack bathroom I had shimmied into through a window across the riverbed. The advantage to these bathrooms was the cement floor. But the odor of old urine and feces in the corners would make it very difficult for me to urinate. Somehow, I found a way to make that happen because I could not face the possibility of peeing in my bus seat.

I hung the two bags on the little hook in the stall, hoping they would hold, pulled down my pants with Marco on my chest and aimed for the toilet.

He grunted hard and I knew the diarrhea had hit once again. A bottle of Pepto-Bismol had not made my survival gear list and was not to be had at the station. I washed my hands and found a space on the counter where I could change his diaper again, worried because I only had a few left. I cleaned his bum quickly and carefully to prevent a rash. But I knew I had to get back to the bus as quickly as I could. We pushed our way back to the bus platform only to see it pull away without us. I ran fast after it and was amazed to watch men running along with me and jump, one by one, onto the back and sides of the bus. They were parasites latching onto a large host animal trying to get away from them.

The driver saw us and stopped. He opened the doors and shook his head in anger. I panted, "I'm so sorry. Thank you for stopping!" I don't think my apology or gratitude had any effect, but I tried to be polite. We sat in the closest available seat, settled in and looked down. Shit. Marco's diaper was beside my feet. As we departed the station, it rolled behind my seat. I never saw it again.

The driver announced that we *should* arrive in Panama City in three hours. I was elated. I could endure three more hours, maybe. But that was *all* I could handle. Well — it wasn't.

I closed my eyes and slouched back. Marco snuggled on my chest. An alarm went off overhead. We slid forward hard. The bus slammed to a quick stop. Shouting and excited voices behind me made me turn to look. A group of people huddled over a passenger. They carried an elderly woman past me and out of the bus. She shook and foamed at the mouth. They put her down on the ground, just outside the doors of the bus. I stood up and looked out the window to see. She was having a seizure. I wanted to help, but there were others already doing what they could. Without any explanation, we waited on the bus on the side of the road until help arrived. I wished I had taken the "Regular" bus. The "Express" bus was not.

An hour passed before an ambulance came. I don't know if the woman was alive or dead. I was surprised that we waited and glad that we didn't just leave her there. But the selfish part of me wanted to move on. I felt terrible.

When we finally drove away, I knew we would arrive in Panama City very late. It was dusk when we came to the bridge over the canal. It was heavily guarded and United States soldiers stepped onto the bus and looked around. I think they may have counted heads, and in the meantime, I heard quick footsteps on the roof of the bus. I imagined that those passengers were quickly disembarking.

We crossed the bridge over the canal about as slow as a bus can move and still be moving. I looked down at the canal and was completely amazed. I had studied the history of how the canal was built, but never appreciated the engineering that allowed two oceans to meet and vessels to pass between them. The expanse of the canal was so great, I could only see the sections on either side of the bridge as we crossed. I will never forget the sight of something that took nearly a century to construct and took the lives of so many of the people that built it.

I knew we were close to the city and yet it had taken hours longer than I expected. I was done with this part of our journey. Marco was done with being strapped to my chest. I stayed calm to keep him calm, but it was his witching hour.

The sun was beginning to fall behind the mountains just beyond the city. I threw my hand up to hail the first taxi I saw. It worked, just like in the movies.

A white Corolla pulled up beside me and I reached for the handle and opened the door. I climbed into the back seat with Marco still on my chest. The driver was a young African man with long dreadlocks. I felt the car floor bend downward and quickly lifted both of my feet. Through a hole about the size of a bread plate, I saw the pavement.

"Miss, where are we going?" he asked.

I laughed nervously, "Airport please." I wanted to say, "and step on it" but didn't want my feet to go through the floor.

"Okay," he said.

It was still very hot in the early evening hour. "Is your taxi air-conditioned?"

"No," he replied.

I wanted to open the window but saw no handle. Only a small metal nub stuck out where the handle should have been.

"I need to open the window," I said to the driver.

"Okay, Miss," he responded.

In one smooth movement, he bent over and grabbed something from underneath the front seat, leaned over the back with a large metal tool, wrenched the nub and pushed the tool up. I sat back afraid he was going to hit us. He had opened the window halfway down without a word and without slowing the taxi.

I was happy to have some air and relieved when we arrived at the airport without injury.

At the ticket counter, the agent told me there were no more flights to the U.S. until 9:00 a.m. the next morning. The only seats available were first class until 2:00 p.m. tomorrow afternoon when I could buy a coach ticket. I laughed and asked, "How much for the first-class ticket in the morning?"

She replied, "Will your baby need a seat, or will he be on your lap?" "I will keep him on me," I replied with a smile, trying to look like I had everything under control.

"The first available first-class ticket will be 1,300 dollars, on American Airlines leaving at 8:40 a.m. going to Miami." She looked at me doubtfully. I know she wondered if I had enough money or if I am wasting her time. I couldn't tell if she could see my muddy jeans and sneakers from behind her counter.

"Okay," I quickly responded. "I will take it."

I reached for some cash from my socks, my bra, Marco's sling and one of the bags with food. The money was wet and crumbled and smelly, but it would spend so I stacked it on the counter and counted out 1,300 dollars. The agent watched me closely. I don't know if she was surprised, interested or dismayed. I didn't really care but I needed her to take the money and give me a ticket. I looked up at her and she was smiling. I saw her name tag, Alisa Ortega. *What a pretty name*, I thought. I believed that she was concerned rather than alarmed. I knew I looked like a refugee and reinforced that image when I pulled cash from my clothes and things.

"Well," she said, "I see you do have the funds."

I nodded and said, "Yes." And just stood there as the agent printed out my receipt and ticket.

She paused and asked, "Do you have somewhere to stay tonight?"

I replied, "No, can we sleep in the airport?" She laughed a little and replied. "There is a hotel next door to the right when you leave this building. You will see it. You can walk over. Do you want me to call them for you?"

"No thank you. I will go on over. I am absolutely starving. And he needs a bath."

"Buenas noches," She offered.

"Igualmente," I replied as I walked back out of the airport.

It wasn't a far walk and the hotel looked clean. I got a room, closed the door behind me and too tired to smile, was glad to see that room service was available. I decided to wait to order dinner until after Marco and I had a bath.

After the most delicious hamburger and fries I had ever eaten (with lots of ketchup), and the most delicious strained carrots topped with chicken and rice Marco had ever eaten, I placed a collect call to Dawn in Atlanta. We were safe and out of Costa

Rica. I told her about my flight reservation to Miami and she told me to take another flight from Miami to Atlanta.

Dawn promised to send an email to Juliana to let her know that we would be arriving in the United States tomorrow.

I pushed the double bed against the wall and put Marco down. I cried soft tears of joy, relief, and sheer exhaustion. We were on our way home now. And nothing was going to stop us.

The Fulcos had no idea where we were or where I was going. My life, my son's life, and our future were in my hands for the first time since I had said "yes" to Tomas's proposal.

We checked out after a quick breakfast at the hotel restaurant. I walked outside with Marco in his sling and started to walk toward the airport, past an old black limo. A tall man in a chauffeur uniform watched me. As I got closer, he cleared his throat and said, "Perdon, Señora." I stopped and looked at him, wondering what now? He smiled politely and tipped his cap. "I am here to take you to the airport. You are Señora Devold?"

I frowned confused. How would he know my name?

"I have a request from American Airlines to pick you up and take you to Departures. You have a first-class ticket?"

"Oh, yes, I do, but I did not call for a limo," I said slowly.

He replied, "Your agent, Señora Ortega, called for it last night. May I take your bags?"

"No, gracias. I will keep them with me." I cautiously approached the limo. The chauffeur opened the back door for me, and I leaned in to make sure there was no one else in the car. A part of me thought that this could be a trap, but he did mention the agent's name and didn't seem suspicious. In fact, I felt more at home being picked up by a limo because I had a first-class ticket. It felt good and I needed to feel good. He drove us a half mile to departures, opened my door, and waited until I had collected my bags from the back seat.

I reached around to get some cash to tip him, but he put his gloved hand up and shook his head no with a smile. "That's all right Señora, I was happy to drive you and your son this short distance. Have a wonderful flight." With that, he turned on his heel, got in the driver's seat and drove away.

Now, I turned to face my final check point. Getting my boarding pass depended on my ability to raise no questions, no doubts as to why I was carrying a minor child into the U.S. without his father's written permission. This was a sophisticated, orderly check point, unlike the chaos the first time I entered Panama without Marco.

I stepped up to the departure counter and kissed my baby's head and bounced him a little bit as I hoped the movement would distract the agent. A tired-looking, middle-aged man with a large stomach and thin hair looked at me with a slight smile.

I waited for his instruction. "Passaportes y boletos porfavor," he stated. I handed him my Swiss passport and ticket receipt. He flipped open my passport and looked at me, then flipped the page, looked at Marco's photo and said, "Ah. Señora. Did you enjoy your stay in Panama?"

"Yes, I used to live here as a child. It was so good to see everyone again," I said with a big smile on my face. "I can't wait to see our pictures."

He looked at me as if he wanted to ask a question. My chest tightened and I tried to remember the story I was going to tell if I was asked for the required permission letter of a minor leaving a country or the story I would tell if they asked me how I got into Panama without it.

The agent next to him, a young man, stepped over to ask him a question. He said, "Un momento por favor" to the young man. He turned to me and said, "I don't want to hold you up." He stamped my passport and printed my boarding pass. He handed it to me and said, "You may go to the first-class lounge. It is at concourse A right next to your gate. Have a wonderful flight."

I smiled and said, "Thank you, Señor, and you have a wonderful day!" I took my passport and boarding pass, picked up my bags and hurried down the hallway letting out a deep sigh but trying not to call attention to myself. I followed the signs to Concourse A and was glad to see the first-class lounge, where I enjoyed a Mimosa made with freshly squeezed orange juice, some pan dulce, and Marco enjoyed his bottle of apple juice with a teething cookie. I took another sip of the most delightful Mimosa I had ever tasted.

CHAPTER 35

A Moment in Haven

With our first-class tickets I got my favorite seat with Marco on my chest. Before takeoff, the warm towel served to me with silver tongs made me feel at home and at rest. The flight attendant offered me a Mimosa and I happily accepted. Marco was ready for a nap. I was ready to take off. The pressure said to my body, I am almost home. It's been a long journey and I was almost ready to think of it as an adventure. But not yet. Zoryia had to meet me on the other side of freedom.

No one sat next to me, so I put Marco there and reclined his seat. He sighed and relaxed back. I giggled and stretched. It was time to write. Zoryia was in peril. She had to go home. Her son belonged in Antarvia.

"Zoryia dragged her body, baby in his sling, up the rocky river side. Her breaths were heavy, deep. The bruises on her legs were sore. There was no one to help her get out of this place. No sight of Rangi. No sound from anything. She lay still. Her son wanted to get up. She couldn't let him.

The ground trembled just a little. A white flash flew over her with a whinny she knew so well. Her precious horse, Andor!"

Our Antarvia, the Main Kingdom Land, lay ahead. Miami, Atlanta, wherever we would live would be our home. I realized in that moment that all the power I had written into Zoryia had to be my own. I could not have thought of or written about her strengths if they were not my own. The men, the women, the family, the friends I had believed to be more than they were, turned out to be only human. Each of us has our own life to live, our own path to walk and to learn from, should we choose to learn from them. I was ready to choose a different reality and I knew then that I could.

In Miami I bought a ticket to Atlanta and called Dawn to let her know my arrival time. She said she would be happy to pick me up at the airport and would have warm jackets for both of us.

Atlanta was in the midst of a cold front that hit us as we walked through the gateway. I shivered in my short-sleeved shirt and jeans. Marco at least had his blanket.

Dawn greeted me from her car at the arrival pick-up. She jumped out and hugged us tightly. "You made it, Sydney!" She stepped back but held my shoulders with Marco between us. "Shit, he's huge. How did you carry this big baby all the way from San Jose?"

I laughed, exhausted and said, "I have no idea. I guess I just had to."

"Let's get home and get some nice cocktails. You have to tell us everything. Henry will be home by the time we get there."

Marietta Country Club Estates was an affluent community of successful doctors, lawyers, and business owners. We wound through streets of manicured lawns, gleaming cars, and massive windows surrounded by stacked stones, brick, and lines of trees groomed to unnatural perfection. I had to make myself focus and remember what I was looking at. This was another reality so removed from where I had escaped that I wasn't sure I recognized, at first, what I was looking at.

Henry came out to car and looked at me. As surreal as their world seemed to me at that moment, I must have looked just as strange to him. No makeup, no jewelry, hair a pony-tail mess, about 90 pounds of jeans and white T-shirt, holding a baby almost bigger than I was.

"Shit, Sydney, what the hell happened to you? Where have you been and what the hell have you been feeding this little monster?"

I just looked at him, rolled my eyes, and gave him a big hug. He hugged me back and said, "Let's get you inside, and a cocktail in your hand."

I said, "Oh, please."

All I wanted to do was get Marco to sleep and lie down myself. My shoulders were sore, my head hurt, and finally, I was on home soil.

Dawn had a crib waiting for Marco. As soon as his head hit the mattress he was out.

Henry waited downstairs with my gin and tonic with a twist. He sat down with his scotch on the rocks and crossed his legs. I sat across from him and sipped my drink with plans to go to bed as soon as I could.

"Do you want the good news or the bad news first?" he asked.

"Well, I've had a lot of bad news lately, so please, give me the good news."

I looked at Dawn to try to read her expression. She quickly looked down at her own cocktail and twirled it with her finger.

"The good news is that your mom has arranged for you and Marco to stay with her friend, Clair. You know her, right?" he asked.

"Uh, sure I met her before. But I can't stay with you?" my voice trembled a little.

"Well, that's the bad news. My friend, Morris Franklin, advised me that you shouldn't stay with family. He is a family lawyer and I trust his judgment. You have to understand that we could be implicated as accomplices if you stay here — should it come to that. You broke the law in Costa Rica."

I took another sip and put the glass down. I understood what my uncle was saying and that he was on my side. At the same time, I felt betrayed.

I nodded and said, "I am tired, and I need to go to bed now. I will call Clair in the morning. Thank you for letting me stay tonight."

CHAPTER 36

The Hague

Juliana emailed me good news. My father had arranged to pick us up on his private jet at the McCollum airport in Kennesaw. We were going to meet with a high-powered international firm in New York City. These attorneys would guide me through the chaotic waters that comprised international law as concerned Costa Rica and the U.S. I was thrilled that he was going to take a role in our future. Apparently, I needed more help than I thought would be necessary in the U.S. People had told me that Costa Rica could extradite us at any time. This kind of fear was more intense because I was home, but still not free of the Fulcos' influence. I struggled to understand how this kind of threat could continue.

Mateo was cordial and happy to see his grandson. I cannot say that he was happy to see me, but it didn't matter. What did matter was that he was doing something to help us. Something that only he had the power to do, or so it seemed.

We landed in New York, a limo picked us up and we headed straight to the law offices on Park Avenue. We were greeted by two young, slender woman wearing pencil skirts and white starched blouses. I liked the way they looked and made a note that one day I would wear the same. They looked very professional.

The young woman with long straight dark hair pulled into a tight French Twist offered us water and said, "Mr. Achilles, they are waiting for you and your daughter if you will follow me."

With Marco in his stroller, we followed where she led.

The conference room was beautiful. Floor-to-ceiling windows along the outer wall was breathtaking from the 50th floor. I wanted to look through the glass and forget what I was afraid to hear. Three men sat at the end of the conference table. Two of them stood up and looked at us expectantly. Only the man at the end of the table, a small, bald, older gentleman with thick rimmed glasses, smiled at us and gestured for us to take a seat. Before he sat down, my father took his hand and they shook briefly.

"I see that you have some water. Is there anything else that we can get for you?" he looked directly at me.

"Oh, thank you. We are fine." I replied. My father said nothing.

"Good. Let's get started. Hand me all the documents that you were able to bring with you from Costa Rica. Have they been translated?"

I shook my head, no.

He touched the phone in front of him. In response to "Yes, Mr. Simon?" he said, "Please send Serena in to translate some documents for us."

"Yes, sir."

He leaned back in his big leather chair and crossed his arms in a relaxed manner. There was nothing about this man that seemed hurried, concerned, or tense in any way. He was in command and I was glad he was going to help me. The other two men sat quietly and looked at the documents in front of them.

Mr. Simon looked at me and said, "Now, Sydney, tell me everything from the beginning. Don't leave out any details."

"Okay, where do you want me to start?"

"I want to know everything. How did you end up in Costa Rica? Why did you marry, uh, what's his name?"

"Tomas" I said. "It's a very long story." I looked at my father. He was paying by the hour, I was sure.

"Go ahead and tell him all the details. It's necessary and we are here for this purpose," My father said reassuringly.

It took several hours to tell Mr. Simon what he needed to know. Serena returned with a stack of papers and put them in front of Mr. Simon. He smiled, nodded at me, and said, "We have ordered lunch for you. Please enjoy it, tend to your baby and I will see you at 2:00 p.m."

I looked at my father. His expression was blank but that was better than an expression of disappointment. We took a break and had lunch. My father asked me no questions and I let Marco explore the attorney's break room. The women in the office enjoyed playing with him and took turns holding my son. I could not have asked for a better experience in this kind of situation.

The woman with the French Twist opened the breakroom door and said, "Mr. Simon will see you now."

In the next few moments I would learn how the laws of Costa Rica would rule our lives in the United States. As hard as it was to cross that muddy riverbed, the twenty yards to the conference room threatened to change our lives forever. Would I have to change my identity? Would I have to leave my family and hide? Would I have to leave the country? Could we find a way to live in hiding in Switzerland?

I pushed Marco who, thankfully had fallen asleep in his stroller, through the double-glass doors into the conference room, crossing over a threshold that led to another world. It was filled with people watching us. My father was behind me and still said nothing. Mr. Simon gestured to the chairs across from him. He was sitting in the middle chair with papers sprawled in front of him. We took our seats. I pulled Marco up beside me and waited for a cue.

Mr. Simon took off his glasses and the hustle and bustle of the people around us stopped. All eyes were on him, especially mine.

"Have you ever heard of the Hague Treaty?"

I shook my head no and looked at Mateo. Mr. Simon looked back at me and raised his right eyebrow and chewed the right corner of his moustache.

"In 1988, President Reagan signed an extradition treaty with most Latin American countries. In this treaty, each sovereign country had the right to extradite nationals born within their borders that were taken illegally into another country. In other words, if your son was born in Costa Rica and illegally brought into the U.S., you would be legally bound to return the child to Costa Rica."

I looked at him and my heart stopped. All I could see were uniformed arms pulling Marco from my arms, and placing him in the arms of Otto Fulco. I couldn't breathe. I put my hand on Marco's chest. I was completely and fully ready to grab him and run. I knew how to do that and that I could and would.

He rubbed his eyes. I looked at Mateo, wanting some agreement of reality, then looked back at Mr. Simon.

He continued, "I don't believe in miracles, but someone is definitely watching over you. You are an American and Marco is an American. You don't have to run or hide ever again." He paused.

I didn't understand.

He continued, "The only country that did not sign the Hague Treaty, and hasn't to this day, is Costa Rica. You won." Mr. Simon actually cried tears and wiped them away with his handkerchief. Everyone in the room let go a collective breath. We all breathed together. The room changed. My life changed. Marco's life was certain. He was mine. He was here and we had nothing to fear.

CHAPTER 37

Meeting Max

Life with the Witos in Atlanta was a refuge for us for the following year. We had a stable environment, supported by the two most important people who had always supported me. They were retired and looking forward to traveling and visiting family members in Europe, Africa, and Central and South America.

Marco and I were free to live our lives. And we lived as well any single mother and young son could hope, given my financial position. I worked two jobs and studied to be a medical assistant at a local technical college. The Witos were retired, patient, and understanding. They delighted in Marco. He delighted in them and together we grew from being subjected to laws and expectations of a society rooted in a world apart from the reality where we came from. I worked at Marco's daycare three times a week. I loved those babies and I loved working near my son in the toddler room.

My paychecks were $0.00 because everything I made went to his tuition. I could work a second part-time job and go to school. Every waking hour of my life in Atlanta was spent working, studying, or taking care of Marco. I had the energy, stamina, and will to become independent. The last thing on my mind was to get into a relationship. My intention was to never get married again. I was perfectly content to reach for my goals. I would live independently from the Witos. I would be my own woman. I would raise my child on my own. I could do this. I would do this, and I knew it.

By the end of September, I weighed 89 pounds, not because I wanted to be skinny, but I really didn't have time to eat. I'm sure Wita spoke to Juliana about it, so she came to Atlanta to urge me to join her in the Atlanta Whole-Life Fair, an expo for alternative medicine and spirituality awareness.

I was still officially Catholic at the time. Juliana was exploring spiritual alternatives for herself and wanted to expose me to other avenues of health and beliefs. I wasn't open to it at first, but I did need the break and agreed to join her at the expo. The overarching message that year, was on "signs." On Friday, we listened to Deepak Chopra. I was impressed by how this Doctor of Medicine was so spiritual and how he found his spirituality through the signs that he experienced. After listening to Deepak, I was emotionally moved and open to hearing the next speaker. Wayne Dyer took the stage and I never looked back. His message on "signs" broke through every wall I had ever offered against the conventional religion and psychological theory I had been taught.

He closed his lecture with a song that to this day resonates with me. It was the song I sang to Wita twenty-three years later just before she died. It opened my whole being to allow miracles, opportunities, and the flow of Universal Intelligence, All That Is, God, or whatever you want to call it, to guide me. This song reminds me that we are all here to have experiences for the evolution of our consciousness, this thing we call God or energy.

I left that evening completely overwhelmed, feeling as small as a grain of sand. It's a cliché, but that's how I felt. I was emotionally exhausted the next morning and decided to sit in my tiredness. It felt significant. I felt different. Where I was when I woke up, was living in a new place I had only hoped existed. Everything I had gone through was for a greater purpose than I could comprehend or imagine. It seemed remote, as if it had happened to someone else. Yet, it was a story I could share and somehow in the sharing connect with others. It was no longer attached to me. In that moment I realized I was not a victim. I was a survivor with a purpose.

Juliana made me go to the last day of the expo. Reluctantly, I got up and didn't worry about my hair, makeup or what I was wearing. These things were insignificant in the new reality or consciousness to which I had awakened. We were one of the first ones at the expo. Before us was a warehouse filled with New Age and Spiritual healers looking to promote their services and expertise. Juliana flirted with a musician who had a booth. I wandered off to the alternative health side of the building.

Dr. Max Imus, an Atlanta chiropractor, passionate and confident about his purpose in life, was helping a colleague set up his booth. I found out years later, that Max had seen me from a distance and told his colleague, "I'm going to marry her."

I approached the booth. A model of a human spine dangling from a display caught my eye. I knew it wasn't a real spine, but it looked so real I stopped.

Dr. Imus looked at me and smiled. I asked, "Is that a real spine?"

He laughed, "No, that's a model spine I used at school."

I replied, "That's a real-looking spine." Ready to keep walking, I thought nothing more about it.

Halfway down the aisle, I heard him say, "Would you like a free spinal screening?"

I looked at him as if he was absolutely crazy. Given that there were multiple medical doctors in my extended family, I had no desire to entertain whatever this man offered. After all, chiropractors were quacks, it was an accepted truth.

I turned to him and said, "No thanks. I don't believe in chiropractic."

He said, "What don't you believe in?"

I had no answer.

He said, "Sit down here for a moment and let me see if there is anything I can help you with."

I turned and looked at Juliana flirting with the musician down the aisle where I had left her, shrugged my shoulders and said, "Fine. I'm waiting for my Mom to catch up."

I sat down and Dr. Imus put his hand on my shoulder and gently ran his fingers down my spine. Normally, this kind of touching would have made me bolt, but for some reason, his confident manner and assuring attitude were not threatening. I actually relaxed. When he reached my lower back, he said, "Wow, you have had a significant injury in this area. I would say about eight years ago."

I quickly turned around and looked at him as if he was some kind of psychic. "How do you know?" I asked.

He replied, "I'm just that good. I'm assuming I am correct?"

"Yes," I replied astonished. "I fell off a horse at a show when I was fifteen-years old."

CHAPTER 38

Good Fate

Wita woke me up on the brisk morning of Thursday, October 2, 1997.

"Therrr is the sherriff downstairs. He has to give jou documentos. He said he had to give it to jou."

I sat up and my stomach set off an alarm. I knew something was up.

During the past year, no word had been sent from Tomas or the Fulco family to the Witos. Our location was no secret. Our well-being was no secret. We were in Atlanta. Everyone knew.

I opened the front door. A short, round-bellied man in a Cobb County Sheriff's starched black uniform stood on the front porch. I looked at the gun in the holster on his hip. He held out a large legal envelope in both hands and showed me the label.

"Are you Sydney DeVold de Fulco?" I laughed nervously at his southern pronunciation of Fulco. It sounded like "Fuck-o." I laughed and thought of Hugo.

"Yes, I am" I replied.

"You've been served." He handed me the envelope, turned around, and walked back to his patrol car.

"Wita, I've been served," I said, wondering if this was going to be good or bad news. My stomach voted for the latter. I shrugged and voted for the former.

"Ay si, open it," said Wita.

"It's a subpoena. Tomas is suing me for custody of Marco, and he wants a divorce." I was excited at the prospect of being free from the Fulcos once and for all and scared because the subpoena also petitioned to relinquish my rights to Marco, as I had broken Costa Rican law.

Actually, I had absolutely no tolerance at this point for any more demands from this family. Being so far beyond their reach for so long, it seemed almost laughable to me that they could even envision such an aristocratic demand, especially from a single, American mother who had solely taken care of this child for over a year, without help, interest, or inquiry from Marco's father or his family.

"Ay no," Wita moaned, putting her hands to her temples. "I thought dey would just leave us alone now. It's been sooo long. Why do dey care? Dey never call. Dey must have someding up their pantalones!"

I normally would have laughed at that, but the only thing I could think about was finding a damn good lawyer.

So I did.

Early on the brisk morning of Monday, October 6, with documents in hand and my best outfit, makeup and hair in place, I was determined to not only look good to the judge, but to look damn good to my son's asshole father.

I did.

I drank a cup of coffee with the Witos in the kitchen and tried to calm my nerves and my anger. Wito was looking forward to spending the day with his grandson. I asked Wita what she was going to do today. It was hard to tell because she always woke up "ready to go."

"Why, I'm going wit jou, of course," she smiled. I wondered what she had up her sleeve, donned in her best jewelry and finest, favorite wig.

"Wita, I love you, but you cannot come with me. I know how you are."

"Jes, I am. Who helped jou get into jour apartmento in San Jose when Otto locked jou out? Rrrrememberrrrrr? Jou need me."

"Yes, I always need you Wita, but you will be held in contempt the minute you see Tomas. I know how much you want to protect me. But in this situation, I think you might make things worse."

"Ay no! There is no No! I am coming with jou! I have jour keys." She dangled them in front of me.

"Ay no!" I replied laughing nervously. "Okay, you can come, but I'm driving. I don't care what anyone says or does, you have to promise me not to stir the pot."

"Sydney, jou know, I am not cuuking. I can be quiet."

I shook my head, rolled my eyes and grunted, "Uh … I love you so much. If you say anything to Tomas, I will pull your wig off. Get in the car."

We drove to the courthouse in silence. Wita was thinking hard and I was trying not to throw up.

We sat in our car, parked at the historical "Marietta Square" across from the courthouse. Bronze statues, stone walkways, green areas, and big trees framed the park — like setting in front of us.

I took a deep breath to try and calm my nerves and looked at Wita. She placed her small, smooth hand on my shoulder and said "Jou arre going to be okay. I know dat for sure. Wat is di name of jour lawyer?"

I replied, my voice shook a little, "I know it will be okay. My lawyer's name is Crosby."

Wita curled her lip in disgust. "Wat kind of nombre is dat? Isn't jour lawyer a woman?"

"Yes. I don't know what she looks like, but she had a very strong voice on the phone. You know I haven't had time to meet her. Let's go in now. I want to find her before Tomas shows up."

Just before we found the courtroom designated in the subpoena, I saw a tall, sophisticated "bullish" looking woman, standing with her feet wide apart, as if she was supporting a tower. She looked directly at me and, in a way that reminded me of a military commander, thundered through the quiet hallway, "Sydney DeVold! Are you Sydney DeVold?"

My nervous laugh came out. "Mrs. Crosby?"

She said loudly, but not quite as commanding as before, "Yes," and offered her hand.

We shook and she could have dislocated my wrist, her gesture of warmth and greeting was over the top. I stood amazed at the power this woman seemed to possess, and happy she was on my side!

"This is my grandmother, we call her Wita. You can call her that, too." I smiled at my tiny Wita, who seemed even smaller in stature next to my attorney.

"Is nice to meet jou, Mrs. Crosby," Wita said in a strong voice of her own.

"Love the accent. Let's go inside and get down to business," Mrs. Crosby replied, opened the large door and pointed inside the courtroom. We walked in and sat down at the front table on the left side.

Mrs. Crosby told us very matter-of-factly the procedure for this hearing. She explained that it would be a short, discovery hearing to determine whether the judge would decide whether or not kidnapping would be a factor in the custody and divorce case.

She looked at me very seriously. "If he does, I will show him the demand letters they gave you in Costa Rica. We'll counter with the fact that the Fulcos kicked you out of your home, the fact that Tomas kidnapped Marco, and that he used false documentation to accuse you of being an unfit mother and commit you to a mental hospital."

I was speechless and so glad this marvelous woman was on my side. Mentally I thanked Max's friend who had recommended Mrs. Crosby with such short notice, and that she was available to help me, and familiar with international law, especially Central America.

Out of the corner of my eye, I saw the courtroom door swing open. I felt Wita poke my shoulder, alerting me that Tomas was coming in. I caught my breath and wanted to look him directly in eyes. At first it was very awkward, but I forced myself to stare in his eyes and prove to him that I wasn't afraid. Otto was not with him, which made me very happy. This time, Tomas would have to handle things on his own.

Tomas looked the same, but a bit shorter and rounder. He had gained weight.

I secretly snickered to myself and turned back around.

Wita whispered in my ear, "Oye, he is so fat."

"Wita," I whispered back. "Do you want me to pull your wig off? Be quiet."

Mrs. Crosby stood up and offered her hand to Tomas' lawyer. She boomed, "Mr. Franklin. A pleasure." She shook his hand. Mr. Franklin, a tall, slim, middle-aged man with a full head of salt-and pepper-hair and wire-rimmed glasses, smiled and said in a southern gentleman tone of appreciation, "As firm a handshake as ever. It's good to see you again, Mrs. Crosby."

He glanced over her shoulder to look at Wita and me. He turned away, then turned back and looked at us again. I looked at him trying to figure out how tough an opponent he was going to be, but Wita stayed focused on the Judge's Bench.

To be honest in writing this, after I heard "All Rise, Court is in Session," the proceedings were a big blur. I didn't understand the legal jargon and everything Mrs. Crosby had tried to explain to me evaporated. I was scared, but I had faith in my bulldog of a lawyer. What I will never forget is that Tomas' lawyer, Mr. Franklin, leaned back in his chair every few minutes to look across the aisle at us.

Wita mentioned it to me in a whisper, and I knew she was uncomfortable with his attention. It did seem to be strange behavior to me as well, but this was probably an unusual case for him.

I wanted his glances at us to stop and spoke to Mrs. Crosby. She agreed his stares were excessive and asked Judge Davis to allow her to approach the Bench.

They spoke for a moment. Judge Davis looked at Mr. Franklin and waved him to come forward and join their conversation. The three of them spoke quietly and Mr. Franklin turned and looked at us again. Judge Davis and Mrs. Crosby also looked at us. Then everyone in the courtroom looked at us. Wita and I looked at each other.

Mrs. Crosby strode back to our table with a bemused look. She leaned in and said in a very low voice, "Mr. Franklin wants to meet with us in a side room. This is unheard of, but the Judge agreed that in this specific case, it would be an appropriate course of action. It is totally up to you, but I recommend that we comply with his request. What do you want to do?"

"Will Tomas be in the room too?" I asked.

"No. That's the unusual part of this. Mr. Franklin does not want his client in the room. It is for our ears only."

I turned to look at Wita for guidance. She nodded affirmatively, and I said, "Okay," my voice a question mark.

Mrs. Crosby led us through a side door to a small conference room. We stood and waited for Mr. Franklin to join us. A moment later, he came in and walked over to Wita. I was surprised because I thought Mr. Franklin was going to make a settlement offer.

"Jou look familiarr," Wita said looking up at Mr. Franklin.

He smiled and, on an exhale, said, "Yes, I believe we do know each other. Are you Dr. Henry DeVold's mother?"

"Oh, jes!" she acknowledged "I am! And jou arre his friend?"

He smiled, and nodded, "Yes, I actually am his neighbor. We play golf together and, I believe you have played bridge with my wife at the country club."

"Jes, Jes, jes," her head bobbed up and down. "I rremember jou now!"

Mrs. Crosby and I looked at each other in amazement.

Wita paused, cocked her head to the side and pointed a finger at Mr. Franklin's stomach. Slowly she said with puzzlement in her voice, "Arre jou di one who told Henry not to let Sydney stay wit him and Dawn when she escaped with Marco from Costa Rica?"

He frowned and looked at his shoes. "I did, but I did not know the whole story at the time." He looked directly at me and I was surprised to notice that he had very kind eyes.

"Let's all have a seat and Sydney, please tell me in your own words, what happened to you in Costa Rica. I have already heard Tomas's version."

I replied, "It will take some time to tell you everything."

Mr. Franklin replied, "We have until 1:00 p.m. The judge called a lunch recess."

I told him the important details as quickly as I could. It wasn't hard to do. To prepare for the judge's questions, I had rehearsed them in my head many times. Mr. Franklin took off his glasses and put them on the table. "I am going to help you. Tell me what you want, and we will finish this today."

I looked at Mrs. Crosby and she nodded at me and said, "Go ahead."

"First of all, I want a divorce. Secondly, I want Marco to have a relationship with Tomas but for that to happen, he needs to provide financial support."

Mr. Franklin asked, "Are you willing to give Tomas joint custody?"

I replied, "No. I would agree to visitation rights in the U.S. only. I am afraid that the Fulcos would keep Marco in Costa Rica once he was there. And I can never go back to that country."

Mr. Franklin said, "I will explain your concerns to Tomas. I can petition the courts to allocate a large cash bond that would help you hire someone to get him back if that did happen. To be honest, I don't think Tomas would keep Marco away from you at this point."

"How do you know?" I asked.

"I don't for sure, but things have changed for the Fulcos. That's all I can say." He continued, "Let me talk with Tomas and see if we can come to an agreement."

Mr. Franklin left the room. Mrs. Crosby patted the table with both hands and smiled broadly. "I've never seen anything like this with any international case. I thought we had a real fight on our hands. For some people, this kind of thing drags on for years.

"I'm impressed by your courage, Sydney. And frankly, I'm inspired by this turn of events." She winked at Wita and excused herself. "Can I get you ladies some water, something from the vending machines? This will take a while longer."

"Can you get us each a Coke?" I asked.

"Sure thing," she replied.

Wita and I found the restroom down the hall and relaxed for a moment. I felt like I could almost let go of subconscious tension that suddenly became conscious. I took several breaths and before we returned to the conference room, I hugged Wita and she laughed. "I didn't even have to say anyding and look what happened for jou Sydney. I just had to be here."

"Wita," I replied, "this never could have happened had you not been here. Your love and support mean everything to me." I kissed her cheek and she beamed. Proud. Strong. She said, "Wita wins!"

Tomas and Mr. Franklin worked with us with little push back. Tomas seemed happy about our agreement. He would take Marco to San Jose in two days. I would live in hell for two weeks until he returned my son. I was happy but still very scared. Tomas would have to pay child support and lied about his income. But what else was new. We signed the papers that afternoon. The judge approved it and we were technically divorced that day, and it would be official in thirty days. By then I would have Marco back and could expect to receive some financial support.

Outside the courthouse it was a sunny fall afternoon. Not one cloud was in the sky. The air smelled different to me. Or maybe I was different. I felt reborn. Lighter.

Wita and I hugged, and I could tell she felt relieved, as if a chapter in our lives was over.

I heard Tomas clear his throat. He stood directly behind us. I turned. We shook hands. For the first time in over a year he spoke to me.

"I am happy with this outcome. Thank you for letting Marco visit us. I understand it must be difficult for you. But we will be so glad to have him with us again. I know, it's for only two weeks. I promise. You will have our itinerary before we leave. Don't worry, I don't want any trouble. I just want to know my son."

I replied, "I want him to know you, too. And I want him back. I promise you, I got him out once and I will do it again if I have to."

Tomas cocked his head and squinted his eyes. In a low, secretive voice he asked, "How *did* you get out of the country?"

"Well," I said squinting my eyes right back at him. In a low secretive voice, I replied, "It's all in The Journal."

The End

EPILOGUE

Breaking the Pattern

"From struggle comes satisfaction of the purest kind."
— Wito.

We all have a story. We all have pain and put up walls to protect our most vulnerable selves.

We think showing strength gives us strength. In reality, it makes us brittle. It takes inner strength to pull down the walls and be authentic.

It's our insecurities that hook us, and that's okay, as long as we use them to identify and heal the pain that made us insecure in the first place. Observe it in others and, you will see yourself.

The powers I gave to Zoryia were the powers I desperately wanted. Doing nothing to stop the life-altering future we faced in Costa Rica was not a possibility in my heart. Without hesitation, I made the choice to save my son and myself. During these actions, something inside shifted. I began to suspect that Zoryia's powers were actually my powers. Leaving with my son was the only way to break my pattern of fear. It was the only way to create a full and meaningful life.

I married Dr. Nicholas Sudano, whom you know as Dr. Max Imus. I asked him what name he would like me to use in this book and being a strong Italian man, he said, "Maximus, like the guy from the movie *Gladiator*!"

We had our four beautiful, healthy daughters born at home. We made incredible memories. Our dream home, five children, three dogs, two rabbits, a really cool turtle, and our social engagements created chaos, drama, fun, and many sleepless nights. This level of stimulation was what I had always known. I was rarely bored.

Looking back, I believe this part of my life gave me the variety and challenges I needed to continue to learn, experience, and heal. And with my new family, I had a solid foundation and a husband who challenged me and, kept me grounded.

As we built our lives together, I sometimes wondered when the big house, nice cars, membership in a prominent country club, and "keeping up with the neighbors" was going to fill the void inside. Why was I feeling incomplete? Why did I still sometimes feel empty?

In 2008, as many people experienced, our lives changed with the economy. We lost almost everything.

I'll never forget one cold winter morning when we had to leave our home to find a new one. I hit rock bottom and slumped to the floor. I cried because we had worked so intensely to create security and happiness for our family and understood, for the first time, that having expensive things had nothing to do with having a good life. My heart knew I had to make a change and while I didn't know how, I was certain I would find a way to break the pattern.

Weeks later, we moved into a nice, but smaller, rented home, focused on Nick's work and what we had to do to make a family thrive.

It wasn't easy. It was an interesting new world filled with many opportunities to grow and learn for all of us. Our children loved us as parents. To this day, they want to be around us. This new family pattern has given purpose and meaning to our roller-coaster life together. With its ups and downs, our marriage has grown stronger. We made a promise when we married, "We will never give up on each other." I am happy to say, we continue to keep our promise.

No matter what we go through, life can be so beautiful in the mundane moments, through the difficult times, and especially when learning occurs. I continue to do the work and accept that for me, past abuse — whether physical, emotional, or sexual — is a lifelong healing process.

Triggers happen every day. I see them now as opportunities to step away and ask my heart where they come from. It isn't easy to remember the coping tools I've learned, but when I can recognize that I'm in pain, confused, afraid and about to protect myself with a response that will not give me what I ultimately want, I can pause and respond in a healthy way, instead of reacting in non-awareness of what I am doing or why.

The most powerful healing tool in my belt is mindfulness. It is the pause between feeling something and reacting to it. Our moments of mindfulness are gifts we give ourselves and others. It is the difference between acting out how we feel in the moment, and how we can engage others in our truth. Mindfulness is choosing to act in ways that work to our advantage long enough to take a breath, think a better thought and, make a better choice that serves the Self, and everyone involved.

My mentor from the Atlanta Awareness Center, Patricia Zerman, once told me something that continues to help. "When someone points a finger at you, they are pointing three fingers right back at themselves." If I get hooked by a comment, I know I need to look inward and heal it.

Pain is pain. We cannot compare it, quantify it, or judge it. All we have is the present moment. All we can do is be aware of the pain and understand that hurt people — hurt people. In these moments of awareness, we can step aside, see the arrows shooting at us, and make a choice — accept that it's not really about us. In these moments we can allow what is, breathe, grow and understand.

Anyone who tells us we are lesser than, unworthy of, and must do what they want before we can be of value to them — is in the kind of pain that only by making you feel pain, can they connect with you, another human being. This is *their* pattern. It's how they survive in *their* world. And why it must always remain a secret, for *them*. It's never really about us. We may attract it to experience and learn from it, but it's *their* pain.

I've learned to never mistake a kind heart for weakness. A person who is kind, vulnerable, and honest has great strength and empathy. If we truly want to change our lives, we must act from a position of strength, not fear. If we truly want to change the world, *we must be who we really are.*

We each have a voice. Instead of judging and reacting, we can be a light for ourselves, and others who need it.

The greatest agent for change is a loving, compassionate heart that speaks with a clear, transparent voice. We've heard such voices before. They continue to inspire the world.

"Veritas Dat Viribus Alas": Truth Gives Strength to Wings — *Laertes & Isadora*

Laertes stood up, cleared his throat, and took a slow, deep breath.

"Veritas Dat Viribus Alas." In our original language, this means, "Truth Gives Strength to Wings."

No sound followed. His eyes swelled with moistness. He turned and signaled to a distinguished, grey-haired captain waiting in the doorway. In his most dignified and respectful voice, Laertes bowed to Zoryia and called, "Present the Crest!"

Isadora stood and pulled back the silk cloth covering the pillow offered by the captain. She said quietly, "This, too, is your legacy, my child."

Zoryia stood and accepted the shining jeweled shield Isadora fixed to the shoulder of her gown.

"My granddaughter lights up the room!" said Laertes, taking Zoryia's hand. He gazed at the attendant ladies, then continued. "You feel her truth. That is her power. The power of our ancestors flows through each of us. You have gifts inherited through your families. Each of you is unique and necessary. Everyone has gifts and a place in this world. Honor yourselves as you honor my granddaughter now."

Katy Sudano is the wife of Dr. Nick Sudano and the mother of five children. As Vice President of Total Health Solutions and BrainCore Neurofeedback of Milton, she helps people deal with anxiety, depression and PTSD. She also helps individuals find health and success as a certified Robbins-Madanes Coach under Tony Robbins. Katy has written her first book, *Truth Gives Strength to Wings*, her memoir about faith, love, and finding happiness through adversity.

An advocate for preventing child sexual abuse, Katy is a former board member, Spanish spokesperson and workshop facilitator for VOICE Today, a non-profit advocacy for survivors of sexual abuse. She was a model and actor for Real People Models and Talent. Katy is a former member of the Local Advisory Council (LSAC) for Fulton County Schools. She speaks 4 languages and is passionate about inspiring, motivating and helping people.

Ginger studied writing at a local university and contributed articles for student and alumni publications. She was the co-author of *What to Do While Things Are Changing* published in *Physician Executive Magazine*, and a ghost writer for leadership training articles for a performance consulting firm.

As a former senior communications manager and marketing manager for a global human resources consulting firm, Ginger created "countless" articles promoting leadership strategies and marketing incentives for the company's internal and external audiences.

Today she coordinates marketing efforts for a worldwide aviation corporation. Ginger looks forward to retiring from the corporate world and writing creative stories from the heart.

CPSIA information can be obtained
at www.ICGtesting.com
Printed in the USA
LVHW030435030420
652108LV00004B/1071

9 781641 843072